Sadlier

CHRIST IN US™

School Edition 5

"*Christ In Us* Grade 5 cover artwork speaks to the students' discovery of the challenges and opportunities of being missionary disciples to all of creation."

Reverend Donald Senior, C.P., S.T.D.

Sadlier Religion

This advanced publication copy has been printed prior to final publication and pending ecclesiastical approval.

Acknowledgments

This publication was printed with permission pending from the following copyright holders.

Excerpts from the *Catechism of the Catholic Church, second edition*, © 2000, Libreria Editrice Vaticana—United States Conference of Catholic Bishops, Washington, D.C. All rights reserved.

Scripture texts in this work are taken from the *New American Bible*, revised edition © 2010, 1991, 1986, 1970 Confraternity of Christian Doctrine, Washington, D.C. All Rights Reserved. No part of the *New American Bible* may be reproduced in any form without permission in writing from the copyright owner.

Excerpts from the English translation of *The Roman Missal* © 2010 International Commission on English in the Liturgy, Inc. (ICEL). All rights reserved.

Excerpts from the *Lectionary for Mass for Use in the Dioceses of the United States of America, second typical edition* © 2001, 1998, 1997, 1986, 1970 Confraternity of Christian Doctrine, Inc., Washington, D.C. All rights reserved. No portion of this text may be reproduced by any means without permission in writing from the copyright owner.

Quotations from papal addresses, audiences, homilies, speeches, messages, meditations, encyclicals, and other Vatican documents are from www.vatican.va and copyright © by Libreria Editrice Vaticana.

His Holiness Pope Francis, Twitter posts: September 9, 2013, 2:12 a.m., October 17, 2013, 6:45 a.m., and February 28, 2014, 3:28 a.m. http://twitter.com/Pontifex

Excerpt from "Issues and Action: Cultural Diversity—African American—Resources: The Gift of African American Sacred Song," United States Conference of Catholic Bishops, Inc., http://www.usccb.org/issues-and-action/cultural-diversity/african-american/resources/upload/The-Gift-of-African-American-Sacred-Song-Sr-Thea-Bowman.pdf

Excerpt from Thomas McNally, C.S.C., and William George Storey, D.M.S., Editors, *Day by Day: The Notre Dame Prayer Book for Students*, Ave Maria Press, Notre Dame, IN, 1975. Copyright © 1975 by Ave Maria Press.

"One Bread, One Body" © 2018 John Foley, S.J. Published by OCP, 5536 NE Hassalo, Portland, OR 97213. All rights reserved.

Printed in the United States of America.

William H. Sadlier, Inc.
9 Pine Street
New York, NY 10005-4700

ISBN: 978-0-8215-3705-3
123456789 WEBC 23 22 21 20 19

Cover Series Design: Silver Linings Studios; **Cover Series Illustrator:** Jui Ishida

Photo Credits

age fotostock/CSP_jarenwicklund: 185, 289; lev dolgachov: 159; Grzegorz Galazka: 66; Spencer Grant: 20, 41, 253, 287; Jeff Greenberg: 156; Megan Maloy: 40; Rebecca Nelson: 169; Henrik Sorensen: 128; Aflo Foto Agency: 252; Caia Image/Robert Daly: 14; Dinodia Photo: 251; FS Productions: 108; Hero Images: 44; Kidstock: 123, 127; UIG/Godong: 34 *bottom*, 35. Alamy Stock Agency/Godong: 75, 92; Chris Beer: 133; Dimitry Bobroff: 55; Scott Goodno: 46; Richard Levine: 59; Itsik Marom: 130; juan moyano: 78; Anne Rippy: 208; Jozef Sedmak: 261 *bottom*; Marmaduke St. John: 25; Friedrich Stark: 24 *top*; Agencja Fotograficzna Caro: 76, 114; Alamy Live News/Massimo Valicchia: 168; Album: 207; Albuquerque Journal/ZUMAPRESS.com/Jim Thompson: 196; BE&W agencja fotagraficzna Sp. z.o.o.: 265; Blend Images/Kidstock: 129, 148; Godong: 34 *top*; Hero Images Inc.: 269; IanDagnall Computing: 170; imagegallery2: 77; Rawpixel Ltd: 126; robertharding: 94. AP Images/ AP Photo/Andrew Medichini: 118; Associated Press/Bikas Das: 88; Butch Comegys/The Times-Tribune via AP: 103, 105; Imaginechina/Li gang: 85. Art Resource, NY/Erich Lessing: 243. Bridgeman Images/The dream of Saint Joseph (chromolitho), French School, (19th century)/Private Collection/ © Look and Learn: 236; Ms 370 fol.184 The Last Supper (vellum), French School, (15th century) / Bibliotheque Municipale, Abbeville, France : 21; The Solitude of Christ, 1918 (oil on canvas), Denis, Maurice (1870-1943)/Private Collection: 218; The Tree of Knowledge. Adam and Eve in the Garden of Eden, by Karima Ali (born 1945)/Werner Forman Archive: 43. Karen Callaway: 33, 36, 42, 54, 82, 87, 95, 145, 177, 181, 190, 192, 202, 205, 229, 247, 257, 273 *top*, 286. The Crosiers/Gene Plaisted OSC: 32 *top right*, 32 *bottom*, 73, 154, 158, 164, 178, 217, 259, 271. Dreamstime.com/Godfer: 197. Getty Images/boryak: 179; drnadig: 246; kate_sept2004: 175; Maskot: 62 *bottom*; Photos by R A Kearton: 186; Westend61: 124, 227; Dirk Anschurz: 125; Eric Audras: 245; Kathy Collins: 228; Danny Hu: 258; Dan Kenyon: 135; Philippe Lissac: 241; Peter Macdiarmid: 81; Ulrike Schmitt-Hartmann: 134; Jordan Siemans: 235; AFP/FRANCISCO LEONG: 83; AFP/JEAN-FRANCOIS MONIER: 52; Atlantide Phototravel/Guido Cozzi: 264; Caiaimage/Tom Merton: 71; Compassionate Eye Foundation/Martin Barraud: 136; Digital Vision: 115; EyeEm/Zelma Brezinska: 111; EyeEm/Sawitree Pamee: 191; Hero Images: 19, 91; NurPhoto/Emmanuele Contini: 24 *bottom*; Science Photo Library - NASA EARTH OBSERVATORY: 195; Universal Images Group/Godong: 149,187. GoodSalt/Lars Justinen: 51; Lifeway Collection: 53, 267; Providence Collection: 61; Review & Herald Publishing: 104. The Image Works, Inc./Sean Sprague: 62 *top*, 64. iStockphoto.com/aldomurillo: 222; alejandrophotography: 15; andresr: 107; grandriver: 163; jacquesvandinteren: 272-273 *bottom*; jarenwicklund: 112; kali9: 6, 144; PapaBear: 240; RichVintage: 263; zodebala: 153; Steve Debenport: 102; monkeybusinessimages: 117. Greg Lord: 101. Masterfile/jamdesign: 155. Newscom/Album/Oronoz: 50; dpa/picture-alliance/Armin Weigel: 210; GODONG/picture-alliance/Pascal Deloche: 166; REUTERS/Remo Casilli: 198; SIPA/Grzegorz Galazka: 30; TNS/David Maialetti: 56; Zuma Press/Donatella Giagnori: 157. Shutterstock.com/Frippitaun: 63, 291; guteksk7: 184; KemarinSore: 132; Luxerendering: 248-249 *bottom*; Macrovector: 236-237 *top*, 242-243 *top*, 260-261 *top*, 266-267 *top*; PT Images: 29; Redcollegiya: 17 *background*, 69 *background*, 121 *background*, 173 *background*, 225 *background*, 230-231 *background*, 248-249 *background*, 254-255 *background*, 272-273 *background*, 279 *background*; Slanapotam: 18, 70, 122, 174, 226; Thoom: 138; vipman: 142; wideonet: 32 *top left*; R. Daniluk: 288; Nataliya Dolotko: 279; Philip Meyer: 225; Jaroslaw Pawlak: 270; Viktor Petruk: 254-255 *bottom*; Viktoria Pranzhu: 116; David Allen Photography: 234; Syda Productions: 12; wavebreakmedia: 11. Spirit Juice Studios: 45. Superstock/3LH/James Tissot: 23; Spencer Grant: 72, 284; Jose Pelaez: 137; akg-images: 97; All Canada Photos/Glenn Davy: 215; Blend Images/Klaus Tiedge: 160; Caia Images: 150; Compassionate Eye Foundation/Jasper White: 176; Exactostock: 209; Hero Images: 96, 140, 167, 219; Image Source/Rebecca Nelson: 201; Minden Pictures: 239; Oronoz/Album: 86, 212; Radius: 211; robertharding: 31. W.P. Wittman Limited: 7, 22, 39, 60, 65, 74, 93, 106, 113, 139, 143, 146, 164, 180, 182, 188, 189, 199, 200, 206, 216, 221, 231, 233, 285. Wikimedia Commons/SICDAMNOME: 84; Saint Francis of Assissi, 1642 by Jusepe de Ribera: 220; Head of Christ, 1648 by Rembrandt Harmenszoon van Rijn: 49.

Illustrator Credits

Pierre Droal: 17, 69, 121, 173, 275, 276, 278. Robert Kayganich: 282-283. Matthew Laznicka: 10, 13, 26, 36, 46, 56, 66, 78, 88, 98, 108, 118, 130, 140, 150, 160, 170, 182, 192, 202, 212, 222.

Christ In Us was developed in collaboration with the wisdom of the community. The team included respected catechetical, liturgical, pastoral, and theological experts who shared their insights and inspired its development.

With grateful acknowledgment of
William Sadlier Dinger and Frank Sadlier Dinger
for their leadership, vision, and commitment to excellence in the development
of Sadlier's catechetical programs and resources since 1963

Theological and Liturgical Consultants

Most Reverend Christopher James Coyne
Bishop of Burlington, VT

Donna Eschenauer, Ph.D.
Associate Dean, Associate Professor of Pastoral Theology
St. Joseph's Seminary and College

Rita Ferrone, M.Div.

Thomas Kendzia
Sadlier National Consultant for Liturgy and Music

John B. Angotti, M.A.P.S.

Barbara Sutton, D.Min.

Kathleen Dorsey Bellow, D.Min.

Scripture Consultant

Reverend Donald Senior, C.P., S.T.D.
Chancellor and President Emeritus
Catholic Theological Union

Catechetical Consultants

Amy Welborn, M.A.

Susan Stark

Sr. Theresa Engel, O.S.F.
Member of the School Sisters of St. Francis

Maureen A. Kelly, M.A.

Karla Manternach, M.A.

Woodeene Koenig-Bricker, M.A.

Connie Clark

Shannon Chisholm, Ph.D.

Susan M. Sink

Maureen Shaughnessy, S.C.

Lori Dahlhoff, Ed.D.

Andrea D. Chavez-Kopp, M.Ed.

Educational Consultants

Richard Culatta

Heidi Hayes Jacobs, Ed.D.

Jay McTighe

Allie Johnston

Learning Style Inclusion Consultants

Charleen Katra, M.A.

Jennifer Ochoa, M.Ed., LDT/C

Inculturation Consultants

Luis J. Medina
Director, Bilingual Catechesis

Charlene Howard, M.A.

Michael P. Howard, M.A.
Eat the Scroll Ministry

Catholic Social Teaching

Kristin Witte, D.Min.

Genevieve Jordan Laskey, M.A.

Michael Jordan Laskey, M.A.

Media and Technology Consultants

Spirit Juice Studios

Top Floor Productions

Sr. Caroline Cerveny, S.S.J.-T.O.S.F., D.Min.

Reviewers and Contributors

Jennifer Hayhurst

Concetta M. Duval, Ed.D.

Trenton W. Mattingly, M.A.

Debi Mahr, M.A.

Mary Homola, M.A.

Linda Mele Dougherty, M.A.

Mary Jane Krebbs, Ph.D.

Darcy Osby, M.Div.

Hugh M. Keenan

Sadlier Consultant Team

Suzan Larroquette

Kathy Hendricks

John Collins

Writing/Development Team

Diane Lampitt, M.Ed.
Vice President, Product Manager, Religion

Blake Bergen
Vice President, Religion Editorial

Deacon Matthew Halbach, Ph.D.
Catechetical Director

Regina Kelly, M.A.
Editorial Director, Religion

Mary Carol Kendzia, M.S.
Research and Development Director, Religion

Robert Vigneri, M.S.
Executive Editor, Religion

Editorial Staff
Tina Dennelly, Ellen Marconi, Linda Nicholson, Roger Ochoa, Amanda Pisciotta

Publishing Operations Team

Patricia Coryell
Senior Vice President & Publisher

Robert Methven
Vice President, Shared Services

Carole Uettwiller
Vice President, Supply Chain

Vince Gallo
Senior Creative Director

Francesca O'Malley
Art/Design Director

Cesar Llacuna
Senior Image Manager

Roderick Gammon
Director, Digital Strategy

Joanne Rosequist
Instructional Design Director

Toby Carson
Digital Design Director

Cheryl Golding
Production Director

Laura Reischour
Project Manager

Evie Alvarez
Program Manager

Jovito Pagkalinawan
Electronic Prepress Director

Yolanda Miley
Image Rights & Permissions Director

Lucy Rotondi
Business Manager

Design/Image Staff
Kevin Butler, Nancy Figueiredo, Stephen Flanagan, Debrah Kaiser, Gabriel Ricci, Bob Schatz, Daniel Sherman

Production Staff
Robin D'Amato, Carol Lin, Vincent McDonough, Allison Pagkalinawan, Brad Tucker

Contents

Catholic Spirituality 10
Welcome 11

Unit 1: What do we believe?
The Faith Professed
Unit Opener 17

Lesson 1: How do we know God? 19
Prayer: Meditation
Psalm 105:3
• God is truth and love. • We come to know God through Sacred Scripture. • We come to know God through Jesus. • The Church shares her beliefs through Scripture, Tradition, and the sacraments.
Lesson Test: Show What You Know
Partners in Faith: Saint Ignatius Loyola
Mini-Task: How can I show God to others?
At Home: Remembering experiences of God's love

Lesson 2: Who is God? 29
Prayer: Praise
***Catechism of the Catholic Church*, 221**
• We can know God through Creation and the Church. • The Blessed Trinity is a mystery of faith, in which God is revealed as Father, Son, and Holy Spirit. • Jesus' Spirit, present in the sacraments, helps us understand the mystery of the Blessed Trinity. • The Church shares her beliefs through Scripture, Tradition, and the sacraments.
Glory Be
Lesson Test: Show What You Know
Partners in Faith: Juan de Zumárraga
Mini-Task: How do I live out my belief in God?
At Home: Showing respect for all life

Lesson 3: Why did God make us? 39
Prayer: Petition
***Roman Missal*, Eucharistic Prayer IV, 117**
• God created us with a body and a soul. • The Church supports and nourishes our faith. • God created Adam and Eve to live in friendship with him. • Everyone who dies in God's friendship will have the joy of eternal life with him.
Lesson Test: Show What You Know
Partners in Faith: Saint Peter
Mini-Task: How can I grow in holiness?
At Home: Strengthening one another's faith

Lesson 4: Who is Jesus Christ? 49
Prayer: *Lectio* and *Visio Divina*
Pope Francis, *Angelus*, St. Peter's Square
• The Holy Spirit prepared Mary for her work as the Mother of God. • The Incarnation is the mystery that Jesus, the only Son of God, became human. • How do we celebrate the coming of Christ? • Jesus is the Savior who came into the world to save us from sin. • At the Ascension, the Risen Christ was taken up into heaven.
Apostles' Creed
Lesson Test: Show What You Know
Partners in Faith: Saint Catherine Labouré
Mini-Task: How do I come to know Mary, the Mother of God?
At Home: Praying for family members who have died

Lesson 5: What is the Church? 59
Prayer: Intercession
Rite of Baptism for Children
• In Baptism, we become members of the Church. • The People of God are the temple of the Holy Spirit and the sacrament of Christ. • The Church is divinely sent, motivated by love, and guided by the Holy Spirit. • Through our Baptism, we continue Jesus' work in the Church today.
Lesson Test: Show What You Know
Partners in Faith: Blessed Sára Salkaházi
Mini-Task: How does my parish reflect the work of the Church?
At Home: Remembering family baptisms

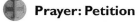

Your Spiritual Journey

Your Grade 5 Saint: Saint Ignatius of Loyola

Christ In Us offers a saint for every grade. As you journey through each unit, remember to pray to your grade's saint. Ask him or her to help guide you to be closer to Jesus Christ.

Saint Ignatius of Loyola was born in the Basque country of Spain in 1491 and was the youngest of thirteen children. Ignatius' mother died soon after his birth.

In his youth, Ignatius developed a passion for military life and enjoyed dressing up as a soldier. He joined the army at the age of seventeen.

Ignatius was a fearless soldier and participated in many battles without injury. His bravery and leadership were recognized by the royal family of his region, and he soon became an important leader.

But Ignatius' streak of good fortune came to an end in 1521, when he was seriously hurt at the Battle of Pamplona. He was hit by a cannonball, injuring his legs. He would limp for the rest of his life. The military career in which Ignatius took so much pride had come to an end.

The injury, however, set the stage for a religious conversion. During the time his legs were healing, Ignatius read Scripture and books about the lives of saints.

In 1522 Ignatius traveled to a monastery, where he confessed his sins. He placed his sword at the altar of the Virgin Mary as a sign that he would now be a soldier for Jesus Christ.

At the age of 48, Ignatius formed the Society of Jesus. It is a religious order better known as the Jesuits. Ignatius wanted the Jesuits to travel around the world as missionaries. He wanted to spread the Gospel of Jesus Christ by establishing schools, colleges and seminaries.

How can you be a missionary for Christ?

Welcome to ***Christ In Us***, an exciting way to grow in your Catholic faith!

Each one of us is on a journey to love and know Jesus Christ. Imagine if every person who met you knew you were a friend of Christ!

Together in this program

we will **ENCOUNTER** Jesus Christ

we will **SEEK** him in our lives

we will **WITNESS** to our faith.

You will use this book as well as your online digital portal as you discover and grow closer to Jesus Christ.

As you journey in your faith, you can think about these questions:

Examine me, Lord, and test me;
search my heart and mind.

Your mercy is before my eyes;
I walk guided by your faithfulness.

Psalm 26: 2–3

Why is it important to have Christ live in you?
What would happen if you did not have Jesus in your life?
How does your faith, the Church, and your family help bring you closer to God?

Every lesson has four Spiraling Main Ideas. Here is an example.

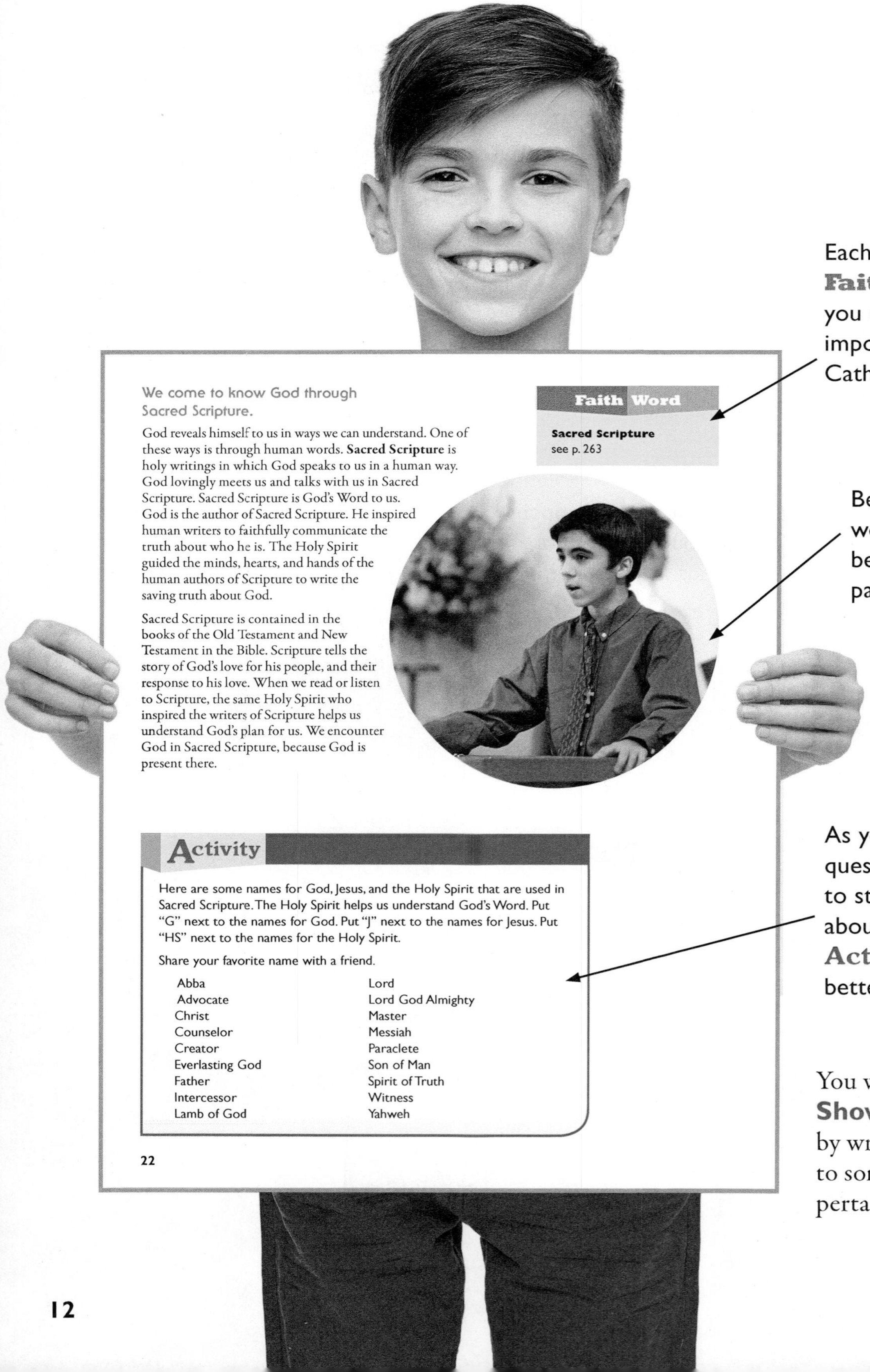

We come to know God through Sacred Scripture.

God reveals himself to us in ways we can understand. One of these ways is through human words. **Sacred Scripture** is holy writings in which God speaks to us in a human way. God lovingly meets us and talks with us in Sacred Scripture. Sacred Scripture is God's Word to us. God is the author of Sacred Scripture. He inspired human writers to faithfully communicate the truth about who he is. The Holy Spirit guided the minds, hearts, and hands of the human authors of Scripture to write the saving truth about God.

Sacred Scripture is contained in the books of the Old Testament and New Testament in the Bible. Scripture tells the story of God's love for his people, and their response to his love. When we read or listen to Scripture, the same Holy Spirit who inspired the writers of Scripture helps us understand God's plan for us. We encounter God in Sacred Scripture, because God is present there.

Faith Word

Sacred Scripture
see p. 263

Activity

Here are some names for God, Jesus, and the Holy Spirit that are used in Sacred Scripture. The Holy Spirit helps us understand God's Word. Put "G" next to the names for God. Put "J" next to the names for Jesus. Put "HS" next to the names for the Holy Spirit.

Share your favorite name with a friend.

Abba	Lord
Advocate	Lord God Almighty
Christ	Master
Counselor	Messiah
Creator	Paraclete
Everlasting God	Son of Man
Father	Spirit of Truth
Intercessor	Witness
Lamb of God	Yahweh

22

Each lesson has one or more **Faith Words** to help you understand the important words we use as Catholics.

Be sure to look at all the wonderful photos and beautiful art found in the pages of your book.

As you explore this question, you might be asked to stop and think more about it and then do a short **Activity** to answer it better.

You will be asked to **Show What You Know** by writing down the answers to some short questions pertaining to the lesson.

You will not be alone as you journey through ***Christ In Us***. You will have lots of **Partners in Faith**—saints and other holy people who lived amazing lives—walking with you.

Along with **Saint Ignatius**, here are some other Partners in Faith whom you will meet throughout the book!

Saint Thomas More

Saint Peter

Saint Catherine Labouré

Rose Hawthorne

Blessed Sára Salkaházi

Saint Andrew Kim Taegŏn

Saint Rose of Lima

Saint Anselm

Next, you will be asked to go to your **Portfolio** to creatively share how you can bring Christ to the world.

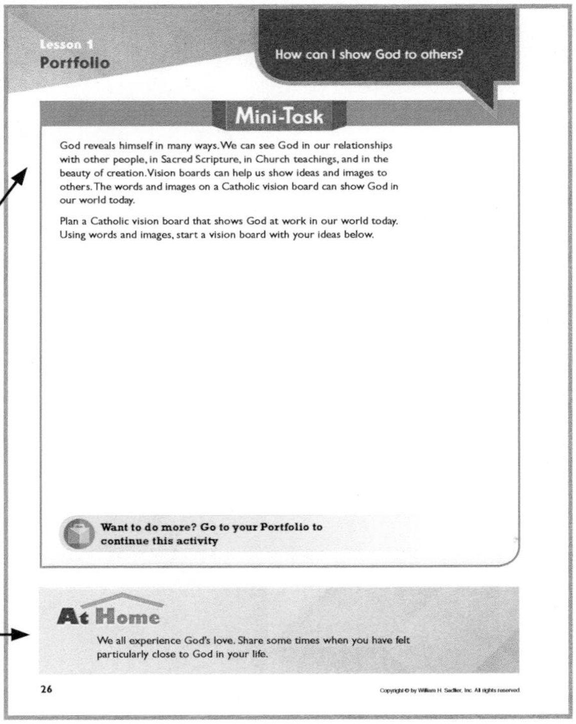

Lesson 1
Portfolio

How can I show God to others?

Mini-Task

God reveals himself in many ways. We can see God in our relationships with other people, in Sacred Scripture, in Church teachings, and in the beauty of creation. Vision boards can help us show ideas and images to others. The words and images on a Catholic vision board can show God in our world today.

Plan a Catholic vision board that shows God at work in our world today. Using words and images, start a vision board with your ideas below.

Want to do more? Go to your Portfolio to continue this activity

At Home

We all experience God's love. Share some times when you have felt particularly close to God in your life.

26

Copyright © by William H. Sadlier, Inc. All rights reserved.

Each lesson ends with a **Mini-Task** that invites you to show ways you can live out your faith as a missionary disciple of Christ.

Finally, you will be given ways to think and talk with your family **At Home**.

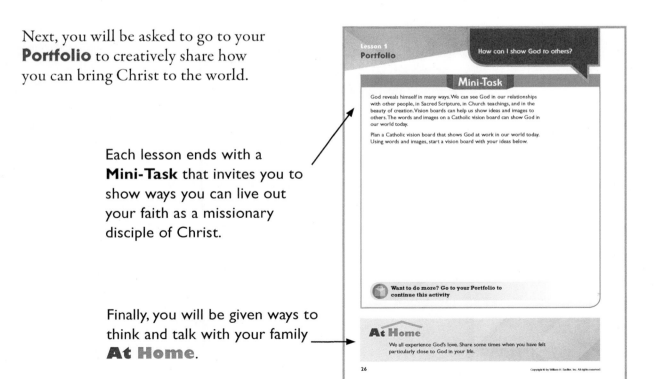

Throughout each lesson you will see interesting icons. They are meant to point you to your online digital portal. Here is what each of these icons means.

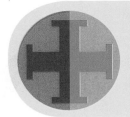

Prayers can be spoken. But did you know that they can also be seen and read? When you see this icon, you will know you can see and read prayers in your digital portal or in the back of your book.

When you see the **Did You Know?** icon, you will know there is more to learn in your digital portal about this subject.

When you see this audio icon, it is time to go to your student portal to read and hear the **Prayer** or **Scripture** so you can learn it by heart.

This icon lets you know that you can hear more about the lesson's **Partners in Faith** in an online video.

Want to do more? There is a lot to do in your **Portfolio**! Items next to this icon are to be done in your digital portal or Portfolio workbook.

Digital discipleship is what identifies who we are as followers of Jesus online. We are called, as disciples of Jesus Christ, to spread his Kingdom wherever we are, and when we are online, we can spread the Kingdom to the whole world. For years you might have read the steps of Catholic Social Teaching and thought, "This is great, but I don't have the time", or "I don't know where to start", etc. Now you can start in your family room, at the dining room table, anytime, anywhere. There are Web sites that can give your family ways to actually show God's love to others in real time. ***Christ In Us*** has some suggestions. Go into your Student portal. And check out your parish Web site. Get involved. You'll feel good. Sharing Jesus makes you and your family feel good, too!

Collect colorful medals as you complete projects, tasks, and play games.

Your Songs for Grade 5

Unit Songs	Liturgical Catechesis Seasonal Songs
Unit 1: We Have Been Told, David Haas	**Lent:** Your Grace Is Enough, Matt Maher
Unit 2: Light of Christ, Tom Kendzia	**The Church Year:** The Lord Has Done Great Things For Us, Jamie Cortez
Unit 3: I Send You Out, John Angotti	**Ordinary Time:** We Are His People, Greg Walton
Unit 4: Here I Am, Lord, Dan Schutte	**Triduum:** I Will Have Faith In You, Sarah Hart
Unit 5: We Are Called, David Haas	

Your journey continues with your login to *Christ In Us* Digital!

Here you can explore all the exciting resources that blend together with your textbook.

Take a look at your personalized online dashboard. Everything you need is at your fingertips!

- Think of your portfolio as your digital backpack! Here you can get your assignments, see reminders, send emails, and even talk to your catechist.
- Interactive Mini-Tasks! Here you will be able to share exciting activities with others. You will be able to get hands on and creative by making videos or interactive posters.
- Go on a game quest! Take your ***Christ In Us*** experience to the next level and earn a medal in the process. Your Grade 5 quest will begin with Saint Ignatius of Loyola.
- Listen with you heart and pray the prayers of *Lectio* and *Visio Divina*, praise, petition, intercession, litany, meditation, blessing and thanksgiving from your lesson.
- Track your progress with digital quizzes and tests.

Have a wonderful year!

Unit 1

The Faith Professed

In this unit you will learn about our Catholic faith and how our belief is revealed both in God's creation and in Sacred Scripture and Tradition. We will see how we share our faith in the Church and with the world.

What do we believe?

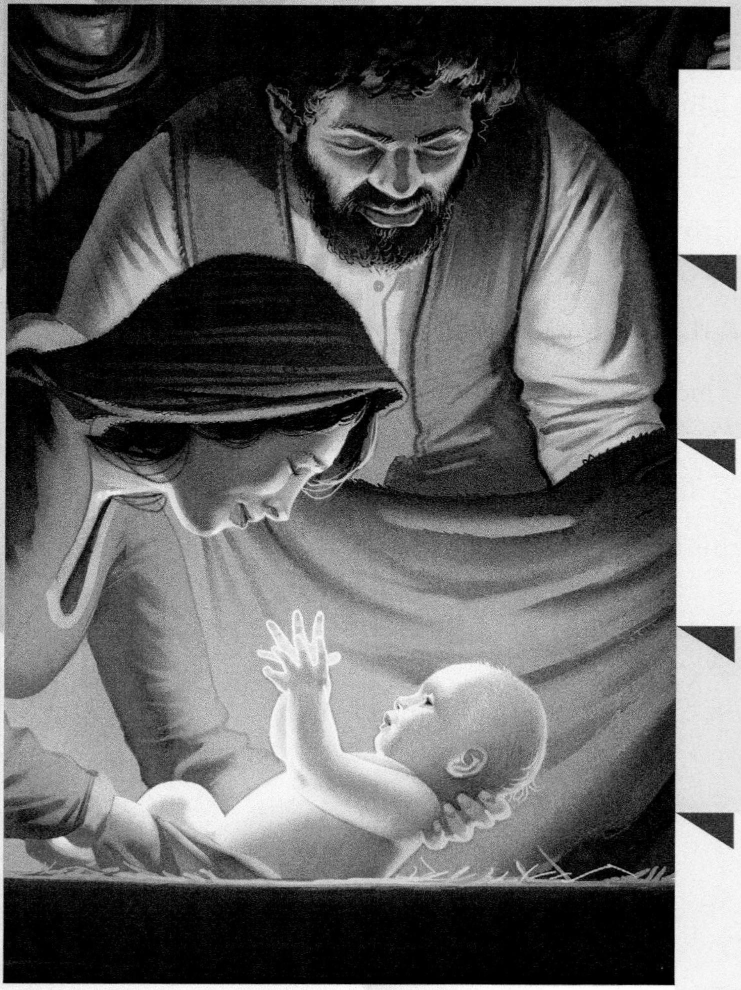

Unit Song:
"We Have Been Told,"
David Haas

Unit Prayer

Leader: Saint Ignatius of Loyola prayed: "Give me only your love and your grace, that is enough for me." Through the sacraments, we discover God's love and grace.

Let us listen to how the sacraments have changed the lives of people among us.

Listen to the stories of Missionary Disciples among us . . .

Leader: Let us pray. Jesus, we receive your love and grace in the sacraments, and through the stories we shared today. In thanksgiving for the gift of the sacraments in our lives, we pray:

Leader: O God, at Baptism we are clothed in your love and sent to be a living sign of Christ.

All: Give me only your love and grace, that is enough for me.

Leader: When you forgive our sins, we celebrate your unconditional love for us.

All: Give me only your love and grace, that is enough for me.

Leader: In the Eucharist you nourish us with your body and blood, filling us with your presence.

All: Give me only your love and grace, that is enough for me.

Leader: With Saint Ignatius we say, "Give me your love and your grace, that is enough for me."

All: Give me your love and your grace, that is enough for me.

End the Unit Prayer by singing the song for this unit.

Missionary Discipleship

How have you been the living sign of Christ with your family and friends? What happened? How did you feel? What are the ways that you are nourished with the Body and Blood of Christ in the Eucharist?

How do we know God?

God has planted in every human heart the desire to know him. God reveals himself to us so that we can share in his life and love. We come to know who God is when we read and listen to Sacred Scripture. We know God when we celebrate and take part in the sacrifice of Jesus at Mass. God reveals himself to us through the Church in Sacred Scripture, in Sacred Tradition, and in the Seven Sacraments.

Meditation

Glory in his holy name;
let hearts that seek the LORD rejoice!
Psalm 105:3

God is truth and love.

God created us out of love. He gave each of us the desire to know our purpose in life, and to discover life's truth and meaning. God never stops calling us to be close to him.

We can never know everything about God, or always understand his plan. God is a **mystery**, which means that he is greater than the human mind's ability to understand. Words will never be enough to describe who God is. But over time, God has gradually revealed the mystery of who he is through his saving words and deeds. **Divine Revelation** is God's making himself known to us. Through Divine Revelation we come to know his plan of salvation for all people.

God is the Truth that all people seek. God is the Love that all people long for. The *Catechism of the Catholic Church* teaches that "God's very being is Truth and Love" (*CCC*, 231).

Faith Words

mystery see p. 294

Divine Revelation see p. 293

God's creation reveals his truth, love, beauty, and goodness. All of creation gives praise and honor to him. We discover that God's love is without limits. Even though the first man and woman turned away from him, God did not end his relationship with humanity. God's covenant with Noah, Abraham, and others shows us that he has never stopped reaching out to us with his saving love.

One way we come to know God is through one another. We are all created in God's image and likeness, so we can see God in each other and in our relationships with others. We have a lot to learn from one another about who God is.

Did You Know?

The Bible writers wrote for different audiences.

What is one way God has reached out to me recently?

Prayer

Meditation

We come to know God through Sacred Scripture.

God reveals himself to us in ways we can understand. One of these ways is through human words. **Sacred Scripture** is holy writings in which God speaks to us in a human way. God lovingly meets us and talks with us in Sacred Scripture. Sacred Scripture is God's Word to us.

God is the author of Sacred Scripture. He inspired human writers to faithfully communicate the truth about who he is. The Holy Spirit guided the minds, hearts, and hands of the human authors of Scripture to write the saving truth about God.

Faith Word

Sacred Scripture see p. 295

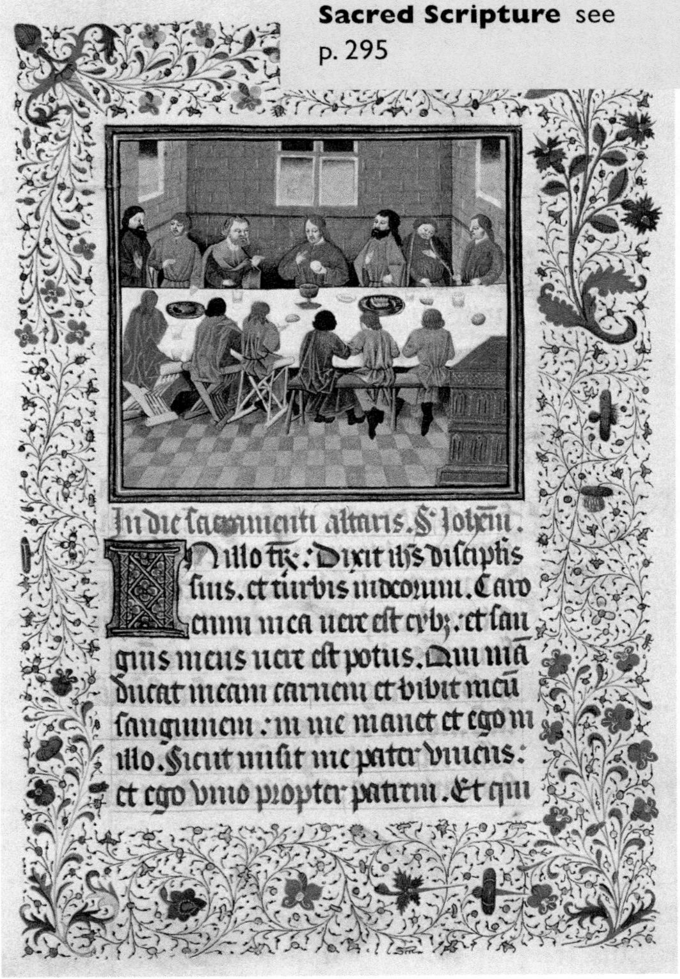

Bibles in the Middle Ages often were illuminated with scenes of stories from Scripture, like this one of the Last Supper from the Gospel of John.

Activity

Here are some names for God, Jesus, and the Holy Spirit that are used in Sacred Scripture. The Holy Spirit helps us understand God's Word. Put a "G" next to the names for God. Put a "J" next to the names for Jesus. Write the letters "HS" next to the names for the Holy Spirit.

Share your favorite name with a friend.

Abba	Father	Messiah
Advocate	Intercessor	Paraclete
Christ	Lamb of God	Son of Man
Counselor	Lord	Spirit of Truth
Creator	Lord God Almighty	Witness
Everlasting God	Master	Yahweh

Sacred Scripture is contained in the books of the Old Testament and New Testament in the Bible. Scripture tells the story of God's love for his people, and their response to his love. When we read or listen to Scripture, the same Holy Spirit who inspired the writers of Scripture helps us understand God's plan for us. We encounter God in Sacred Scripture, because God is present there.

Activity

Name two people who have helped you come to know God. Write a short prayer thanking God for those people in your life.

____

____

____

One Church, Many Cultures

Knowing that we are all made in God's image and likeness can help us understand that we are meant to respect and show kindness to all people. There are people in our communities who may be different from us, but we are all the same in God's eyes. The fact that we are all still made in God's image, despite our differences, reminds us that God is a mystery we can never fully understand. The Church teaches that we can see God's love and care in everyone.

Prayer

Meditation

We come to know God through Jesus.

"For God so loved the world that he gave his only Son, so that everyone who believes in him might not perish but might have eternal life" (John 3:16). This Scripture verse reveals a central truth of Christian faith. God sent his own Son to live among us and to save us. God the Father's love for us is beyond anything we can imagine.

***The Scribe Stood to Tempt Jesus* by James Tissot**

God has never stopped loving us. Even when his people turned away from him, God remained true to his covenant. Jesus Christ is the New Covenant. In Jesus, God fully revealed who he is: always faithful, always loving, and always calling us back to himself.

Jesus tells us that he is the final Word about God. "I am the way and the truth and the life. No one comes to the Father except through me" (John 14:6). We read about the life of Christ in the four Gospels, which begin the New Testament. We know the authors of the Gospels as Matthew, Mark, Luke, and John.

The Gospel writers wanted to share their faith with others. They wanted to share the truth revealed to them by Jesus: "Whoever has seen me has seen the Father" (John 14:9). At the heart of the Gospels is the revelation that Jesus "is the Messiah, the Son of God" (John 20:31).

Every single thing about Jesus' life reveals who God is. Jesus' sacrifice on the Cross and his Resurrection are the fulfillment of Divine Revelation.

Activity

Everything Jesus said and did revealed who God is. Look up the Scripture passages and read them together in small groups.

Luke 5:17–26, Matthew 6:9, John 15:9–14, Mark 4:35–41

Decide which statements below best describe what Jesus is saying about God in each passage.

God is merciful. God is our Father. God is love. God is powerful.

Then choose one of the statements about God. Talk in your groups about how you have experienced this aspect of God in your life. Share your thoughts with a partner.

In the Gospels, we read about how Jesus invited people to follow him. These people became his disciples. Jesus wanted them to live as he did. He taught them to obey God's law and to rely on God, not money, power, or possessions. He invited all people to trust in God and seek God's forgiveness. This was Jesus' mission, to share the life of God with all people and to save them from sin.

Jesus called people to change the way they lived and to love God and others. He told them, "The kingdom of God is at hand. Repent, and believe in the gospel" (Mark 1:15). The Kingdom of God is the power of God's love active in our lives and in the world.

During Mass, we show our reverence for the Good News of Jesus Christ by standing for the proclamation of the Gospel. The deacon or priest kisses the Book of Gospels, which was also honored in the procession at the beginning of Mass. And while the deacon or priest proclaims the Gospel, altar servers often stand on either side of him holding candles. These are a few of the ways we show how important the Gospels are to our lives as Christians.

The deacon or priest then gives a homily that helps us to reflect on the ways in which the Gospel calls us to live as faithful followers of Christ.

Prayer

Meditation

Faith Word

Sacred Tradition see p. 295

The Church shares her beliefs through Scripture, Tradition, and the sacraments.

We also come to know God through the Church. The Church, with the help of the Holy Spirit, guides and teaches us the truth about who God is. At Mass, we read and listen to Sacred Scripture. In the Eucharist, God reveals the depth of his love for us. For in the Eucharist, Christ offers his sacrifice of praise and thanksgiving to his Father. We share in the grace of salvation.

The faith of the Church that has been passed on orally and in writing by the Apostles and their successors is called **Sacred Tradition**. Sacred Tradition is separate from, but closely connected to, Sacred Scripture. Together, Sacred Scripture and Sacred Tradition make the mystery of Christ present in the Church. They shape our faith in Jesus Christ and our life as his disciples.

What Makes Us Catholic?

The things your family does regularly are called "family traditions." The Catholic Church and family has Sacred Tradition. We believe that the Church has passed down teachings and practices. Jesus gave these teaching to the Apostles, who then passed them on to Christ's followers. This Sacred Tradition has been passed down for over 2,000 years. It includes things we still do every time we meet as a Church, like the rituals for the sacraments. When you go to Mass and receive Holy Communion, or attend a Baptism, you are participating in the same practices that have been in the Church from her earliest times.

We especially encounter the Good News of God's love in the Seven Sacraments, which Jesus gave to his Church. The works of creation make Jesus Christ visible in the sacraments. Oil, water, wheat, and grapes remind us of God's powerful work. We share in that work and in God's divine life through the sacraments of the Church, beginning with the new life in Christ we receive in Baptism.

Through Scripture, Tradition, and the sacraments, the Church passes on "to every generation all that she . . . is, [and] all that she believes" (*CCC*, 78). In this way, the knowledge of God reaches the ends of the Earth.

Activity

In the sacraments, we encounter Jesus' presence through word, action, and objects. We, too, are signs of Christ's presence. Choose any of the following ways you will be a sign of Christ's presence for the rest of the week.

Love for the poor, the sick, and the lonely

Love for God

Forgiveness of others

Sharing my gifts with others

Other ideas

Write a journal entry each of next three days, telling how you were a sign of Christ's presence.

____

____

____

Partners in Faith

Saint Ignatius Loyola

Saint Ignatius was a Spanish soldier. He was badly hurt when he was hit with a cannonball. While he was getting better, he read about Jesus and saints. Eventually he founded the religious order called the Jesuits. He helped people know God with his book *Spiritual Exercises*. Saint Ignatius wrote prayers and reflections that we still use. The first Jesuit to be pope was Pope Francis.

Learn more about the life of Saint Ignatius Loyola.

Go forth and set the world on fire.

Prayer

Meditation

Faith Words

mystery **Divine Revelation**
Sacred Scripture **Sacred Tradition**

Show What You Know

Match the terms to the correct definitions.

1. Sacred Scripture
2. Divine Revelation
3. mystery
4. Sacred Tradition

something that is beyond our ability to understand

the way God makes himself known to us

holy writings in which God speaks to us in a human way

the Revelation of the Good News as lived out in the Church, past and present

Live Your Faith

- How can you come to know more about God?

____

____

____

____

____

____

- How can you treat others to show them that they are made in God's image and likeness?

____

____

____

____

____

____

How can I show God to others?

Mini-Task

God reveals himself in many ways. We can see God in our relationships with other people, in Sacred Scripture, in Church teachings, and in the beauty of creation. Vision boards can help us show ideas, and images to others. The words and images on a Catholic vision board can show God in our world today.

Plan a Catholic vision board that shows God at work in our world today. Using words and images, start a vision board with your ideas below.

Want to do more? Go to your Portfolio to continue this activity

At Home

We all experience God's love. Share some times when you have felt particularly close to God in your life.

Who is God?

From the beginning of time, people have searched to know who God is. God gives us ways to enter into the mystery of who he is. Creation is one way we can know God. God also helps us know who he is through the mystery of the Blessed Trinity and through the Church, where God is present in the Seven Sacraments. Jesus' spirit, present in the Church and in the sacraments, helps us understand the mystery of the Blessed Trinity.

Praise

God's very being is love. By sending his only Son and the Spirit of Love in the fullness of time, God has revealed his innermost secret: God himself is an eternal exchange of love, Father, Son, and Holy Spirit, and he has destined us to share in that exchange.

Catechism of the Catholic Church, 221

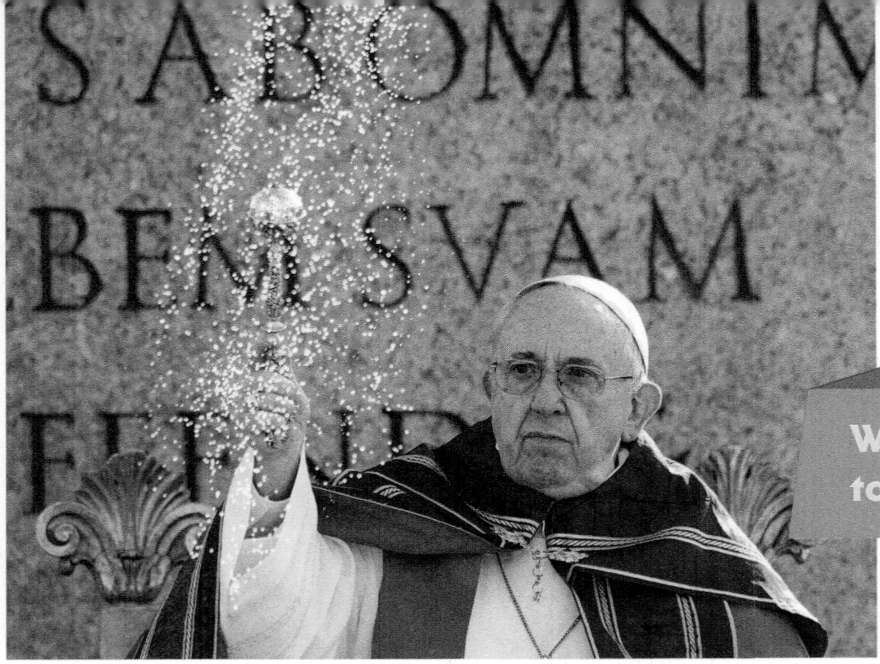

Faith Word

sanctified see p. 295

What has creation taught me?

We can know God through creation and the Church.

God knows that the deepest desire of the human heart is to seek and find him. In his goodness, God has given us ways of coming to know him. One amazing way is through creation. Creation was God's first witness to us of his almighty love and wisdom. In creation, God took the first step toward us. Freely and without any help, God laid the foundation of his loving goodness.

God created us to be open to truth and beauty. When we use this gift of openness, we can look at God's creation and see all that it has to teach us about who God is. A sunset on an autumn horizon might leave us amazed by its beauty. From this experience, we know that God is beauty. When we witness the miracle of new life, such as when a baby bird hatches from its egg or a butterfly emerges from its cocoon, we know that God is life-giving.

The high point of God's act of Creation was the creation of man and woman. God created humans in his image and likeness. He created us with a sense of what is good and right, and with a longing for happiness. God gave us freedom and a conscience and the ability to reason. We can use these gifts to know that God exists.

The Church uses the gifts of creation in her celebration of the sacraments. These gifts, such as water, light, fire, oil, bread, and wine, are **sanctified**, or made holy, in the Seven Sacraments. In the sacraments, we celebrate God's inviting, strengthening, nourishing, healing, forgiving, merciful, just, loving, and serving presence in our lives.

Activity

Think about something that has amazed you about God's creation. What is it? Write down why this is so important to you. Share your thoughts with a partner or with the group.

Did You Know?

There are many ways to bless with holy water.

Prayer

Praise

The Blessed Trinity is a mystery of faith, in which God is revealed as Father, Son, and Holy Spirit.

"In the name of the Father, and of the Son, and of the Holy Spirit. Amen." With these words, we are baptized into the faith of the Church. These words, and the Sign of the Cross marked on the forehead of those celebrating the Sacrament of Baptism, signify the central mystery of the Christian faith: the mystery of the Blessed Trinity. Whenever we pray the Sign of the Cross, we profess an essential belief of the Church.

Through Divine Revelation, God revealed himself as Father, Son, and Holy Spirit. God is the Father, the origin of everything. Together with the creative action of the eternal Word (God's Son), and his Wisdom (God's Spirit), God the Father is the Creator, the author of life. Creation is a joint work of the Blessed Trinity.

Glory Be

The Church teaches these truths about the Blessed Trinity:

- The Trinity is One. We do not speak of three separate gods, but of Three Persons in one God. Each Person of the Trinity is God. They do not share one divinity among themselves.
- God the Father, God the Son, and God the Holy Spirit are distinct from each other. They are not different ways of being God. They are three identifiable Persons. Father, Son, and Holy Spirit are each fully God.
- Father, Son, and Holy Spirit are in relationship with each other, existing in perfect unity and love. They are inseparable in what they are and in what they do.

Activity

Join one of two teams. As your teacher reads the statements, work with your group to decide if each is true or false.

The Blessed Trinity is One.

The Blessed Trinity is three Gods in one Person.

God is the Father, the origin of everything.

The Trinity can only be separated when each Person is doing a particular job, for instance, when Jesus lived on earth.

God the Father and God the Son are the only Persons who are truly God.

Father, Son, and Spirit exist in perfect unity and love.

Creation is a joint work of the Trinity: Father, Son, and Spirit.

The Blessed Trinity is always present in the Church. Most especially, the Trinity is at work in the Seven Sacraments, where we share in God's life. In the sacraments, we encounter Jesus. The gift of the Holy Spirit draws us closer to Christ.

What Makes Us Catholic?

The Blessed Trinity is a very important part of our faith. In A.D. 325, the wording of the Creed was changed to say the Holy Spirit "proceeds from the Father and the Son" (*The Nicene Creed*), not just from the Father. This change helped the Church better understand that the Blessed Trinity is One God in Three Persons. We understand that Saint Patrick used the three leaves of a shamrock to explain the Blessed Trinity to his listeners. Today we can use others symbols to help us understand the Blessed Trinity, like the Trinity Knot, a triangle, or the fleur-de-lis. Which symbol would you use to help you explain the Blessed Trinity?

Prayer

Praise

Jesus' Spirit, present in the sacraments, helps us understand the mystery of the Blessed Trinity.

Think about your best friend's name. What thoughts come to mind when you say it out aloud? Just as when you think of your relationship with your friend, you see that person's face in your mind, or hear his or her voice. Your friend's name, which is simply a series of letters strung together, becomes more important than the word itself. Names are like that. They are much more than what they appear to be, particularly when we know the person.

What thoughts come to mind when you say the name "Jesus"? In the Bible, names often took on significance beyond the actual word. Names signified or described a role a person played in God's plan of salvation.

The name "Jesus" means "God saves." Jesus, in whom God fully reveals himself, is the fulfillment of God's plan of salvation.

Activity

You can probably think of many ways to describe Jesus. Write down five to ten words that describe Jesus for you. They can be things that Jesus said or did, words that describe Jesus, titles of Jesus, qualities of Jesus, or anything you want.

____

____

____

____

____

____

____

When you are finished, choose the three words that are most meaningful to you. Write them on a separate sheet of paper and add them to a classroom word wall.

In order for us to participate fully in God's life, Jesus gave the Church the sacraments. The sacraments, through the power of the Holy Spirit, make Jesus' saving work present.

The *Catechism of the Catholic Church* explains the Spirit's action this way: "The Spirit and the Church cooperate to manifest Christ and his work of salvation in the liturgy. . . . The liturgy is the memorial of the mystery of salvation. The Holy Spirit is the Church's living memory" (*CCC*,1099). The Holy Spirit makes present the mystery of Christ. Every time we gather for liturgy, the Holy Spirit brings us into communion with Christ (*CCC*, 1108). Through the sacraments, "God saves."

Through the sacraments, we share in the very life of God, the Blessed Trinity.

Prayer

Praise

The Church shares her beliefs through Scripture, Tradition, and the sacraments.

From the beginning of time, God's Spirit had been preparing his people for the time of the Messiah. Jesus began his ministry by proclaiming,

"The Spirit of the Lord is upon me,
because he has anointed me
to bring glad tidings to the poor.
He has sent me to proclaim liberty to captives
and recovery of sight to the blind,
to let the oppressed go free,
and to proclaim a year acceptable to the Lord"
(Luke 4:18–19).

These words from the prophet Isaiah meant something important to the people who were gathered in the synagogue listening to Jesus. Through those words, Jesus revealed that his mission and the mission of the Holy Spirit were the same.

From the beginning until the end of time, whenever God the Father sends his Son, he also sends his Spirit. The connection between Jesus and his Spirit is so close that, before he dies, Jesus promises his disciples that he would send the Holy Spirit upon them. The Spirit will be their helper. He would reveal the truth about God.

Then Jesus gives the disciples these instructions: "Go therefore, and make disciples of all nations, baptizing them in the name of the Father, and of the Son, and of the holy Spirit, teaching them to observe all that I have commanded you. And behold, I am with you always, until the end of the age" (Matthew 28:19–20). At that moment, the mission of Christ and the Spirit became the mission of the Church.

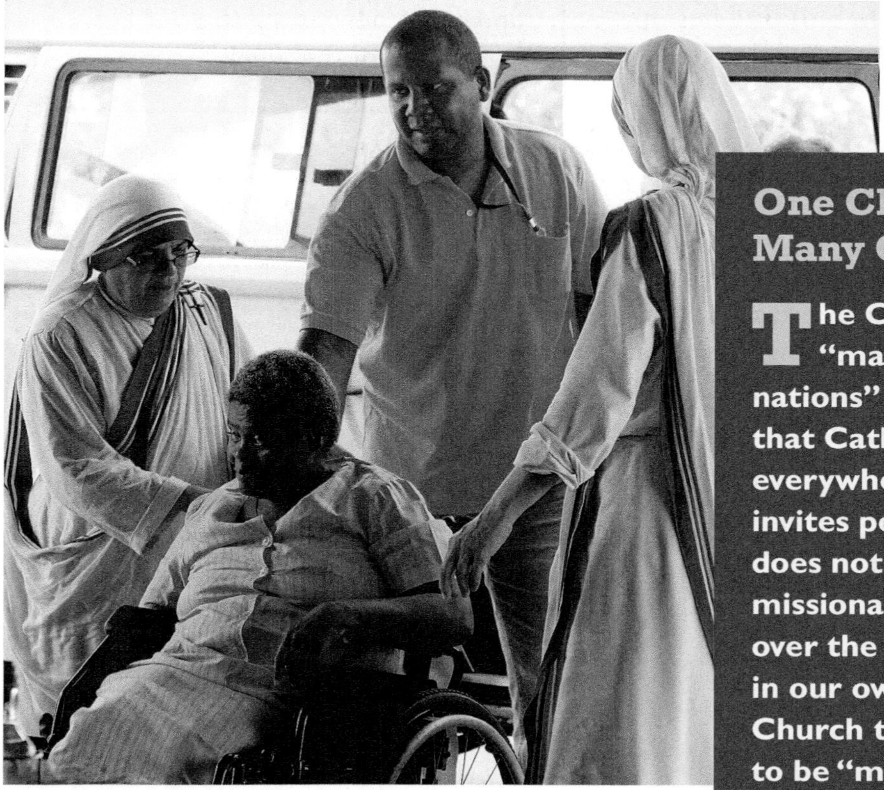

Saint Teresa founded the the Missionaries of Charity to help the poor, sick and disabled. Here they carry out their mission in Brazil.

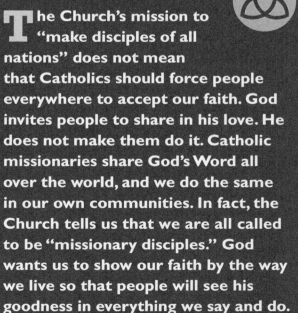

One Church, Many Cultures

The Church's mission to "make disciples of all nations" does not mean that Catholics should force people everywhere to accept our faith. God invites people to share in his love. He does not make them do it. Catholic missionaries share God's Word all over the world, and we do the same in our own communities. In fact, the Church tells us that we are all called to be "missionary disciples." God wants us to show our faith by the way we live so that people will see his goodness in everything we say and do.

In these and other words from the Bible, the love of God as Father, Son, and Holy Spirit is revealed to the Church.

The Church, which is "a communion living in the faith of the apostles which she transmits" (*CCC*, 688), is where we know the Holy Spirit. Some of the ways that we come to know the Spirit are in Sacred Scripture, in Sacred Tradition, in liturgy, and in prayer.

Jesus, more than anyone or anything else, helps us see God's presence in the world. He is the original sacrament. The Church, then, is also a sacrament. Through her sacraments, we experience and celebrate the connection that Jesus made between God and us. The Church is a sign of the unity of the Blessed Trinity and all people. She is Christ's instrument for the salvation of all people.

The Holy Spirit works in the Church to bring her members to Christ and to show us who Christ is. The Spirit opens our minds and hearts to the mystery of Christ's saving love. The Holy Spirit both makes present the mystery of the Blessed Trinity through the sacraments and draws us into communion with God, especially in the Eucharist. The Spirit is always at work in the Church, building her up, bringing her life, and sanctifying her, or making her holy.

Activity

Write a blog entry about the ways the Holy Spirit helps you draw closer to Christ and makes you want to be more like him. Choose one to concentrate on this week, and add a new entry to your blog at the end of the week.

Partners in Faith

Juan de Zumárraga

Juan de Zumárraga was a Franciscan priest in Spain. As a priest, Zumárraga was known for leading a very religious, poor and humble life. With the Spanish king's help Zumárraga became the first bishop of Mexico in 1530. He was given the title "Protector of the Indians." Zumárraga believed his role was to make sure natives in New Spain were not treated poorly. Under his spiritual leadership, he fought for the rights of the people and built the first school, hospital and printing press in Mexico. It was Archbishop Zumárraga who received Saint Juan Diego's cloak with the miraculous image of the Virgin of Guadalupe on December 12, 1531. Zumárraga's fight for the dignity of native peoples helped grow the Church in the New World.

If God does not provide a remedy from his hand, this land will be lost.

Learn more about the life of Juan de Zumárraga.

Faith Word

sanctified

Show What You Know

Complete the sentences.

1. When something is made holy, we say that it is ________________.
2. Water, light, fire, oil, bread, and wine are made holy in the ________________.
3. The Blessed Trinity is a ________________ of faith.
4. The ________________ is a sacrament that reveals the Trinity to God's people.

Live Your Faith

- How would you describe the Blessed Trinity to a friend who does not know God?

____
____
____
____
____
____
____
____

- How can spending time with creation help you know God better?

____
____
____
____
____
____
____

How do I live out my belief in God?

Mini-Task

We are created in the image and likeness of God. And just as the Persons of the Blessed Trinity–Father, Son, and Holy Spirit–are in relationship with each other, we are called to be in relationship with our friends and family.

Bio-poems tell about a person in a special way, using seven lines that describe the person. On the lines below, write a bio-poem about one of your relationships.

First Name:	
Friend of:	
Son/Daughter of:	
Student at:	
Working on:	
Grateful for:	
Last Name:	

Want to do more? Go to your Portfolio to continue this activity.

At Home

God is life-giving. We are called to be life-givers, too. Choose one way your family can show respect for all life.

Why did God make us?

God created us to share in his life and love forever. God created us with a body and a soul, to experience his presence and the wonders of the created world. Through the gift of faith, supported and nurtured through our families and through the Church and the sacraments, we come to know God's plan of holiness and justice. We see the gift of God's grace active in our lives. We grow in holiness, and we look forward to eternal life and friendship with God.

Petition

We give you praise, Father most holy,
for you are great
and you have fashioned all your works
in wisdom and in love.

Roman Missal, Eucharistic Prayer IV, 117

God created us with a body and a soul.

Faith Word

soul see p. 295

God created the universe and everything in it. The greatest of all God's works is the human person. Humans alone, out of all of God's creatures, are able to know and love God.

> *Yet you have made [them]*
> *little less than a god,*
> *crowned [them] with*
> *glory and honor.*
>
> *Psalm 8:6*

God created us to share in his own life. How does this great mystery and miracle happen? At the moment of our conception, our parents join together to form a unique physical body–us! At the exact same moment, God breathes his very life into us. We read about this in the second account of Creation, in which "the LORD God formed the man out of the dust of the ground and blew into his nostrils the breath of life, and the man became a living being" (Genesis 2:7). This breath of life from God refers to the soul. The **soul** is the invisible, spiritual reality within each of us. The soul is immortal. It will never die.

God created humans as a union of a visible, physical body and an invisible, spiritual soul. Every human being is unique. We are given the physical DNA of our parents (our body) and the spiritual DNA of God (our soul). Because we are physical beings, we can see, taste, smell, touch, and hear. We can experience God's creation all around us. But the soul is the spiritual "breath of life" that makes us uniquely human. We have the spiritual ability to know and to love because we each have a soul.

The whole human person, body and soul, is meant to become a temple of the Holy Spirit. One day we will die, but our souls, the breath of God in us, will live forever. At the end of time, our bodies and souls will be reunited when Christ comes again at the Last Judgment.

What is something I have felt deep in my soul?

Did You Know?

Catholics care for themselves, body and soul.

Prayer

Petition

The Church supports and nourishes our faith.

Blaise Pascal, a French mathematician and Catholic theologian, described our desire for God as an "infinite abyss," or space, that only God can fill. God always takes the first step to fill that space. Faith is our response to God's invitation to share in his life, and the way we respond to his call.

For Christians, having faith means believing that God has revealed himself to us through his words and actions, and most especially through Jesus Christ. Faith is a gift from God that guides how we live every day. It is necessary for our salvation. We freely choose to have faith. It is our free response to God, who reveals himself. God does not force it on us.

Faith is also an action–something we do. It is not, however, something we do on our own. No one can believe alone. Faith is not something we can give to ourselves. Faith comes to us in many ways, beginning with God and in our families. Do you remember the first prayers your prayed with your family? Do you remember your first experience of Church–going to Mass, or celebrating a holy day with your family? Our families help the seed of faith grow in us.

Activity

Write about a faith memory that happened in your family. It might be your first Holy Communion, something that happened on your way to Mass, a family celebration of a feast day, or something else entirely. Describe what happened and what this special memory means for you.

____

____

____

____

____

____

____

Share your memory with a partner or your class.

We also experience faith in the Church. The Church teaches us about God, helps us to grow in our knowledge and love of God, and, most especially, nourishes us through her sacraments. In the sacraments, we profess and celebrate everything that we believe and know to be true about God. Through the sacraments, we come to know that God loves us completely, and without limit.

- In the Sacrament of Baptism, we receive faith and new life in Christ.
- In the Sacrament of Confirmation, the outpouring of the Holy Spirit strengthens us to live our faith and be witnesses to God's love in the world.
- In the Sacrament of the Eucharist, we are fed by Christ's Body and Blood.
- In the Sacrament of Penance and Reconciliation, God heals the wounds of sin and division with his forgiveness.
- In the Sacrament of Anointing of the Sick, God heals us spiritually and gives us hope during times of illness and infirmity.
- In the Sacraments of Holy Orders and Matrimony, which are the Sacraments at the Service of Communion, God calls men and women to a life of service and commitment to the gospel.

The Church lives her faith through what she believes and through what she celebrates. We respond to God by faith when we profess, "I believe."

What Makes Us Catholic?

You might think of the word *nourish* in terms of the food you might eat every day, like bread. As Catholics, we are nourished in a special way during the Communion Rite at Mass. Bread and wine are changed into the Body and Blood of Christ. The bread must be made of wheat and without yeast, which would make it rise. The wine has to be made entirely from grapes, with nothing else added. We are not nourished because these items are food and drink. We are nourished by them because they become Christ's own Body and Blood. We recall Christ's sacrifice and pray for the strength to do his work in the world. When you receive Holy Communion at Sunday Mass, think about what this strength helps you to do.

Prayer

Petition

Faith Words

original holiness see p. 294

original justice see p. 294

God created Adam and Eve to live in friendship with him.

When you read the word "paradise," what images come to mind? Images of the Garden of Eden in Scripture help us to imagine the paradise that God created for Adam and Eve:

"The LORD God planted a garden in Eden, in the east, and placed there the man whom he had formed. . . . The LORD God then took the man and settled him in the garden of Eden, to cultivate and care for it" (Genesis 2:8, 15).

God created Adam and Eve to live in friendship and happiness with him forever. We call this state of being **original holiness**. Original holiness is the state of sharing in God's grace, or God's life. This is what God wanted for humans from the beginning.

God created Adam and Eve to live in harmony with themselves, with each other, and with creation. This state of living in harmony is called **original justice**. Original justice was God's plan for humanity, but it was lost by the sin of our first parents.

Through the Sacrament of Baptism, we are freed from Original Sin. God invites us to share in his life. Through the sacraments, most especially the Eucharist, we receive the gift of holiness and the grace to live holy lives.

Tree of Knowledge, Adam and Eve in the Garden of Eden **by Karima Ali.**

God created the first human family in a state of total and complete happiness with God, and in perfect harmony and friendship with one another. God continually calls us back to friendship and harmony with him and with each other. Our own families help the seed of faith grow in us. This happens when family members:

- believe in God and that God cares for them. They turn to God in times of trouble and give thanks to God when all goes well.
- never stop loving and believing in the value of each other.
- spend time together and accept each other.
- profess their faith in God and practice Gospel values. Families recognize God's presence all around them!
- learn about the faith and about Christian values and live them!
- pray together, thanking God for blessings, asking for guidance, and fostering an awareness that God is always present with them.
- serve others, looking for ways to help people who are in need.
- forgive and ask for forgiveness, over and over again!
- celebrate together–birthdays, weddings, births and deaths, graduations, first days of school, family reunions, holidays, and holy days.
- welcome the stranger and practice hospitality.
- act justly in their communities by treating others with respect and dignity.
- affirm life as a precious gift from God.

Activity

In a small group, discuss what it might be like to live in original justice. Together, brainstorm ideas for how everyone in your class can live in harmony with each other–before, during, and after school

Share your ideas with the class. Based on these ideas, develop some classroom rules and guidelines to help everyone live in greater harmony with each other.

Faith Word

particular judgment
see p. 294

For we must all appear before the judgment seat of Christ, so that each one may receive recompense, according to what he did in the body, whether good or evil.

2 Corinthians 5:10

Prayer

Petition

Everyone who dies in God's friendship will have the joy of eternal life with him.

The Church teaches that when we die, Christ will judge us at the moment of our death by comparing our lives to the Gospel message (see Matthew 25:31–46). This is called the **particular judgment**.

At the time of particular judgment, Christ will reward a person either with life with God in heaven; a time of purification, or cleansing; or eternal separation from God in hell.

Our greatest hope as Christians is that we may have eternal life with God. We prepare for this by remaining in relationship with God, following his Commandments, and showing love to others. At the particular judgment, those who have lived holy lives will immediately share in the joy of eternal life in God's presence, or heaven. The Church honors those who now live with God in heaven on All Saints' Day, one of the Holy Days of Obligation.

Activity

The death of a loved one is a sad time for that person's family and friends. Design a sympathy card that could be sent to comfort someone who has lost a loved one. Add a personal message if you have someone specific in mind. Be sure to include a short prayer.

One Church, Many Cultures

The Church celebrates November 2 as All Souls' Day. But on November 1 and 2, many Latin American Catholics celebrate Día de los Muertos, or the Day of the Dead. Families often visit the graves of their relatives. They bring crosses, flowers, candles and other items, and they sometimes play music or read poetry. Afterward, families share a meal to celebrate, remember, and pray for those who have died. In some communities, there are parades with dancers in costumes. The holiday has grown in several countries to include festivals of Latin American culture and the arts.

Those who need to grow in holiness will prepare for heaven in Purgatory. Purgatory is a state of cleansing after death and before heaven. Those in Purgatory have not broken their relationship with God, but they are not yet ready for heaven. As a Church, we are encouraged to pray for souls in Purgatory, especially on All Souls' Day. We pray that they will be prepared for eternal life with God.

Those who have chosen to turn away from God and have refused God's mercy and forgiveness will remain separated from God forever. This eternal separation is called hell.

However, God wants all of his children to respond to his grace in their lives. One important way that Jesus helps us live holy lives is in the sacraments of the Church. These seven celebrations are special signs of God's love and presence. Jesus instituted, or began, the sacraments so that his saving work would continue for all time.

Partners in Faith

Saint Peter

Saint Peter was once a fisherman named Simon. One day, he met Jesus and became his follower. Jesus changed Simon's name to "Peter," which means "the rock." After Jesus' Resurrection, Peter became the head of the Church. He is remembered as the first pope. He was martyred in Rome and is buried at the Vatican.

Learn more about the life of Saint Peter.

"You are the Messiah, the Son of the living God."
Matthew 16:16

Prayer

Petition

Faith Words

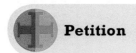

soul **original sin** **original holiness**
original justice **particular judgment**

Show What You Know

Complete the sentences.

1. The judgment by God that each person will face at the moment of death is the
   ______________________ judgment.
2. Original ______________________ is the original state in which humans were created, of being with God in total and complete happiness.
3. The ______________________ is the invisible spiritual reality that makes each of us human and that will never die.
4. ______________________ sin is the sin of the first humans.

Live Your Faith

- How can you take care of your body?

____

____

____

____

____

____

- How can you take care of your soul?

____

____

____

____

____

____

How can I grow in holiness?

Mini-Task

Prayer is our main way to communicate with God.

Talk with a partner about why is it important to take time out of our busy lives for quiet, reflective prayer.

Follow the instructions below to connect with God right at this moment or at any time.

Breath Prayer

God has breathed life into us. . . .
Close your eyes and take a deep breath.
Exhale and breath slowly in and out.
Begin by telling God three things you are grateful for in your life right now.
Ask God to help with any needs, hurts, or worries.
Be silent for a few moments.
Conclude by reciting the Lord's Prayer.
Amen.

Want to do more? Go to your Portfolio to continue this activity.

At Home

Talk with your family members about how you can strengthen one another's faith.

Who is Jesus Christ?

As part of his divine plan of salvation, God sent his Son, Jesus, to become human like us. Through the power of the Holy Spirit, God prepared Mary to be the Mother of his Son. Mary is our model of holiness. The Incarnation is the mystery that Jesus, the only Son of God, became human. He is the Savior who came into the world to save us from sin. We share in the new life that Christ won for us.

Lectio and *Visio Divina*

Apostles' Creed

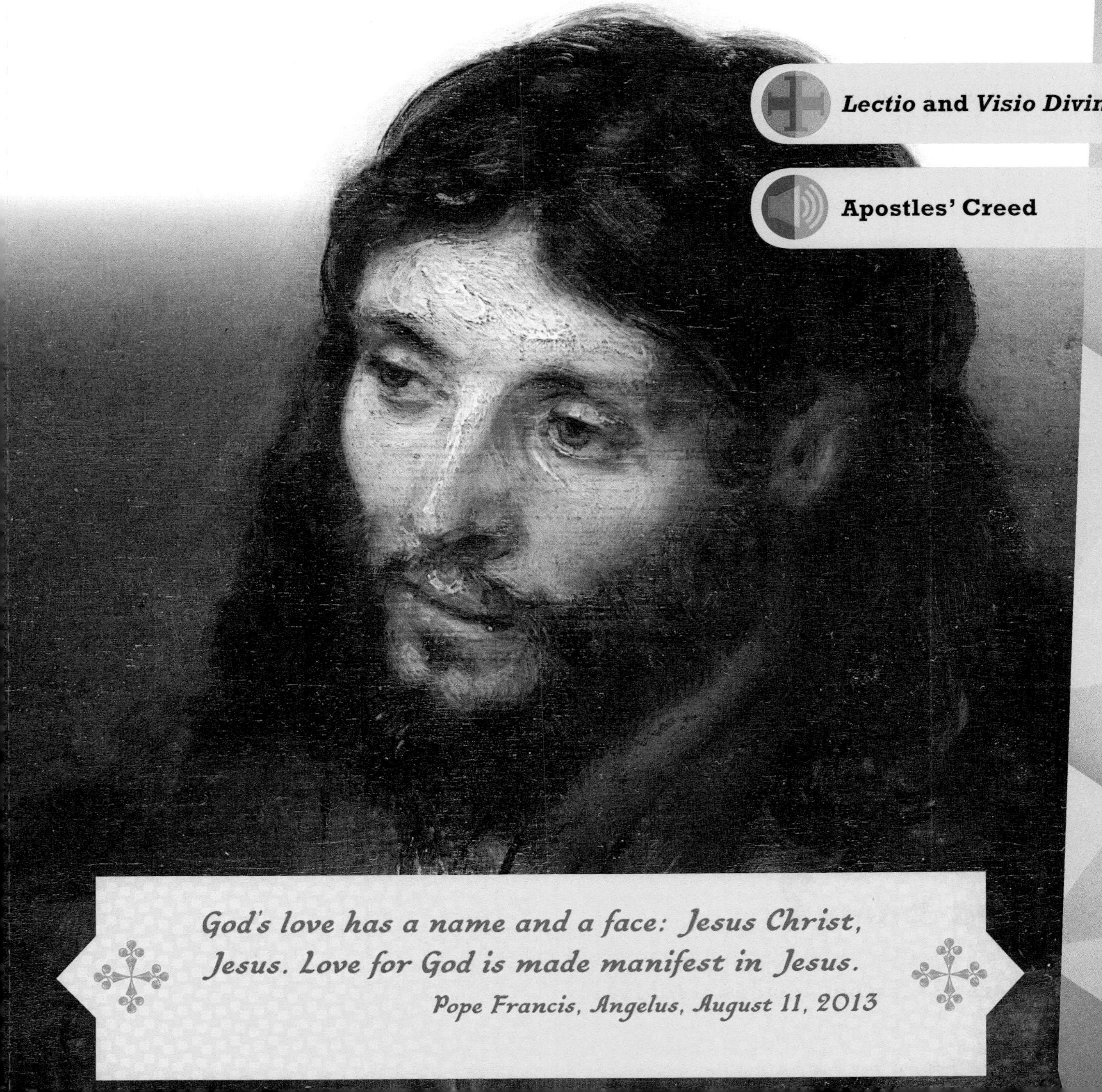

God's love has a name and a face: Jesus Christ, Jesus. Love for God is made manifest in Jesus.

Pope Francis, Angelus, August 11, 2013

The Holy Spirit prepared Mary for her work as the Mother of God.

Since the beginning of time, the mission of God the Son and God the Holy Spirit has been at work in God's divine plan of salvation. Mary, the Mother of God, is the masterwork of this mission.

By grace, the Holy Spirit prepared Mary to be the Mother of God's Son. From the moment Mary came into being, she was immaculate, without sin. Because of her Immaculate Conception, Mary was able to welcome the "gift of the Almighty" (*CCC*, 722).

In what way is Mary a model for me?

Faith Word

Assumption see p. 293

The Holy Spirit fulfills the plan of God the Father's loving goodness in Mary. Mary helps to make the Word of God human. People were able to see and touch Jesus. The Holy Spirit, through Mary, gives the world Emmanuel, God with us.

We honor the Blessed Virgin Mary as the Mother of God. She was fully united with Jesus her Son from the moment of his conception in her womb. She is a model of faithfulness. The **Assumption** of the Blessed Virgin marks the event where Mary, at her death, was taken up by God, body and soul, into heaven. In heaven she shares in the glory of her Son's Resurrection.

One Church, Many Cultures

Latino and Latin American Catholics in the United States have a special connection to Mary as the Blessed Virgin and Mother of God. That connection includes sayings such as *¡Virgen Santísima!* (Holy Virgin) and special Masses to honor Mary. The Cathedral of Our Lady of Divine Providence in Puerto Rico is dedicated to her, and there is a popular devotion to Mary as Our Lady of Guadalupe, whose shrine is in Mexico City. Our Lady of Guadalupe is also the patroness of the Americas.

Activity

Assumption means "to be taken up." *Ascension* means "to rise." Jesus ascended into heaven but Mary was assumed into heaven. Have a panel discussion to talk about the differences between these two words.

Did You Know?

There are various images of Mary.

Prayer

Lectio and *Visio Divina*

Faith Word

Incarnation see p. 293

The Incarnation is the mystery that Jesus, the only Son of God, became human.

The **Incarnation** is the mystery of the union of the divine nature and human nature in one Person, God's Son. We can never totally understand its meaning: that Jesus had both human knowledge and human will, as we do, *and* a divine knowledge and a divine will.

The Incarnation does *not* mean that Jesus was part God and part man. He was not a mixture of human and divine. The Incarnation is the mystery that Jesus became truly human while also remaining truly God.

The events of Jesus' Crucifixion and Resurrection help us understand why this truth is so important. If Jesus was only divine, then his Death on the Cross would not have even been a death as we understand it, because how can God die? There would have been no Resurrection.

Jesus had to be fully human, just like us, to freely choose to die for our sins. If these events only involved God, then they would not have saved us. On the other hand, if Jesus was only human (not divine), he would have simply been like any other good man who died for preaching an unpopular message.

Jesus, the only Son of God, became human to make us sharers in God's own life.

Activity

In the space below, create a mind map of the titles of Jesus. Write a title on the main line and then write words that describe that title. Explain your mind map to a partner.

How do we celebrate the coming of Christ?

The Church celebrates the Incarnation on December 25, the Solemnity of the Nativity of the Lord (Christmas). The Church has four options for the liturgical celebration of Christmas Mass: Christmas Vigil, Mass at Midnight, Mass at Dawn, and Mass During the Day. Each liturgy has a different set of readings.

How are the Eucharist and Jesus as our Savior connected? At the Last Supper, Jesus gave us the gift of his Body and Blood. He said to his disciples, "Do this in memory of me" (Luke 22:19). In the Sacrament of the Eucharist, we join in Jesus' sacrifice. Saint Paul tells us, "For as often as you eat this bread and drink the cup, you proclaim the death of the Lord until he comes" (1 Corinthians 11:26).

The Church's Eucharistic Prayers acknowledge that when we celebrate the Eucharist, we celebrate the memorial of Jesus' Passion, his Resurrection, and his Ascension into glory. Here are examples of two versions of the prayer we pray with the priest after the consecration:

"Therefore, O Lord,
as we celebrate the memorial of the blessed Passion,
the Resurrection from the dead,
and the glorious Ascension into heaven
of Christ, your Son, our Lord,
we, your servants and your holy people,
offer to your glorious majesty
from the gifts that you have given us,
this pure victim,
this holy victim,
this spotless victim,
the holy Bread of eternal life
and the Chalice of everlasting salvation."

Roman Missal, Eucharistic Prayer

"Therefore, as we celebrate
the memorial of his Death and Resurrection,
we offer you, Lord,
the Bread of life and the Chalice of salvation,
giving thanks that you have held us worthy
to be in your presence and minister to you."

Roman Missal, Eucharistic Prayer II

Prayer

Lectio* and *Visio Divina

Faith Word

Paschal Mystery see p. 294

Jesus is the Savior who came into the world to save us from sin.

Jesus' victory over death in the Resurrection teaches us that death is not final. Pope Francis described it this way:

"Death stands behind us, not before us. Before us is the God of the living . . . the final defeat of sin and death, the beginning of a new time of joy and of endless light. But already on this earth, in prayer, in the Sacraments, in fraternity, we encounter Jesus and his love, and thus we may already taste something of the risen life" (*Angelus*, November 10, 2013).

Belief in Jesus Christ and his Resurrection changed the disciples' whole way of looking at life. They encountered the Risen Lord after the Resurrection. In that encounter, they knew that death is behind us. Belief in Jesus and his Resurrection changes our whole way of looking at life, too. The life that we now live is not all there is.

The Seven Sacraments nourish and strengthen us to live as disciples of Jesus. In the Sacrament of the Eucharist, we share in the **Paschal Mystery**: the life, Death, Resurrection, and Ascension of Jesus Christ. At every moment somewhere in the world, the People of God are celebrating the Sacrament of the Eucharist. This means that the Church is always gathering to celebrate Jesus, the Savior who came into the world to save us from sin.

What Makes Us Catholic?

Can you imagine a series of events that makes you want to celebrate all year long? The Paschal Mystery informs our whole year in the Church. In every season, the Church celebrates and remembers events in the birth, life, suffering, Death, Resurrection, and Ascension of Christ. We celebrate in the Mass and on special occasions, including holy days and feast days. Every time we gather together for these celebrations, we share our belief in Christ and in his return in glory. We never run out of reasons to celebrate his life and his love for us.

How are the Eucharist and Jesus our Savior connected? At the Last Supper, Jesus gave us the gift of his Body and Blood. He said to his disciples, "Do this in memory of me" (Luke 22:19). In the Eucharist, we join in Jesus' sacrifice. Saint Paul tells us, "For as often as you eat this bread and drink the cup, you proclaim the death of the Lord until he comes" (1 Corinthians 11:26).

Every time we celebrate the Eucharist, we are made sharers in Jesus' Death and Resurrection. This is a great mystery of our faith: Christ is made present again. We share in the life of God, the Blessed Trinity.

Christ gave himself in thanksgiving to God the Father when he offered himself on the Cross. Jesus experienced death so that we might experience divine life with God forever. He poured out the grace of salvation on the Church. We celebrate God's saving action present in the world today.

Activity

With a team, go on a scavenger hunt for the following words on pages 52–54 in your book. The first team to find the word gets one point. The first team who can correctly define the word for the other team, or use it in a sentence, gets five points.

Incarnation	dawn
memorial	salvation
nourish	encounter
Paschal Mystery	chalice

Prayer

Lectio and *Visio Divina*

At the Ascension, the Risen Christ was taken up into heaven.

God revealed himself to us fully in his Son, Jesus Christ. Jesus is our full and complete encounter with God. When we gather as Church to celebrate the sacraments, we encounter Jesus Christ. Through the power of the Holy Spirit, we experience God's saving grace.

Jesus experienced death so that we might experience divine life with God forever. His sacrifice restored us to new life. When we celebrated our Baptism, we began to share in the Death and Resurrection of Jesus. We were freed from sin and reconciled to God and to each other. In and through Jesus, whose Body and Blood we receive in the Sacrament of the Eucharist, we share in the hope of the Resurrection. Jesus' Resurrection holds the promise of our own resurrection, body and soul, into heaven.

After his Resurrection, Jesus reminded his disciples of their mission to teach and baptize. He told them to spread the Good News of salvation to the ends of the earth (see Matthew 28:18–20). But forty days after his Resurrection, the time came for Jesus to return to his Father. At his Ascension, Jesus entered God's Kingdom completely. He opened the way so that one day we can enter into God's life and eternal happiness. The glory of Jesus, "seated at the right hand of the Father," is the glory we will see at the end of time, when Christ comes again.

The Chapel of the Ascension is a shrine located on the Mount of Olives in Jerusalem. It was built on the site Christians believe to be the spot Jesus ascended into heaven forty days after his Resurrection.

Activity

Use Pope Francis' words as a guide for prayer reflection. Pope Francis asks, "How many times do we say 'Thank you' in our family, our community, and in the Church?"

Write about someone in your family for whom you are grateful.

___

___

___

Pope Francis asks, "How many times do we say 'Thank you' to those who help us, to those close to us, to those who accompany us through life?"

Write about someone who has helped you accomplish something.

___

___

___

Partners in Faith

Saint Catherine Labouré

Saint Catherine Labouré loved Mary. She became a nurse to take care of the sick. One day, Mary appeared to her. She wanted Saint Catherine to make a medal. Mary promised that everyone who wore the medal would be blessed. Saint Catherine made the medal, called the Miraculous Medal. It shows Mary as the Immaculate Conception. Millions of people still wear the medal today.

Learn more about the life of Saint Catherine Labouré.

See the face of God in everyone.

Prayer

Lectio* and *Visio Divina

Faith Words

Assumption **Incarnation** **Paschal Mystery**

Show What You Know

Complete the sentences.

1. Paschal Mystery

2. Incarnation

3. Assumption

4. Ascension

Live Your Faith

- What does Christ's Resurrection and Ascension mean to you?

- How would you describe the importance of Jesus' humanity and divinity to a friend who does not know him?

How do I come to know Mary, the Mother of God?

Mini-Task

There are many titles for and descriptions of Mary.

Review the truths about Mary found in this lesson. From what you know, write your own title for Mary in the top box below. Add three descriptions of what that title means in the spaces provided, and how it can help share a message about Mary with others.

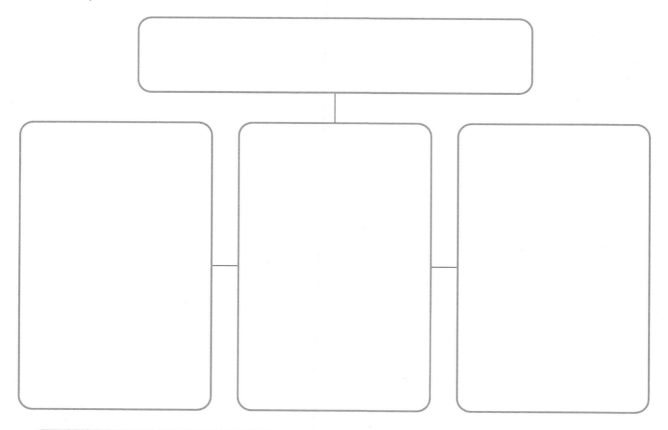

Want to do more? Go to your Portfolio to continue this activity.

At Home

Fearing death is natural, but Christ gives us hope of eternal life. Pray for members of your family who have died.

What is the Church?

The Church is the temple of the Holy Spirit and the sacrament of Christ. The Church is made holy by the Holy Spirit. At Baptism, we become members of the Church. The Church has a mission from God to proclaim to all people everything that Jesus taught and did. She is guided by the Holy Spirit, motivated by love, and united in celebration of the sacraments, where the saving work of Jesus continues until Jesus comes again in glory.

Intercession

This is our faith. This is the faith of the Church. We are proud to profess it, in Christ Jesus our Lord.

Rite of Baptism for Children

In Baptism, we become members of the Church.

Before he returned to his Father in heaven, Jesus sent his Apostles out to all nations to baptize believers. At Pentecost, the disciples told the crowds that Jesus had died and risen to new life. They shared their belief that Christ is the Son of God. Peter told the crowds, "Repent and be baptized, every one of you, in the name of Jesus Christ for the forgiveness of your sins; and you will receive the gift of the holy Spirit" (Acts of the Apostles 2:38).

Many people who heard the Good News of Christ were baptized and became disciples. Baptism is the foundation of Christian life. It is upon Baptism that we build our lives as followers of Christ. Baptism is the sacrament in which we are freed from sin, become children of God, and are welcomed into the Church.

Faith Words

People of God see p. 294

Church see p. 293

grace see p. 293

In Baptism, we enter into the **People of God**. We become members of the **Church**, a community led by the Holy Spirit. In this community, no one is more important than anyone else. God sees us all as his children.

When we are baptized, we receive a share in God's life, called **grace**. The grace of Baptism helps us to believe in God the Father and to love him. It gives us the power to live and act as Christ's disciples in the world.

What makes me feel welcomed?

Did You Know?

The People of God gather together in many ways.

Prayer

Intercession

The People of God are the temple of the Holy Spirit and the sacrament of Christ.

How would you describe the Catholic Church to a friend who is not Catholic? What would you say? As a start, you can look to the saints for guidance. Saints Peter and Paul used images such as the People of God, and the temple of the Holy Spirit, to help the first Christians understand the mystery of the Church.

The people of Israel had long understood themselves to be the People of God, God's chosen ones: "I will take you as my own people, and I will be your God" (Exodus 6:7). Peter helped the first Christians understand that they were Christ's chosen ones, the people through whom God would save the world through Christ and the Spirit.

Saint Peter's message was a new one: No one is excluded from the People of God. The Church is open to everyone, no matter who you are or where you come from. People are invited to become members of the Church through Baptism and their profession of faith in Jesus Christ.

Activity

Each of us is a "temple of the Holy Spirit" (1 Corinthians 6:19). This means that we need to take good care of our bodies so that they will be a worthy place for the Spirit to dwell. Write four ways you take care of your body.

1. ____________________
2. ____________________
3. ____________________
4. ____________________

Now choose something you can do to take even better care of your body. Make a plan to do it.

But you are 'a chosen race, a royal priesthood, a holy nation, a people of his own, so that you may announce the praises' of him who called you out of darkness into his wonderful light.

1 Peter 2:9

The Syro-Malabar Catholic Missionary Sisters of Mary Immaculate help carry out the Church's mission to spread the Good News of salvation through their work at an orphanage in Kerala, India.

Saint Paul described what it meant to be the People of God. He asked Jesus' followers, "Do you not know that you are the temple of God, and that the Spirit of God dwells in you?" (1 Corinthians 3:16).

Paul was telling the people of Corinth that through Jesus Christ, who has poured out his Spirit, God lives in the Church. His Spirit is the breath of life in the Church and is the source and soul of the Church. The Spirit brings unity to the Church and animates, or brings to life, the gifts of the People of God.

The Church is a sacrament of Christ. The Church is a sign of the unity between God and humanity. The Church helps us see God's presence in the world. Through the Church, we can come to know God and share in God's plan of salvation.

The Church continues the mission that Jesus gave to his Apostles: to share the Good News of salvation. Through the Church, we share the message of God's truth and love with all people, everywhere.

Prayer

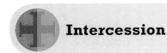

Intercession

The Church is divinely sent, motivated by love, and guided by the Holy Spirit.

Here are some more important things you might tell a friend about the Catholic Church.

- **The Church is divinely sent.** The Church has a missionary mandate. This means that Jesus Christ has sent the Church out into the world to preach the Gospel to all people.
- **The Church is motivated by love.** Christ's saving love is at the heart of the Church's mission. The Church proclaims the fullness of faith, completely and without hesitation. The Church proclaims to all people that life with God forever has been made possible through the life, Death, Resurrection, and Ascension of Jesus. The Church is motivated by the love and unity of the Blessed Trinity.
- **The Church is guided by the Holy Spirit.** Guided by the Holy Spirit, the Church lives Christ's mission to bring the Good News to all people. The *Catechism of the Catholic Church* describes how the Church, "urged on by the Spirit of Christ, must walk the road Christ himself walked" (*CCC*, 852).

Activity

Gather in teams to play a trivia game using questions and answers about your parish. Some questions you might ask include:

What saint is my parish named after? How many Masses does my parish celebrate each week? How many people belong to my parish?

Research the answer to the questions in advance, and then play the game with another team.

The Church is all those who believe in Jesus Christ, have been baptized in him, and are called to follow his teachings. With Christ as its head, the Church is the seed of the Kingdom of God on earth. Through the Church, the power of God's life in the world increases. The Kingdom of God grows when we:

- have faith in Jesus Christ and share our belief.
- live as Jesus did and follow God's will for us.
- seek to build a better community, a more just nation, and a peaceful world.

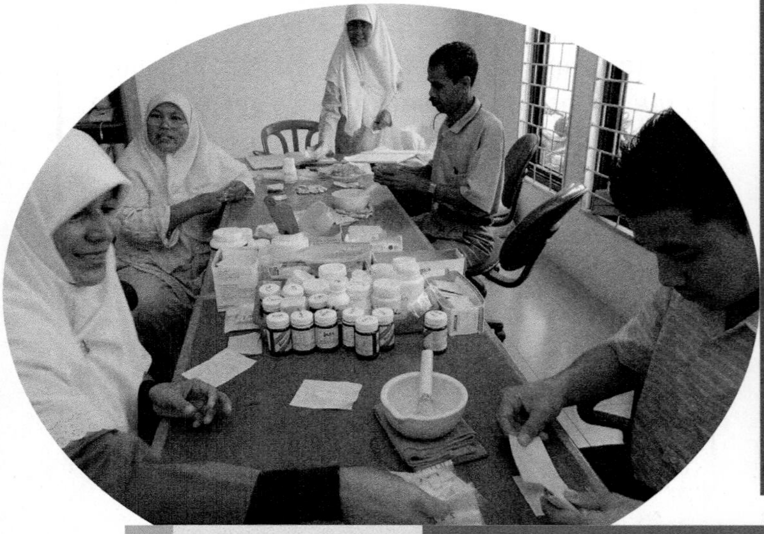

One Church, Many Cultures

Often when there is a natural disaster or another crisis, the Church sends her members to help people all over the world. Catholics bring their skills, talents, and prayers to work in rebuilding homes and businesses, feeding people, and sharing with those in need. For over seventy years, Catholic Relief Services (CRS) has responded to emergencies and helped communities around the world. CRS provides health care, education, and assistance with farming and agriculture, construction, and access to clean water. Wherever the Church goes, she is motivated by God's love. Her members show respect and kindness to everyone, regardless of age, race, or beliefs.

Activity

Each of us is called to help the Kingdom of God grow. In the first circle, write one way you are doing this now. In the each of the other circles, write a new way you would like to build the Kingdom of God.

How I am building the Kingdom of God now

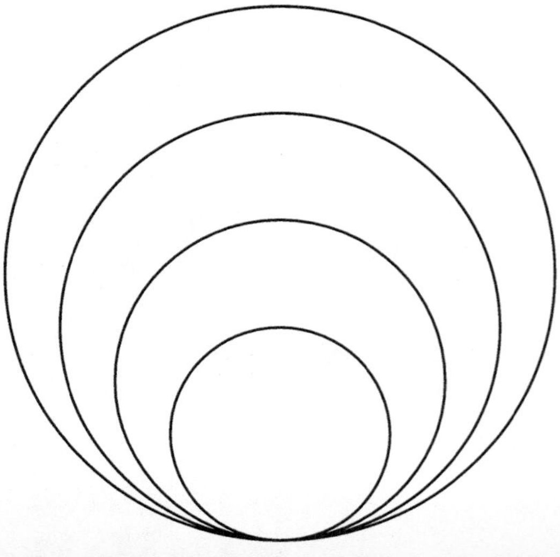

New ways I would like to build the Kingdom of God

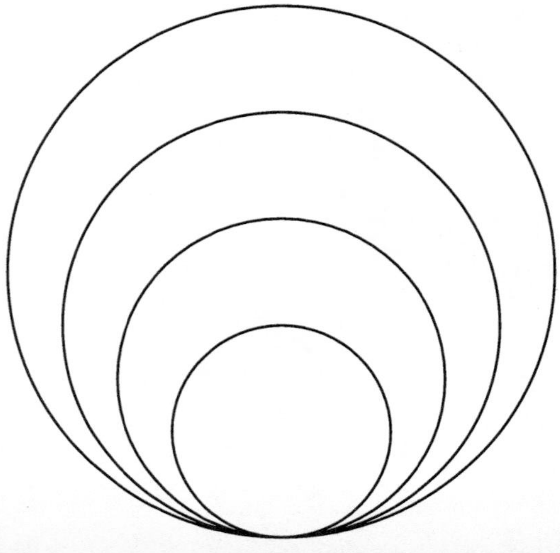

Prayer

Intercession

Through our Baptism, we continue Jesus' work in the Church today.

Everything Jesus said or did pointed to God's love for us. Jesus treated all people with kindness and mercy. How does the work of Jesus continue in the Church today?

Jesus instituted the sacraments so that his saving work would go on for all time. The sacraments link Catholics all over the world with Jesus and with one another. The Church is a sign of God's love and care, and of the unity of the Blessed Trinity.

Jesus sent his Apostles and their successors out into the world to proclaim the faith. He gave them a share in his own mission and the power to act in his name. Bishops, together with the priests and deacons, serve the Church by teaching the faith and celebrating the sacraments.

At Baptism, we are freed from sin. But what about the sins we commit after Baptism? Jesus sent his Apostles to preach repentance and forgiveness of sins in his name. Now, bishops and priests have the power to forgive sins through Christ in the Sacrament of Penance and Reconciliation. In this sacrament, those who are truly sorry confess their sins to a priest and are forgiven. We also promise to repair the harm caused by our sins. When we receive this sacrament, our relationship with God and the Church is made whole again.

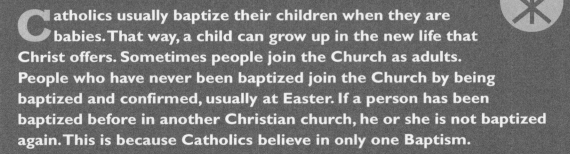

What Makes Us Catholic?

Catholics usually baptize their children when they are babies. That way, a child can grow up in the new life that Christ offers. Sometimes people join the Church as adults. People who have never been baptized join the Church by being baptized and confirmed, usually at Easter. If a person has been baptized before in another Christian church, he or she is not baptized again. This is because Catholics believe in only one Baptism.

When children who were not baptized as infants are preparing to receive the Sacraments of Christian Initiation, they celebrate the Rite of Acceptance into the Order of the Catechumens. A part of this Rite is the signing of the forehead and other senses with the Sign of the Cross. The signing reminds people that they are called to carry out the work of Jesus in the world.

Christ has called you to be his friends. Always remember and be faithful to him.

Therefore, I mark your forehead with the Sign of the Cross. It is the sign of Christians; let it remind you always of Christ and how much he loves you.

I [we] mark your ears with the Sign of the Cross; hear the words of Christ.

I [we] mark your eyes with the Sign of the Cross: see the works of Christ.

I [we] mark your lips with the Sign of the Cross: speak as Christ would speak.

I [we] mark the sign of the cross over your heart: make your heart the home of Christ.

I [we] mark your shoulders with the Sign of the Cross: be strong with the strength of Christ.

I [we] mark your hands with the Sign of the Cross: touch others with the gentleness of Christ.

I [we] mark your feet with the sign of the cross: walk in the way of Christ.

Rite of Christian Initiation of Adults

Activity

Use the baptismal prayer to think about how Jesus works in your life.

What are some words of Jesus that come to your mind right now?

Partners in Faith

Blessed Sára Salkaházi

Blessed Sára Salkaházi was a Hungarian nun who died during World War II. As a young woman, she became a journalist and then joined the Sisters of Social Service. Blessed Sára did charity work, ran a religious bookstore, and established a college for women. She tried to protect young Jewish women from persecution by the Nazis in Hungary by hiding them in a home. Blessed Sára's work was discovered, and she was killed by the Nazis.

Learn more about the life of Blessed Sára Salkaházi.

Prayer

Intercession

Faith Words		
People of God	Church	grace

Show What You Know

Unscramble the words to complete the sentences.

hchcru **eepltm** **eeoppl** **tiisrp**

1. ______________________ is a share in God's life.
2. We are the ______________________ of God.
3. Saint Paul called the Church the ______________________ of the Holy Spirit.
4. The Holy ______________________ guides the Church.

Live Your Faith

- What does it mean to you to be a member of the Church?

____

____

____

____

____

____

____

- How do you continue Jesus' work in the Church today?

____

____

____

____

____

____

____

Portfolio

How does my parish reflect the work of the Church?

Mini-Task

The Church is more than a building. Guided by the Holy Spirit, the Church is made up of members, the People of God, who believe in and follow the teachings of Jesus. That includes you!

Part of being a member of the Church is inviting others to share your faith. On the lines below, write a one-minute commercial for your parish. Your commercial should be about 100 words long. Be sure to include what is special about your parish, how being a member helps you, and why everyone is welcome to join.

Want to do more? Go to your Portfolio to continue this activity.

At Home

Discuss stories of baptisms in your family. Talk about why it was important to your family to baptize your children.

Unit 2

The Faith Celebrated

In this unit you will learn about some of the special celebrations of the Catholic Church, especially the Mass and the sacraments. We will see how these celebrations show God's love for us through the Church.

How do we celebrate what we believe?

Unit Song:
"Light of Christ," Tom Kendzia

Unit Prayer

Leader: As we learn to celebrate God's love in the world, Saint Ignatius told us that love is shown more in deeds than in words. We tell people how much we love them by the way we act. Through the Mass and sacraments we learn how to show this love and are able to let the love of Christ live and speak through us.

Let us listen to the stories of Missionary Disciples among us who show God's love through their lives.

Leader: Let us pray:
O God, your love surrounds us, and we especially know your love through your Son Jesus. Help us to celebrate your love in the sacraments you have given us.

Leader: O God, helps us to celebrate the gift of our Baptism.

All: Help us to be the light of Christ in the world.

Leader: We thank you for your forgiveness.

All: Help us to be the light of Christ in the world.

Leader: Help us to celebrate your love by praying and singing at Mass.

All: Help us to be the light of Christ in the world.

Leader: With Saint Ignatius we pray, "Let our lives be a sign of your love."

All: Let our lives be a sign of your love.

End the Unit Prayer by singing the song for this unit.

Missionary Discipleship

In what way has part of the celebration of the Mass helped you to show God's love to others? What was it? How did you act? How did you feel?

How does Jesus share God's life with us?

So that we would be able to share in God's life and grace, Jesus Christ gave the Church the sacraments. Jesus is with us when we celebrate the liturgy, and the Holy Spirit prepares us to receive Christ in the sacraments. We receive special graces from the Seven Sacraments. Sacramentals help us respond to God's grace we receive in the sacraments. They are sacred signs that help us on the journey to holiness.

Litany

The grace of the Lord Jesus Christ and the love of God and the fellowship of the Holy Spirit be with all of you.

2 Corinthians 13:13

Faith Word

liturgy see p. 294

What is a special memory I have from a Mass I have attended?

Jesus is with us when we celebrate the liturgy.

You may wonder, "Why do we have to go to Mass?" A better question might be, "Why would we *not* want to go to Mass?" Jesus is there in the most special way. He is waiting to fill us to the brim with his love.

Every time the Body of Christ, the Church, gathers to celebrate the **liturgy**, the prayer and work of the Church, Jesus is there. In fact, Jesus is at work in every liturgy, drawing us closer to God the Father, through the power of the Holy Spirit. Jesus is with us, making present his Paschal Mystery. Through the power of the Holy Spirit, we participate in this mystery of our salvation–the Death, Resurrection, and Ascension of Jesus.

Christ acts through the liturgy, particularly the sacraments, to communicate God's grace. He is always present, pouring out God's life upon us.

Did You Know?

Mass is celebrated in various languages.

Prayer

Litany

Faith Word

sacraments see p. 294

The Holy Spirit prepares us to receive Christ in the sacraments.

The power of the Holy Spirit makes possible Jesus' presence in the liturgical celebrations and **sacraments** of the Church. The Holy Spirit calls us together and prepares us to meet Christ. In the liturgy of the Church, the Holy Spirit is our teacher. The *Catechism of the Catholic Church* calls the Holy Spirit the "artisan of 'God's masterpieces,'" the sacraments (*CCC*, 1091).

In the sacraments, the Holy Spirit recalls the mystery of Christ. Together with the Church, the Spirit manifests, or makes known, Christ and his work of salvation. This is why the Church teaches that "the Holy Spirit is the Church's living memory" (*CCC*, 1099).

The Holy Spirit prepares our hearts and minds to encounter Jesus when we celebrate the sacraments. This preparation is the joint work of the Holy Spirit and all those gathered, especially the ministers. The Holy Spirit works within us to awaken our faith, turn our hearts to God, and give us the grace to know what God wants for us.

Activity

The following are some of the roles of the Holy Spirit in the Church. Write what they mean to you.

Teacher ______________________________

Advocate ______________________________

Life-giver ______________________________

Opener of hearts ______________________________

What role do you want the Holy Spirit to have in your life right now? Share your answer with a partner.

How is the Holy Spirit at work in the sacraments? When we celebrate the sacraments, we are not simply recalling the events that saved us—the Death, Resurrection, and Ascension of Jesus. Rather, through the outpouring of the Holy Spirit, these events are made present.

For example, in the Liturgy of the Word during the Mass, the Holy Spirit is present in the Word of God. The Holy Spirit opens our hearts and helps us to understand the meaning of what we hear so that we may live out that meaning in our daily lives. The Holy Spirit awakens our memory of everything that Christ has done for us.

During the Liturgy of the Eucharist, the priest asks God the Father to send the Holy Spirit so that the offerings of bread and wine may become the Body and Blood of Christ. This calling, or "invocation upon" the Holy Spirit, is at the heart of each sacramental celebration, especially the Eucharist.

The Holy Spirit is present in every sacrament, working to bring us into communion with Christ and to form his Body.

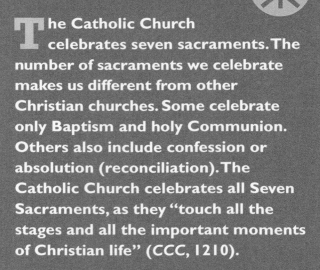

What Makes Us Catholic?

The Catholic Church celebrates seven sacraments. The number of sacraments we celebrate makes us different from other Christian churches. Some celebrate only Baptism and holy Communion. Others also include confession or absolution (reconciliation). The Catholic Church celebrates all Seven Sacraments, as they "touch all the stages and all the important moments of Christian life" (*CCC*, 1210).

Activity

In small groups, create storyboards to show what happens during one of the parts of the Mass listed below. Put together each group's storyboard to create a picture book. Share it with younger children to help them understand the Mass. You can use the Roman Missal to help you get started.

- Introductory Rites
- Liturgy of the Word
- Liturgy of the Eucharist
- Communion Rite
- Concluding Rites

Prayer

Litany

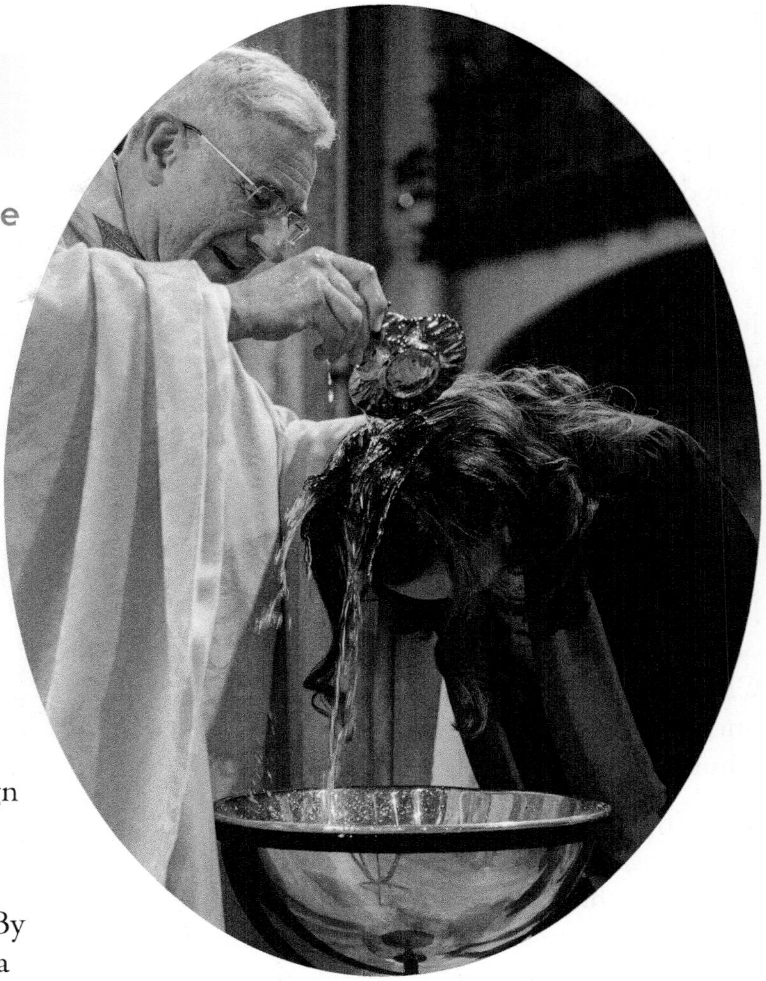

The Church shares signs of God's grace through the sacraments.

A sign stands for or tells us about something. A sign can be something that we see, such as a stop sign. A sign can be something that we do, such as shaking hands or hugging someone. An event or a person can also be a sign.

The world is filled with signs of God's love. Jesus Christ is the greatest sign of that love. Everything that Jesus said or did pointed to God's love for us. Jesus treated all people fairly. He welcomed people whom others neglected. He fed those who were hungry and he forgave sinners. Jesus is the greatest sign of God the Father's love because he is the Son of God.

The Holy Spirit helps us to be signs of Jesus. By continuing Jesus' work, the Church herself is a sign of God's love and care.

The Church's Seven Sacraments are celebrations that are special signs of God's love, presence, and saving power. Jesus instituted, or began, the sacraments so that his saving work would continue for all time.

The sacraments are different from all other signs. Sacraments truly bring about what they represent. For example, in Baptism, we not only celebrate being children of God, we also actually become children of God. This is why we say that a sacrament is an effective sign given to us by Jesus through which we share in God's life.

Christ is at work in the sacraments. We receive the gift of sharing in God's life, or sanctifying grace. This grace helps us to trust and believe in God. It strengthens us to live as Jesus did. We receive special graces from each of the sacraments when we celebrate them properly.

Activity

The Seven Sacraments are celebrations of God's love and presence. As a group, talk about what comes to mind when each of the sacraments is named.

- **Baptism**
- **Confirmation**
- **Eucharist**
- **Reconciliation**
- **Anointing of Sick**
- **Holy Orders**
- **Matrimony**

In the Sacrament of Baptism, we are cleansed from Original Sin and become children of God. We become members of the Church.

In the Sacrament of Confirmation, we are sealed with the Gift of the Holy Spirit. Confirmation strengthens us to live as Christ's followers.

In the Sacrament of the Eucharist, we receive the Body and Blood of Christ. Our community of faith is nourished by God's life. We are called to become the Body of Christ in the world.

The Sacrament of Penance and Reconciliation reconciles members of the Church with God and with the Church. When we receive this sacrament, our relationship with God and the entire Church is made whole again.

The Church offers the Sacrament of the Anointing of the Sick to those who are very sick or near death. God gives those who receive this sacrament the grace to respond to their illness with hope. The sacrament can strengthen their faith in a loving God.

The Sacraments of Holy Orders and Matrimony strengthen those who receive them to serve God and the Church through a particular vocation–the ministerial priesthood and married life.

Activity

Which sacraments have you received? List them here. Then, think about what receiving these sacraments means to you. How do they bring you closer to God and to others?

Sacraments I have received	How they bring me closer to God and others

Prayer

Litany

Faith Word

sacramentals see p. 294

Sacramentals give us grace to share God's love and mission.

What might you find in a Catholic home, on the walls or in other places? A crucifix, a Bible, a statue of Mary, a Guardian Angel plaque, an icon of a saint? And why would you find these particular items in a Catholic home? Each of these objects are **sacramentals.**

Sacramentals are blessings, actions, and objects that help us respond to God's grace. Blessings are the most important sacramentals. Not only is the blessing itself a sacramental, but what is blessed can also become a sacramental. Every blessing praises God and prays for God's gifts.

Here are two blessings you can pray every day:

In the morning, trace a small cross on your lips and say:

> Lord, open my lips,
> and my mouth will proclaim your praise.

When going to bed at night, pray:

> Protect us, Lord, as we stay awake;
> watch over us as we sleep,
> that awake, we may keep watch with Christ,
> and asleep, rest in his peace.

from *Catholic Household Blessings and Prayers*

Activity

Choose from one of the following people or situations and write a blessing for it.

- Leaving for school and/or work for the day
- For safety while traveling
- For sick friends and relatives
- For a team preparing for practice
- For people who have no one to pray for them

____

____

____

One Church, Many Cultures

Many Filipino-American Catholics participate in a devotion to Santo Niño de Cebu, the Holy Child Jesus. Dating back to 1565 in Cebu, in the Philippines, a statue of Jesus as a child has been the site of the largest gathering for this devotion. There is a copy of this statue in St. Augustine Catholic Church in Philadelphia. In the United States and other countries, a statue representing the Santo Niño is dressed in bright clothing for the Feast of Santo Niño, or *Sinulog*. The nine-day devotion begins with a parade and ends with a Mass. It includes a closing procession with members of the assembly holding images of the Santo Niño.

Sacramentals are used in the liturgy and in personal prayer. Here are some examples of sacramentals:

- blessings of people, places, foods, and objects
- objects such as rosaries, medals, crucifixes, blessed ashes, and blessed palms
- actions such as praying the Sign of the Cross and sprinkling blessed water.

Many sacramentals remind us of the sacraments and of what God does for us through the sacraments. Sacramentals also make us more aware of God's presence in our lives and keep us focused on God. In particular, they prepare us to receive God's grace and cooperate with it. Sacramentals can help make every event in our lives holy. Blessing the food we eat, praying the Sign of the Cross as we enter or leave a church, and seeing a crucifix in our home are all reminders that God is with us.

Partners in Faith

Saint Elizabeth Ann Seton

Saint Elizabeth Ann Seton is the first saint born in the United States. She was raised as a Protestant in New York. After her husband died, she joined the Church. She founded the first girls' school for Catholics in the United States. Soon other women joined her, and she started the Sisters of Charity to work with poor children.

Learn more about the life of Saint Elizabeth Ann Seton.

Pay attention to the suggestions of grace.

Prayer

Litany

Faith Words

liturgy **sacraments** **sacramentals**

Show What You Know

Complete the sentences.

1. Blessings, actions, and objects that help us respond to God's grace in the sacraments are called ______________________.
2. ______________________ are effective signs given to us by Jesus through which we share in God's life.
3. The ______________________ prepares our hearts and minds to encounter Jesus when we celebrate the sacraments.
4. The ______________________ is the work and prayer of the whole Church.

Live Your Faith

- What does the gift of grace that you receive in the sacraments do for you?

____

____

____

____

____

____

- How are you a part of the liturgy?

____

____

____

____

____

____

Where do I meet Jesus?

Mini-Task

Jesus is really and truly present in the celebration of the liturgy. He is present in the Eucharist, in the priest, in the Word, and in us, the People of God gathered to celebrate.

How are you changed by encountering the real presence of Jesus at Mass?

How do you share his love on an average day?

Plan a one-minute video testimonial about the way or ways you feel changed by meeting Jesus.

On the lines below, write a brief script for your video.

Want to do more? Go to your Portfolio to continue this activity.

At Home

Through the Holy Spirit's action, we are drawn close to Jesus and receive grace. We are drawn close to each other, too. The next time your family goes to Mass, take a minute to look around. Remember that every person there is your brother or sister in Christ.

How do we praise and thank God?

The Church praises and thanks God all year long with sacramental celebrations. Those celebrations include the Mass, where we learn about God's love for his people in the Liturgy of the Word. Throughout the year, we participate in liturgical celebrations and in the Church's blessings and devotions, when we worship God and honor models of holiness.

Petition

The celebration of Mass, as the action of Christ and of the People of God . . . is the center of the whole of Christian life for the Church . . . moreover, during the course of the year, the mysteries of redemption are celebrated so as to be in some way made present.

Roman Missal, 1.16

We learn about God's love for his people in the Liturgy of the Word.

Faith Word

Liturgy of the Word
see p. 294

Liturgy is the gathering of the Church, the Body of Christ, to worship God. It is the official, public prayer of the Church. We gather to bless and adore God the Father, who is the source of all the blessings of creation. We worship and adore God who offers us salvation, blesses us with his Son, and invites us to be his children.

The most important liturgy of the Church is the Mass, in which we gather to celebrate the Eucharist. Through the power of the Holy Spirit, we join with Jesus in giving thanks and praise to God the Father.

An essential part of the Mass is the **Liturgy of the Word**. This is the part of the Mass in which we listen and respond to God's Word.

On Sundays, we listen and respond to three Scripture readings. We hear about God's great love for his people in the first reading, from the Old Testament. We hear about the life and teaching of Christ in the second reading, from the New Testament. The proclamation of the Gospel is the high point of the Liturgy of the Word because it includes the words of Jesus himself. After the Gospel, the priest or deacon helps us to understand God's Word and apply it to our lives. We profess our faith and pray for all people in need.

How does listening to Scripture at Mass help me?

Did You Know?

The Liturgy of the Word is proclaimed in many ways.

Our Lady of Kamelan is the patron saint of Guam.

Faith Word

liturgical year see p. 294

Prayer

Petition

We worship God and honor our models of holiness throughout the liturgical year.

The Church has special days and times of the year that are important. We remember these times in the celebration of the liturgy. In the liturgy throughout the year, we remember and rejoice in the saving actions of Jesus Christ. The calendar that guides the liturgies and celebrations of the Church year is called the **liturgical year**.

During the liturgical year, we recall and celebrate the whole mystery of Jesus Christ. We celebrate the birth of the Son of God and his younger years, public ministry, suffering, Death, Resurrection, and Ascension into heaven. We celebrate the coming of the Holy Spirit upon the Apostles at Pentecost. And during the year, we venerate, or show devotion to, Mary, the Mother of God, and all the saints.

The Church honors the Blessed Virgin Mary, Mother of God, with a special love. Because she is so closely connected to the saving work of Jesus, the Church admires and raises her up as a model of discipleship. Everything Mary says and does points us to her Son: "Do whatever he tells you" (John 2:5). This is why, throughout the liturgical year, we celebrate the Marian holy days and feast days.

Activity

Use the definitions to identify seasons of the liturgical year. Write the season below each definition. Break into groups to discuss why certain colors are associated with the seasons.

Celebration of Resurrection

____

Coming of Holy Spirit

____

Third Sunday of Advent

____

Time for growing and learning

____

Time of penance

____

Time of waiting before Christmas

____

Marian Feasts and Holy Days

Feast	Event	Date
The Virgin Mary's Nativity	The birth of Mary	September 8
The Presentation of Our Lord	Mary and Joseph present Jesus in the Temple.	February 2
The Visitation of the Virgin Mary	Mary visits her cousin Elizabeth.	March 31
Holy Days	**Event**	**Date**
Immaculate Conception	Mary is conceived without Original Sin.	December 8
Holy Mary Mother of God	Mary is the Mother of God.	January 1
The Annunciation	The Angel Gabriel appears to Mary, announcing that God has chosen her to be the Mother of God.	March 25
Assumption	Mary is assumed into heaven.	August 15

The Church also honors saints during the liturgical year. The saints are holy men and women who have suffered and been glorified in Christ. Their lives of holiness show us what it means to enter into the Paschal Mystery. The Church holds up the saints as models of faithfulness. They teach us what it means to live the Gospel. Their lives draw us closer to God the Father, through Christ.

Our Lady of Kamelan

Activity

Talk in small groups about things that happen during the changing of seasons. You can discuss the weather, activities, holidays, and other events. Do you feel more connected to Jesus during any particular season?

Prayer

Petition

The Church's worship and celebrations are connected by the Apostolic Tradition.

If you visit a parish for Mass on the other side of the world, you will likely experience liturgical traditions different from your own. This is because churches in different areas of the world celebrate the mystery of Christ in ways that are unique to their cultures. They celebrate the same truth–the same Paschal Mystery–just a bit differently! These liturgical differences actually enrich the Church. The *Catechism of the Catholic Church* tells us: "The mystery of Christ is so unfathomably rich that it cannot be exhausted by its expression in any single liturgical tradition" (*CCC,* 1201).

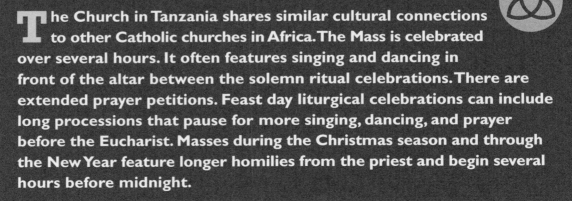

At the same time, many things about the celebration of Mass on the other side of the world will be familiar to you. This is because the Church celebrates the same Paschal Mystery: the Passion, Death, Resurrection, and Ascension of Jesus. From the first Pentecost to today, we celebrate the one faith received from the Apostles and passed down through the Apostolic Tradition.

One Church, Many Cultures

The Church in Tanzania shares similar cultural connections to other Catholic churches in Africa. The Mass is celebrated over several hours. It often features singing and dancing in front of the altar between the solemn ritual celebrations. There are extended prayer petitions. Feast day liturgical celebrations can include long processions that pause for more singing, dancing, and prayer before the Eucharist. Masses during the Christmas season and through the New Year feature longer homilies from the priest and begin several hours before midnight.

We read in the Acts of the Apostles that the first Christians gathered in their homes to study the teachings of the Apostles and to break bread and pray together (see Acts of the Apostles 2:42–47). The earliest account of the institution of the Lord's Supper appears in Saint Paul's letter to the Corinthians.

> For I received from the Lord what I also handed on to you, that the Lord Jesus, on the night he was handed over, took bread, and, after he had given thanks, broke it and said, 'This is my body that is for you. Do this in remembrance of me.' In the same way also the cup, after supper, saying, 'This cup is the new covenant in my blood. Do this, as often as you drink it, in remembrance of me.' For as often as you eat this bread and drink the cup, you proclaim the death of the Lord until he comes.
>
> 1 Corinthians 11:23–26

***La Ultima Cena (The Last Supper)* by Carducho Bartolome was painted in 1605. Notice that the bread is leavened, unlike the flat unleavened bread in Jewish tradition.**

Blessed be the God and Father of our Lord Jesus Christ, who has blessed us in Christ with every spiritual blessing in the heavens.

Ephesians 1:3

Prayer

Petition

Blessings and devotions honor God and our models of holiness.

Of all the many different kinds of sacramental–blessings, actions, and objects that help us respond to God's grace in the sacraments–blessings "come first" (*CCC*, 1671). In other words, blessings are the most important sacramental. Many blessings call on the Blessed Trinity with a sign of the cross and often involve a sprinkling of holy water.

A blessing is a prayer that praises God and prays for his gifts. Through Jesus Christ, Christians are blessed by God the Father.

Activity

Blessings are the most important sacramentals. Write a short blessing for a friend, and another for one of the following:

- Your mother
- Your father
- Your teacher
- Your friend

What Makes Us Catholic?

At some Masses, the priest blesses us during a Sprinkling Rite. He uses a sprinkling of holy water from an *aspergil*, a liturgical item that looks like a silver ball on a stick or a brush. The priest waves the aspergil as he walks through the Church, sprinkling himself, any other ministers, and the assembly. This rite is called the Asperges. In some cultures, the water may contain salt that has also been blessed. This sprinkling reminds us of our Baptism. The Sprinkling Rite is often part of the Mass during the season of Easter.

Every person is called to be a blessing, and every person is called to bless. We can bless others and receive blessings from others! Blessings for students at the start of a new school year, for the teenager who just received his or her driver's license, or for the young adult moving away from home–all these are blessings for new beginnings. There are blessings for just about every situation in life.

Devotions and forms of popular piety draw us closer to God, the way blessings do so. Many devotions honor holy men and women whose lives are models of discipleship. Devotions such as the Stations of the Cross, the Rosary, pilgrimages, processions, and lighting candles at church nourish our faith and prepare our hearts and minds for celebration of the sacraments.

Activity

Have you ever taken part in one of the devotions mentioned above? Or another devotion, such as Divine Adoration? How did this affect your faith? Write a few sentences about it.

____

____

____

Is there another devotion you would like to start practicing? Learn more about this devotion and start making it a practice.

Partners in Faith

Blessed Victoire Rasoamanarivo

Victoire Rasoamanarivo was a member of the royal family of Madagascar. Her parents sent her to Catholic school, where she learned about Jesus. She became a Catholic when she was fifteen, even though her parents disapproved. She married a man who was cruel to her, but she prayed for his conversion. After his death, she cared for the poor and sick.

Learn more about the life of Blessed Victoire Rasoamanarivo.

My soul belongs to God.

Prayer

Petition

Faith Words

Liturgy of the Word **liturgical year**

Show What You Know

In your own words, write definitions for the terms.

liturgical year

Liturgy of the Word

Which of the following is a devotion?

a. Stations of the Cross

b. liturgy

c. Paschal Mystery

Live Your Faith

- Why are many aspects of the Church's celebrations around the world the same?

- Who in your life needs to receive a blessing? Why?

How does faith connect me with others?

Mini-Task

Imagine that you are starting a blog for Catholic young people all over the world. Part of your blog will be a forum in which visitors are invited to share their faith stories and experiences in the Church.

Organize the structure of your forum. Develop five questions that will lead the forum. Write them below. Make them interesting and pertinent to young people's lives to spark conversation and response. Share your forum questions with the group.

Want to do more? Go to your Portfolio to continue this activity.

At Home

With your family, find the readings for next Sunday's Mass in a Bible or online. Try to find time to read together and pray about those Scriptures before Mass.

How do we become members of the Church?

The Sacraments of Initiation–Baptism, Confirmation, and Eucharist–are the foundation of the Christian life. These sacraments begin, strengthen, and nourish our life of faith. Through Baptism, we share in the work of Jesus and are freed from Original Sin. We become members of the Church. The Sacrament of Confirmation seals us with the Gift of the Holy Spirit. In the Eucharist, the memorial of Christ's sacrifice, we are nourished by the Real Presence of Christ.

Petition

Lord God,
. . . Bless all your adopted children
and add these chosen ones
to the harvest of your new covenant. . . .
may they rejoice in eternal life,
won, not by the power of nature,
but through the mystery of your grace.

Rite of Christian Initiation of Adults

The Sacraments of Christian Initiation begin, strengthen, and nourish our life in the Church.

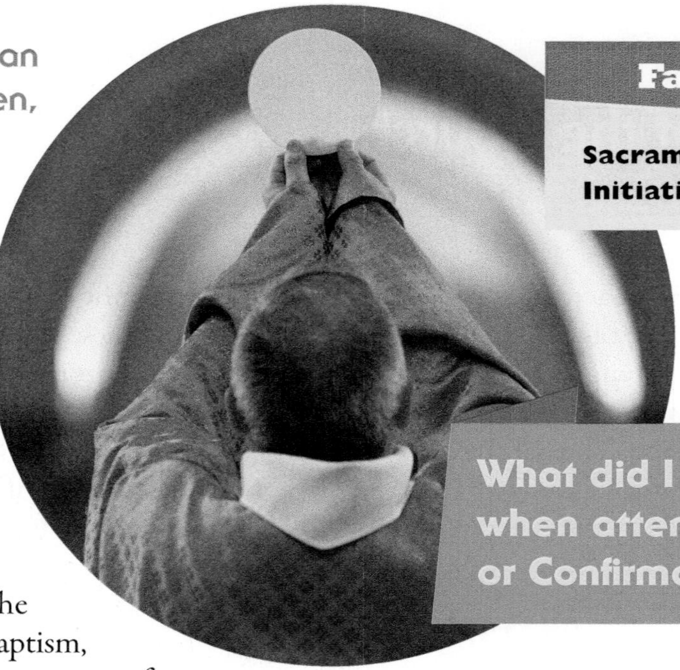

Christian initiation is the process of becoming a member of the Church. The Sacraments of Baptism, Confirmation, and Eucharist initiate us into the Church. They are the **Sacraments of Christian Initiation**.

Faith Word

Sacraments of Christian Initiation see p. 294

What did I experience when attending a Baptism or Confirmation?

The Sacrament of Baptism is the first sacrament we receive. In Baptism, we are united to Christ and become part of the Body of Christ and the People of God. The celebration of this first Sacrament of Christian Initiation is very important. In fact, we are unable to receive any other sacrament until we first have been baptized. Baptism is our welcome into new life in Christ and into the Church.

In the Sacrament of Confirmation, we are sealed with the Gift of the Holy Spirit. Confirmation continues what Baptism has begun. We are strengthened to live as Christ's followers.

The Sacrament of the Eucharist is the Sacrament of the Body and Blood of Christ. The Eucharist is connected to our Baptism, too. Each time we receive Holy Communion, our bonds as the Body of Christ are made stronger. Our community of faith is nourished by God's life.

What Makes Us Catholic?

After we celebrate the Liturgy of the Eucharist at Mass, any hosts that remain or are reserved for those who will receive it outside of Mass are placed inside a container or cabinet called the Tabernacle. The Real Presence of Christ remains true and real in the consecrated hosts. We can spend time with the Real Presence in this way during Eucharistic Adoration. This is a devotion in which we visit the Tabernacle and pray in front of it, focusing our thoughts on Christ and his sacrifice for us.

Did You Know?

In the Rite of Election, it is God who chooses us.

Prayer

Petition

Faith Word

Baptism see p. 293

Baptism gives us a special grace to share in the life and work of Jesus.

Baptism is the foundation of Christian life. It is the very first sacrament that we celebrate. Baptism leads us to the other two Sacraments of Christian Initiation: Confirmation and Eucharist. It is upon Baptism that we build our lives as followers of Christ. We receive the Gift of the Holy Spirit and share in God's own life, which is God's grace. The grace of Baptism helps us to believe in God the Father and to love him. It gives us the power to live as disciples of Christ in the world.

Jesus said, "No one can enter the kingdom of God without being born of water and the spirit" (John 3:5). The *Catechism of the Catholic Church* tells us that Baptism is "necessary for salvation, as is the Church herself, which we enter by Baptism" (*CCC*, 1277).

There are situations in which a person can be saved without receiving the Sacrament of Baptism. The Church teaches that people who die for the faith without ever being baptized can be saved. People who are preparing for Baptism but not yet baptized can be saved. And people who do not know Christ but who are living lives of virtue and grace can be saved. The Church teaches that these people would likely have wanted to be baptized if they had known about its importance for salvation. In the case of children who die without Baptism, we trust in God's mercy and pray for their salvation.

There are times when a person may want to be baptized but a priest or deacon is not available. In that case, any person, even someone not baptized, can baptize. He or she must intend to do what the Church does. The person must follow the essential rite of the sacrament, which is the pouring of water three times on the person's head, with the words "I baptize you in the name of the Father, and of the Son, and of the Holy Spirit" (*Rite of Baptism*, 60).

One Church, Many Cultures

In Baptism, the parents of the baptized infant name godparents for their children. Godparents ensure that the child will be protected and raised to know God. Godparents have a special significance in the Latino Church, remaining involved in the lives of the godchildren well past the teenage years. *Padrinos* typically buy a christening gown and candle for the infant, and they also offer their godchildren special gifts over the years, including items that promote and encourage their faith. Padrinos also serve as *compadres*, or co-parents, offering advice and love.

The Church welcomes all people everywhere to be baptized. Not everyone begins or completes Christian initiation at the same time. Many people are baptized as infants or young children. They celebrate the remaining Sacraments of Christian Initiation when they are older. Other people are baptized as older children or adults. They participate in the Rite of Christian Initiation of Adults (RCIA) and enter the *catechumenate*, which is a time of Christian formation. It includes prayer and liturgy, religious instruction, and service to others. Those who enter this formation are called *catechumens*. They celebrate the three Sacraments of Christian Initiation in one celebration, usually at the Easter Vigil.

The whole parish takes part in the formation of the catechumens. Some parish members serve as sponsors. Others teach the catechumens about the Catholic faith. The catechumens participate in prayer celebrations that introduce them to the symbols of the sacraments. And the catechumens usually join the assembly for part of the Sunday celebration of the Mass.

When infants or young children are baptized in the faith of the Church, the parents choose godparents for the child. The godparents are to be role models of Christian life. Along with the parents and parish community, godparents agree to help the child grow in faith. An ideal day to celebrate Baptism is on Sunday, the Lord's Day and the day of Jesus' Resurrection. The celebration of Baptism on Sunday highlights the fact that we rise to new life as Jesus did. It also allows the parish to welcome the newly baptized.

Through the Sacrament of Baptism

- We are freed from sin.
- We become children of God.
- We are joined to Christ and rise to new life in him.
- We become members of the Church, the Body of Christ.
- We are united with all others who have been baptized.
- We are justified, which conforms us more closely to the justice of God.

Activity

In an emergency, if a person wants to be baptized but a priest or deacon isn't available, you can baptize the person.

Put the following steps in the correct order.

☐ Pour water on the person's head three times.

☐ Ask if the person wants to be baptized.

☐ Say the words from the Rite of Baptism.

Prayer

Petition

The Sacrament of Confirmation seals us with the Gift of the Holy Spirit.

God the Holy Spirit is always with the Church. We first receive the Gift of the Holy Spirit at our Baptism. In the Sacrament of **Confirmation**, we are sealed with the Gift of the Holy Spirit. We become more like Christ and are strengthened to be his witnesses.

Come, Holy Spirit

On Pentecost, the Holy Spirit came upon the Apostles (see Acts of the Apostles 2:1–4). The Holy Spirit strengthened and guided them to give witness to Christ. They baptized many believers. Those people received the strengthening power of the Holy Spirit when the Apostles placed their hands on them. The **laying on of hands** was a sign of God's blessing. By this action, authority and grace were given in God's name.

The laying on of hands by the Apostles was the beginning of the Sacrament of Confirmation. As the Church's understanding of the sacrament developed, an anointing was joined to the laying on of hands. The word "**anoint**" means "to apply oil to someone as a sign that God has chosen that person for a special mission." Like the laying on of hands, anointing is an ancient practice. Anointing was an important part of Jewish life during Jesus' time.

The anointing that happened with the laying on of hands was a sign of the Holy Spirit's outpouring upon the person. In time, the anointing became the essential sign of the Gift of the Holy Spirit. **Sacred Chrism**, oil blessed by a bishop, was used in this anointing. Today, in the Sacrament of Confirmation, the anointing with Sacred Chrism is done as the celebrant anoints the forehead of the person being confirmed.

Faith Words

Confirmation see p. 293

laying on of hands see p. 294

anoint see p. 293

Sacred Chrism see p. 294

The Sacrament of Confirmation completes Baptism. And like Baptism, it imprints on our souls a character, an indelible spiritual seal. We receive it only once. However, the time in a person's life when it can be received varies.

In the Roman Catholic Church, people who were baptized as infants generally receive Confirmation between the ages of ten and fifteen. The Eastern Catholic Church celebrates Confirmation at the time of Baptism (infancy), followed by the Eucharist. This tradition highlights the unity of the three Sacraments of Initiation. Adults and older children who are preparing for Baptism receive the Sacrament of Confirmation as a part of the Rite of Christian Initiation.

The Sacrament of Confirmation deepens the grace we first received at Baptism. In Confirmation

- We are sealed with the Gift of the Holy Spirit.
- We become more like Jesus and are strengthened to be active witnesses.
- Our friendship with God the Father is deepened.
- Our relationship with the Church is strengthened.
- We are sent forth to live our faith in the world.

Activity

Using what you have learned about the Sacrament of Confirmation, create a greeting card for someone preparing for the sacrament. You might remind that person of the many wonderful effects of the sacrament. You might also say you support him or her in prayer. Sign the card with your first name.

Prayer

Lectio and *Visio Divina*

The Last Supper by Fedor Bruni, 1849.

In the Eucharist, we are nourished by the Real Presence of Christ.

At the Last Supper, Jesus gave us the gift of himself in the Eucharist. Through the Eucharist, Jesus remains with us forever. The Eucharist is the Sacrament of the Body and Blood of Christ. Jesus is truly present under the appearances of bread and wine. It is the only Sacrament of Christian Initiation that we receive again and again. We honor Jesus by remembering what he did for us, share in the Last Supper, and remember his Crucifixion.

Jesus often blessed and broke and ate bread with his disciples. It was not until the Last Supper, on the night before he died, that this simple act took on a special meaning. At the Last Supper, Jesus' breaking of the bread and sharing of the cup was an offering of himself for our salvation. Jesus told his Apostles to "do this in memory of me" (Luke 22:19).

When we gather and break bread, we remember the new life we have because of Jesus' Death and Resurrection. In this way, the Eucharist is a memorial. But, it is much more than just remembering past events. In the Eucharist, Christ is really present.

By the power of the Holy Spirit, the Paschal Mystery of Christ's suffering, Death, Resurrection, and Ascension is made present to us. We join Jesus in offering ourselves to God the Father. We offer our joys, worries, and willingness to live as Jesus' disciples.

Jesus acts through the priest to offer the sacrifice of the Eucharist. A sacrifice is a gift offered to God by a priest in the name of all the people. Through this sacrifice, we are saved. We are reconciled to God and one another.

Activity

Imagine you are having a conversation with Jesus. Respond to Jesus by sharing what is in your heart.

Jesus: In the Eucharist, I am really and truly with you.

Me: ______________________________

Jesus: The Eucharist is my gift to you.

Me: ______________________________

Jesus: What will you do today to respond to this gift I have given you?

Me: ______________________________

In the Eucharist, Jesus also offers his Father the gifts of praise and thanksgiving. This thanks and praise is for all the gifts that God has given us in creation. In every celebration of the Eucharist, the whole Church offers thanks and praise. We join Jesus in offering ourselves to God the Father. We offer to God all of the joys and concerns that we have. We offer our willingness to continue to live as Jesus' disciples.

The priest celebrates the Eucharist for and with the People of God. At the Consecration, by the power of the Holy Spirit and through the words and actions of the priest, the bread and wine become the Body and Blood of Christ. This process is called transubstantiation. This is the Real Presence of Christ–Body and Blood, soul and divinity. When we receive Holy Communion, we are nourished by the Body and Blood of Christ. Jesus lives in us and we live in him.

The words of Consecration, also called the words of Institution, are at the heart of the Liturgy of the Eucharist.

In the Sacrament of the Eucharist

- We are nourished by the Word of God and receive Jesus Christ in Holy Communion.
- We are joined more closely to Christ and one another.
- The grace received in Baptism grows in us.
- We are strengthened to love and serve others.

Faith Words

Consecration see p. 293

transubstantiation see p. 295

Real Presence see p. 294

Take this all of you, and eat it,
For this is my body,
Which will be given up for you.

Take this, all of you, and drink from it
For this is the chalice of my blood,
The blood of the new and eternal covenant,
Which will be poured out for you and for many
For the forgiveness of sins.

Do this in memory of me.

Eucharist Prayer II, Prayer of Consecration

Activity

Use all three Faith Words in sentences. With a partner, share what each of the Faith Words means in order to tell others why Holy Communion is one of the greatest gifts God has given us.

Partners in Faith

Saint Teresa of the Andes

Saint Teresa of the Andes is the first saint from Chile. As a child, she had a temper and fought with her brothers and sisters. After her First Communion, she changed and began to think of others first. She read about Saint Thérèse of Lisieux and wanted to be a nun like her. She entered the convent but died when she was only nineteen.

Learn more about the life of Saint Teresa of the Andes.

In the shadow of the Cross, every kind of bitterness fades.

Faith Words

Sacraments of Christian Initiation **Baptism**
Confirmation **laying on of hands**
anoint **Sacred Chrism** **Consecration**
transubstantiation **Real Presence**

Show What You Know

Match the terms to the correct definitions.

1. Confirmation	the process by which the bread and wine become the Body and Blood of Christ
2. transubstantiation	the event at Mass in which the bread and wine become the Body and Blood of Christ
3. Sacraments of Christian Initiation	oil blessed by the bishop
4. Sacred Chrism	the sacrament in which we receive the Gift of the Holy Spirit in a special way
5. Consecration	Christ's true and real presence in the Eucharist in the form of bread and wine
6. Real Presence	these welcome us into the Church

Live Your Faith

- What do the laying on of hands and anointing show about us in the Sacrament of Confirmation?

____

____

____

____

- What does the Eucharist give you the strength to do?

____

____

____

____

Portfolio

How do I grow as a child of God?

Mini-Task

Baptism is the foundation of our faith. It is the first of the Sacraments of Initiation, in which we are welcomed into the Church.

You probably do not remember your Baptism if you were a baby, but you have experienced many graces as a child of God since that time.

On the lines below, design a spiritual timeline with moments when you have experienced the grace of God in your life.

Want to do more? Go to your Portfolio to continue this activity.

At Home

Talk with your family members about what's going on in your lives right now. Be respectful of one another. Include the good and the bad. Offer a prayer of love and comfort for everyone in your family.

How do we celebrate God's forgiveness and healing?

In the Gospels, Jesus showed that God has power over sickness and sin. The Church celebrates God's healing and forgiveness in the Sacrament of Penance and Reconciliation and the Sacrament of Anointing of the Sick–the Sacraments of Healing. In the Anointing of the Sick, God's healing grace is given to those who are sick, suffering, or near death.

Lectio* and *Visio Divina

Make this oil a remedy for all who are anointed with it; heal them in body, in soul, and in spirit, and deliver them from every affliction.

Pastoral Care of the Sick, 123

We celebrate and receive God's healing in a special way.

Many people grew to believe in Jesus because of his healing. Jesus' healing was a sign of God's presence and action in the lives of people.

Jesus cared about the needs of all people. However, he had a special concern for those who were sick and suffering. He did not ignore people who had diseases or disabilities. He listened to them and treated them with respect.

Jesus also wanted to heal people from sin. Often when he cured the sick, he also forgave their sins. Jesus forgave the sins of people because he knew that sin kept them from loving God and living life to the fullest.

The healing and forgiving actions of Jesus showed others that he was the Son of God. They showed that the Kingdom of God was close at hand. Jesus' actions showed that God has power over sickness and sin. Jesus' healing of the sick and forgiveness of sin are signs of his power to save us and bring us God's life.

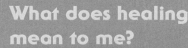

What does healing mean to me?

Did You Know?

Oil has been used throughout the centuries.

Faith Word

Anointing of the Sick see p. 293

Prayer

Lectio* and *Visio Divina

When we are sick, we can call on God.

In the Sacrament of the **Anointing of the Sick**, God's grace and comfort are given to those who are seriously ill or are suffering.

The Church community does two very important things in this sacrament. We support those who fight against sickness, and we continue Jesus' saving work of healing. This sacrament should be celebrated by all the faithful who need it. Children, adults, and the elderly are invited to be strengthened by God's grace in times of serious sickness.

At one time or another in our lives, we will probably get sick. We will catch a cold or come down with the flu. We may be injured while playing sports. Sometimes we may even need surgery. During these times of sickness, we may become lonely or worried. We may even become discouraged and wonder if God remembers us.

Yet God always remembers those who are sick and suffering. As Christians, we believe that when we are suffering, Jesus is with us, sharing our pain. He understands our pain and suffering because he suffered and died on the Cross.

Activity

Think about those in your parish who are sick. Write a short prayer asking God to help them. If possible, do something special for someone who is sick this week. You might call, visit, or send out a card.

____

____

____

When [Jesus] entered Capernaum, a centurion approached him and appealed to him, saying, 'Lord, my servant is lying at home paralyzed, suffering dreadfully.' He said to him, 'I will come and cure him.'

Matthew 8:5–7

When people are very sick, they may become anxious and discouraged. They need the special help of God's grace to stay strong and keep their faith alive. In the Sacrament of the Anointing of the Sick, Christ comforts them and suffers with them.

In the Anointing of the Sick, we proclaim our faith in God's mercy. We support those who are sick and encourage them to fight against illness. In this sacrament, we recall that by his own suffering, Death, and Resurrection, Jesus saves us. We ask God to save those who are suffering. Anointing of the Sick can be celebrated more than once. If people recover after being anointed but becomes sick at another time, they may celebrate the sacrament again. When someone is preparing to have surgery, he or she can celebrate the sacrament with family, friends, and parish.

What Makes Us Catholic?

The Anointing of the Sick often takes place outside the celebration of the Mass. As a result, the sacrament usually begins with a Liturgy of the Word and is followed by Holy Communion. In this way, those being anointed are further strengthened and nourished by the Word of God and by the Body and Blood of Christ. Holy Communion also joins those who are suffering to their parish community, even when they are unable to celebrate Mass.

Prayer

Lectio and *Visio Divina*

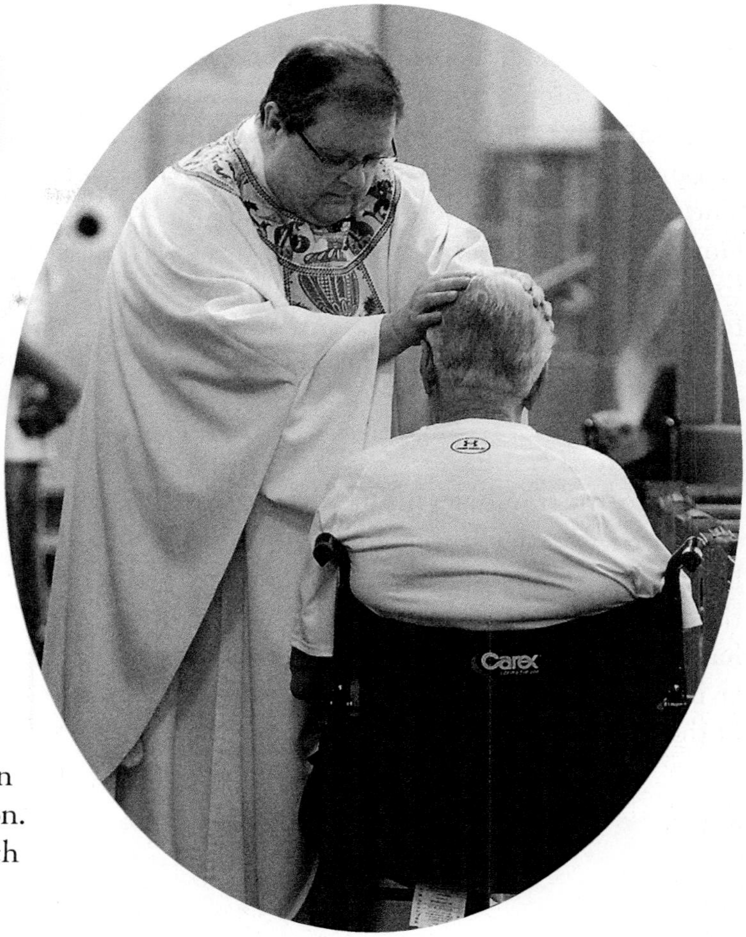

In the Sacrament of Anointing of the Sick, the Church offers strength and healing to those who are suffering.

From the time of the Apostles, the faithful have turned to the Church for healing and comfort.

Jesus wanted all people to know and feel God's power and presence, so he shared his ministry with the Apostles. Sometimes the Apostles were with Jesus as he preached and healed. At other times, Jesus sent them to different towns and villages to share the message of the Kingdom of God. He sent them out to preach repentance and to cure the sick.

This healing ministry of the Apostles took on even greater meaning after Jesus' Death and Resurrection. After his Resurrection, Jesus told them to preach the Gospel to the whole world. He told them that they "will lay hands on the sick, and they will recover" (Mark 16:18).

Like all sacraments, the Sacrament of Anointing of the Sick is a celebration with the whole community of the faithful. Those present from the parish offer comfort and support to those who are sick.

Sometimes the sacrament is celebrated during Mass. More often, it is celebrated in hospitals, homes, at the site of an accident, or wherever someone is in need of it.

One Church, Many Cultures

Pope Benedict XVI said that God can reveal himself "by using languages, imagery and expressions that are bound to different cultures." The Church is made up of many cultures. Yet we may not always reflect an attitude of acceptance and welcome to others. We need to find ways to express healing and reconciliation for the times we have excluded other cultures and people, or been dismissive of them. Pope Francis has asked forgiveness for any harm caused to native peoples, among other groups, especially during the time of early missionary work in the Americas. Today, Native Americans and other diverse groups work within the Church to promote healing and reconciliation as well as celebration.

Prayer of faith

Jesus often healed people because of their belief and faith in him. The prayer of faith has been an important part of the Church's celebration of the sacrament from the beginning of the Church. The whole Church is represented by the priest, family, friends, and other parish members gathered to pray. Trusting in God's mercy, they ask for help for those who are sick. Several intentions are offered. After each intention, those present answer, "Lord, have mercy."

Laying on of hands

In silence, the priest lays his hands on the person who is sick. The laying on of hands is a gesture of healing used by Jesus and the early Church. Many times, Jesus healed the sick by the laying on of his hands or by simply touching them. The priest's laying on of hands is a sign of blessing and a calling of the Holy Spirit upon the person.

Anointing with oil

Because the oil has been blessed, the anointing with oil is a sign of the power and presence of the Holy Spirit. It is also a sign of healing and strengthening. Oil has been used for centuries to restore those who are weak and tired. It is known to soothe and comfort those who are sick.

Activity

Think of the different types of oil that are used in everyday life, such as to cook, run a car, fix squeaky doors, and soften your skin. Talk with a classmate or two about the ways oil makes our lives better. How is this similar to anointing with oil in the Anointing of the Sick?

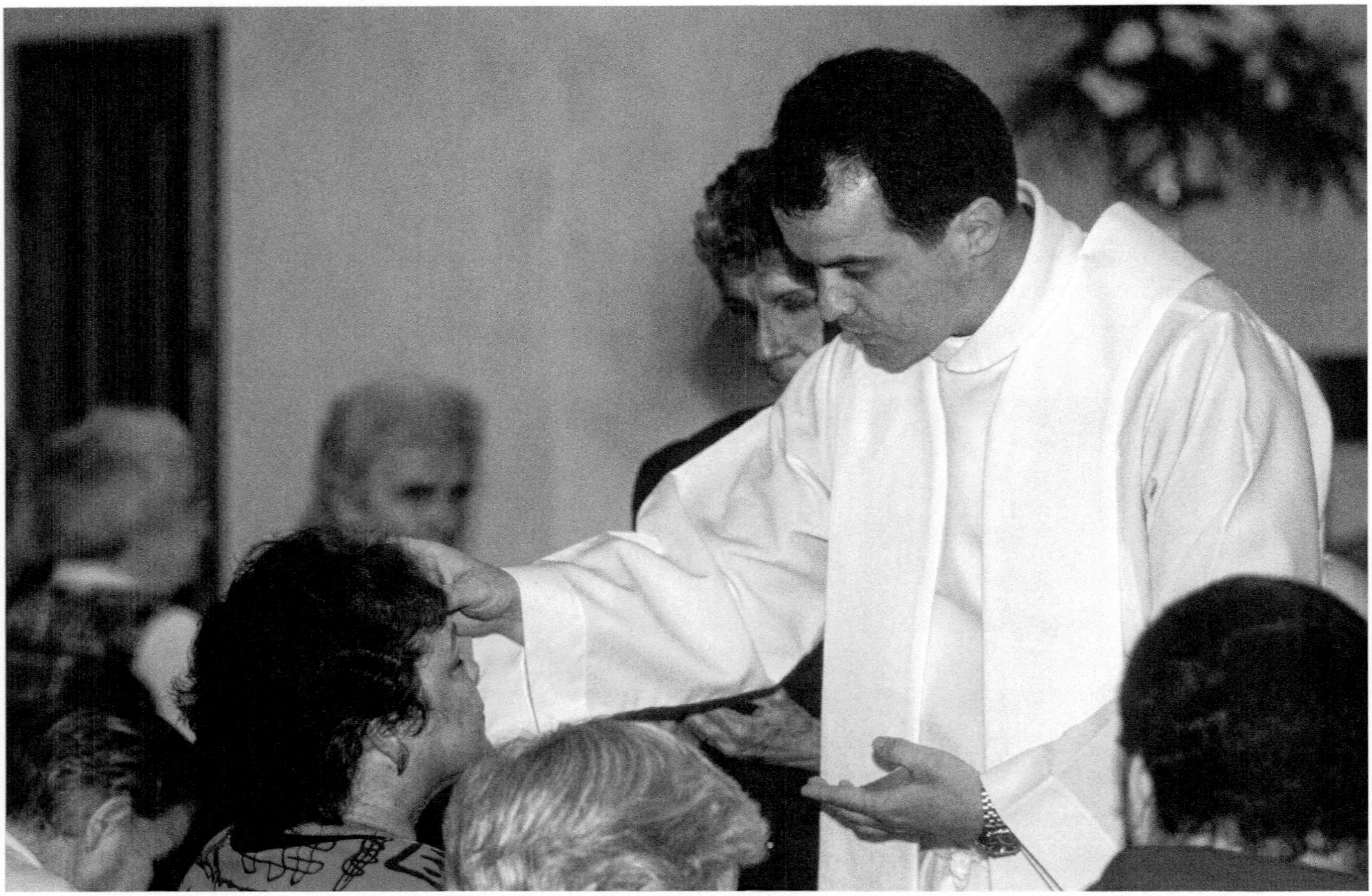

The Sacrament of Anointing of the Sick is sometimes celebrated at Mass.

Prayer

Lectio and *Visio Divina*

The Sacrament of Anointing of the Sick continues Jesus' mission of healing.

When we care for members of the Church who are sick, we are caring for the Body of Christ. We serve Christ himself.

Out of love for Christ and his Body, we work to help others feel better. We try to provide them with the things they need. We join them in the celebration of the sacraments. These actions are a way to share in Jesus' healing work.

Those who are sick have different needs. Sick children may want us to read to them or play with them. Parents who are ill may need us to perform chores around the house. An elderly person may enjoy a short visit and the chance to talk to someone. Our concern for them is a way to support them on their road to recovery. The whole Church remembers in prayer those who are sick, especially when we gather at Sunday Mass.

A special ministry within your parish community is the ministry to the sick and homebound who unable to attend Mass. The ministers can help them to pray and can pray with them. They can share God's Word from the Sunday's Liturgy of the Word and other Scripture such as the psalms, which might bring comfort to the one who is sick. Often, when appropriate, the ministers to the sick bring Holy Communion to the people they visit.

Activity

Think of someone in your school or parish who needs comfort and support. What can your class do to help that person? Make a plan to do this.

____

____

____

____

____

____

____

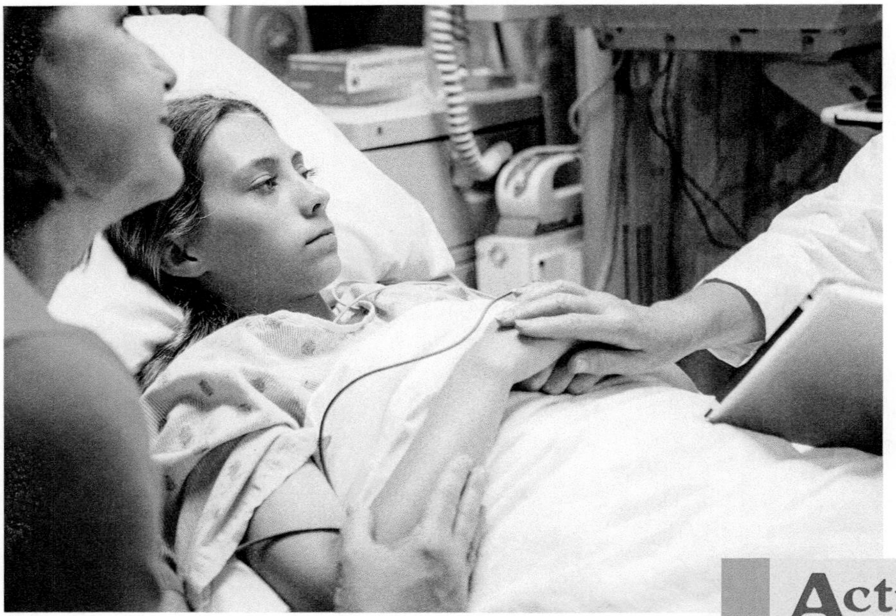

For those who receive the Sacrament of Anointing of the Sick, it

- renews their trust and faith in God
- unites them to Christ and his suffering
- prepares them, when necessary, for death and the hope of life forever with God
- may restore them to health.

Activity

In the Gospel account of Jesus and the centurion, Jesus tells him that his servant has been healed because of the centurion's great faith. Read one or two healing stories from the Bible, and look for the connection between faith and healing. Discuss this connection with your classmates or with your family.

The Church has special prayers for visits to the sick. Here is a blessing that the minister might pray with the person who is sick.

All praise and glory is yours, Lord our God,
for you have called us to serve you with love.
Bless N,
so that he/she may bear this illness
in union with your Son's obedient suffering.
Restore him/her to health,
and lead him/her to glory.
We ask this through Christ our Lord.
Amen.

Blessing, from *Pastoral Care of the Sick*

Partners in Faith

Rose Hawthorne

Rose was a child of the writer Nathanial Hawthorne. In her early years, she lived in Massachusetts, London, and Rome. Rose had trained as a nurse, and when her husband died in 1898, she decided to devote her life to the care of the sick. Rose's case for sainthood was opened in 2003, and she is now known as Servant of God.

Learn more about the life of Rose Hawthorne.

I am for God and the poor.

Prayer

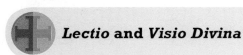

Lectio and *Visio Divina*

Faith Word

Anointing of the Sick

Show What You Know

In your own words, give a short definition of each part of the Sacrament of Anointing of the Sick. Write your definition on the lines below, or discuss it with a partner.

Prayer of faith

Laying on of hands

Anointing with oil

Live Your Faith

- How does the Sacrament of Anointing of the Sick show God's forgiveness and healing?

- Give an example of how you have experienced God's healing in your own life.

How can I help others know God's forgiveness and healing?

Mini-Task

Celebrating the Sacrament of Anointing of the Sick can bring comfort and strength to all who are ill in body, mind, or spirit. God's grace is a powerful gift, one that is available to us in a special way when we celebrate the sacraments.

Imagine you are being asked to plan a Healing Service for your school or parish. Consider when and where you would hold the service, who will be invited, and ways to let people know about the Healing Service. Use the chart to guide you.

Healing Service	Planning
Environment	
Music	
Opening Prayer	
Reading from Psalms	
Reading from the Gospel	
Intercessions	
Blessing	

Want to do more? Go to your Portfolio to continue this activity.

At Home

Jesus works through his Body, the Church, to bringing healing and comfort to the suffering. Your family is part of that Body. Are there people you know who are suffering? How can your family share Jesus' love with those people, even in small ways, today or tomorrow?

How are we strengthened for service to God and others?

The Sacraments at the Service of Communion give us special grace to serve God and others. In the Sacrament of Holy Orders, the Church calls baptized men to serve the Church by teaching, leading the faithful in worship, and living as disciples of Christ. In the Sacrament of Matrimony, a man and a woman are given the grace to love each other as Christ loves the Church. Together they form a Christian family which is a community of faith, grace, and prayer.

Meditation

In happiness may they praise you, O Lord,
in sorrow may they seek you out;
may they have the joy of your presence
to assist them in their toil,
and know that you are near
to comfort them in their need;
let them pray to you in the holy assembly
and bear witness to you in the world.

Roman Missal, Nuptial Blessing

The Sacrament of Baptism calls us to service.

Through Baptism, Confirmation, and the Eucharist, we share a common vocation, or calling, with all of the faithful. We share a call to holiness and to spread the Good News. The Sacraments of Initiation give us the grace we need to share in God's life and in his divine plan to share eternity with him.

Faith Words

common priesthood of the faithful see p. 293

Sacraments at the Service of Communion see p. 294

When Jesus was baptized, the Holy Spirit marked Jesus as priest, prophet, and king. Our anointing at Baptism makes us sharers in Christ's role as priest, prophet, and king. We share in Christ's priestly mission. This is known as the **common priesthood of the faithful**. In the common priesthood, each of us is called to worship God, spread the Good News of Jesus Christ, and serve one another and the Church.

How do I serve others?

We share in God's kingly mission–not a kingship of power over others, but of service to others. Jesus told his followers:

"'Whoever wishes to be great among you shall be your servant; whoever wishes to be first among you shall be your slave. Just so, the Son of Man did not come to be served but to serve'" (Matthew 20:26–28).

Two other sacraments call those who celebrate them to serve others. Their service helps the Church grow in holiness through the ministerial priesthood and through married life. Holy Orders and Matrimony are the **Sacraments at the Service of Communion**. They are directed toward the salvation of others.

Did You Know?

The laity are members of the common priesthood of the faithful.

Faith Word

Holy Orders see p. 293

Prayer

Meditation

The Sacrament of Holy Orders gives special authority to teach and lead the faithful.

One of the ways that God calls baptized men to serve him through the Church is in the Sacrament of **Holy Orders**. In this sacrament, men are ordained to serve the Church as deacons, priests, and bishops. It is a Sacrament at the Service of Communion. Those who receive Holy Orders take on a special mission in leading and serving the People of God.

In the Sacrament of Holy Orders, men are ordained by the bishop's laying on of hands and prayer of consecration. Those who are ordained receive the grace necessary to carry out their ministry to the faithful. They are imprinted with an indelible sacramental character, a permanent spiritual seal on their souls.

Activity

Priests and deacons receive the Sacrament of Holy Orders. Write their names and some of the ways they serve your parish or school. In small groups, brainstorm some ways your class might help these people serve. You might want to contact them and ask if they have any suggestions for what you can do to help.

____

____

____

____

____

____

____

____

The solemn blessing at the end of the conferral of Holy Orders for priests summarizes the mission and ministry of the newly ordained priest. The bishop extends his hands over the newly ordained priests and the people, and he says:

May God, who founded the Church and guides her still, protect you constantly with his grace, that you may faithfully discharge the duties of the Priesthood.(All) Amen.

May he make you servants and witnesses in the world to divine charity and truth and faithful ministers of reconciliation. (All) Amen.

And may he make you true shepherds to provide the living Bread and word of life to the faithful, that they may continue to grow in the unity of the Body of Christ.
(All) Amen.

The bishop concludes by blessing all of the people, adding:

And may almighty God bless all of you, who are gathered here, the Father, and the Son, and the Holy Spirit.

(All) Amen.

—*Roman Missal,* Solemn Blessing at the End of Mass, For the Conferral of Holy Orders,

The Church, through its ordained ministers, continues the mission that Jesus Christ first gave to his Apostles (see John 20:20–23). The ordained act as representatives of Christ, as Head of the Church, and in his office as priest, prophet, and king. Through the grace of the Holy Spirit, men who celebrate this sacrament serve the faithful through teaching, worship, and leading.

Activity

Write down three questions you would like to ask about what it is like to be either a priest or a deacon.

Share your questions with the group. What do your group's questions tell you about your group's understanding of the Sacrament of Holy Orders?

"The disciples rejoiced when they saw the LORD. [Jesus] said to them again, 'Peace be with you. As the Father has sent me, so I send you.' And when he had said this, he breathed on them and said to them, 'Receive the holy Spirit. Whose sins you forgive are forgiven them, and whose sins you retain are retained.' "

John 20:20–23

Prayer

Meditation

Faith Word

Matrimony see p. 294

The Sacrament of Matrimony gives a man and woman grace to love each other as Christ loves the Church.

In the Sacrament of **Matrimony**, a man and woman become husband and wife. They promise to be faithful to each other for the rest of their lives. They

- promise to love and be true to each other always
- lovingly accept their children as a gift from God, not preventing themselves from having children using unacceptable methods
- are strengthened by God's grace to live out their promises to Christ and each other.

The Sacrament of Matrimony is about God first. God calls a man and woman into a sacred covenant. Together they will bring God's love to the world in a way greater than either of them could do alone. The Church is known as the Bride of Christ. The love between husband and wife is a sign of Christ's love for his Church. It is a love that is generous, faithful, and complete.

The Sacrament of Matrimony gives a married couple the grace

- to bring God's love to the world together
- to live the Paschal Mystery in their marriage together
- to live the adventure of discipleship together.

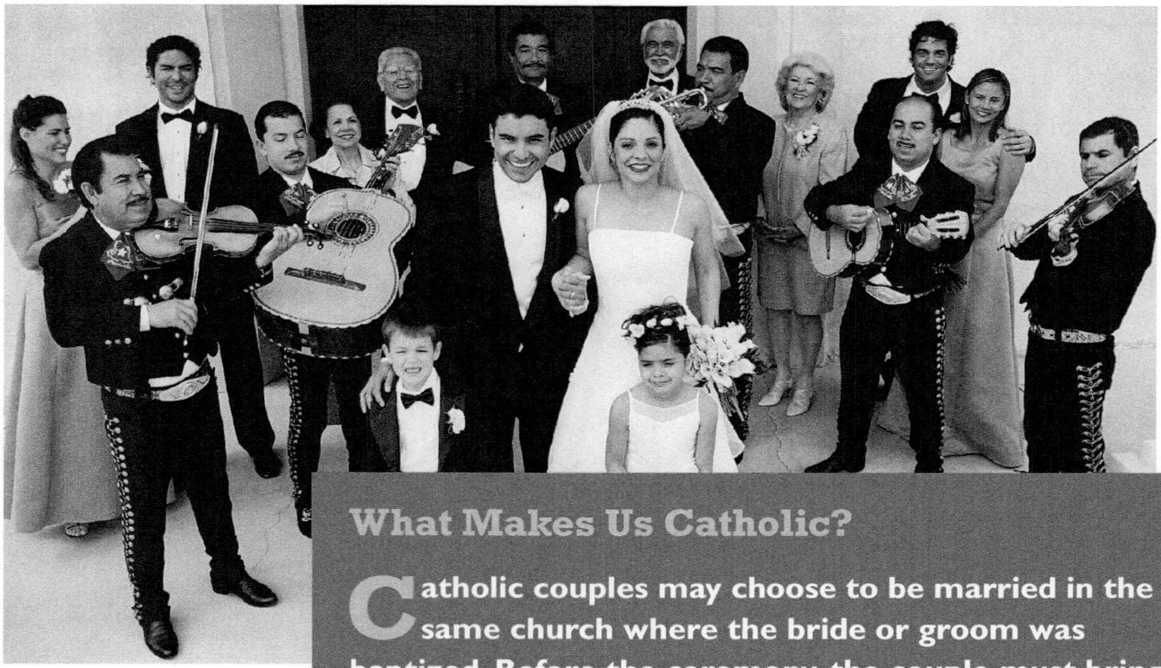

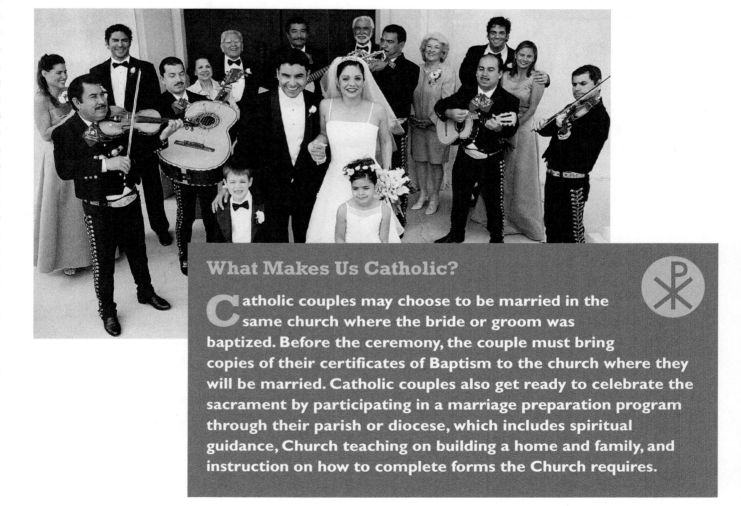

What Makes Us Catholic?

Catholic couples may choose to be married in the same church where the bride or groom was baptized. Before the ceremony, the couple must bring copies of their certificates of Baptism to the church where they will be married. Catholic couples also get ready to celebrate the sacrament by participating in a marriage preparation program through their parish or diocese, which includes spiritual guidance, Church teaching on building a home and family, and instruction on how to complete forms the Church requires.

When a man and a woman celebrate the Sacrament of Matrimony, they, not the priest or deacon, are the celebrants of the sacrament. They give themselves to each other. Jesus acts through the couple and through their promise to always love and be true to each other.

The love the bride and groom have for each other is blessed and strengthened by the grace of the sacrament. The couple is also blessed by the members of the Church community. The bride and groom *together* become a sign of God's love to the Church and the world. They act as a sign of Christ's presence and saving grace as husband and wife.

God's participation in the marriage gives the couple what they need to build a relationship that gives them life and joy, and challenges them to be witnesses together to God's faithful love.

One Church, Many Cultures

In the Latin, or Roman, Catholic Church, the married couple are the celebrants, or ministers, of the Sacrament of Matrimony. In the Eastern Catholic Church, the priest is considered to be the celebrant. In the Eastern Church, some marriage ceremonies also include a "holy crowning" of the bride and groom. During the Mass, the priest prays a blessing and places crowns on their heads to mark the couple as part of the Kingdom of God and as king and queen of their home and family.

Prayer

Meditation

The Christian family is a community of faith, grace, and prayer.

God's creation of man and woman was the beginning of the human family. God told the first man and woman to "Be fertile and multiply" (Genesis 1:28). In this way, God blessed the first man and woman to bring new life into the world. He wanted them to have children and to share in his plan for creating the human family.

Married couples express their love by creating a loving family, with or without children. When they share the goodness of their love with others, their own love for each other and for Christ grows. The Christian family is a community of faith, hope, and charity. It is a sign of the love and unity of the Blessed Trinity.

The family is a community of faith. The family grows in faith when its members learn to be disciples of Jesus and members of the Church. The family grows in faith when it celebrates the sacraments together, especially Sunday Eucharist. Its members grow in faith when they learn and practice Christian virtue.

Activity

Like many Catholic schools and parishes, your school is probably named for a saint. This saint was probably chosen as a patron for specific reasons. Looking through your textbook, choose a patron saint for your family. Write about the saint you have chosen and tell why he or she is a good example to help your family follow Jesus.

____

____

____

Pope Francis has explained the importance of families and faith.

How do we keep our faith as a family? Do we keep it for ourselves, in our families, as a personal treasure like a bank account, or are we able to share it by our witness, by our acceptance of others, by our openness? We all know that families, especially young families, are often "racing" from one place to another, with lots to do. But did you ever think that this "racing" could also be the race of faith? Christian families are missionary families. . . . They are missionary . . . in everyday life, in their doing everyday things, as they bring to everything the salt and the leaven of faith! Keeping the faith in families and bringing to everyday things the salt and the leaven of faith.

Holy Mass for the Family, October 27, 2013

As a community of grace, the family shares God's life and love with its members and with the community in acts of loving service. It shares God's grace and experiences Jesus' love when family members forgive and are forgiven, and when they take care of one another.

And the family is a community of prayer. When a family includes prayer in their everyday life, they acknowledge the presence of God in every moment.

Activity

The family is a community of prayer. Choose one of these events in everyday life. Write a short prayer for your family to pray at these times. Teach it to your family members.

- Before homework
- before a practice or activity
- In the car
- After school

Partners in Faith

Saint Thomas More

Saint Thomas More was a lawyer. In 1529, King Henry VIII made him the Chancellor of England. He helped the king rule England. Thomas loved his family very much. He made sure that his daughters had the same education as his son. When the king wanted to divorce his wife and marry someone else, Thomas opposed the marriage. King Henry eventually had him beheaded.

Learn more about the life of Saint Thomas More.

I die the king's good servant, but God's first.

Prayer

Meditation

Faith Words

common priesthood of the faithful
Sacraments at the Service of Communion
Holy Orders **Matrimony**

Show What You Know

Choose the correct word to complete the sentences.

1. In Matrimony, a ________ man and woman become husband and wife and promise to be faithful to each other for the rest of their lives.

   baptized | beatified

2. The sacrament in which baptized men are ordained to serve the Church as deacons, priests, and bishops is called Holy ________.

   Communion | Orders

3. The common ________ is Christ's priestly mission in which everyone who has been baptized share.

   good | priesthood

Live Your Faith

- What do the two Sacraments at the Service of Communion have in common?

____

____

____

____

____

- How do you share in Christ's priestly mission?

____

____

____

____

____

How do I share Christ's love through service?

Mini-Task

Helping people is at the core of our faith. Catholic Relief Services (CRS) is an international organization committed to helping people meet their basic needs. Whether providing access to clean water, healthy food, or education, CRS sends thousands of volunteers to do the work of Christ around the globe.

One the lines below, write five things you consider basic needs. How can you help provide them for others?

Basic Needs

Want to do more? Go to your Portfolio to continue this activity.

At Home

Jesus tells us that he came not to be served but to serve. Over the next week, find a way to serve another person with love, as Jesus serves us. Involve your family in this project.

Unit 3

The Faith Lived

In this unit you will learn about the ways God shows his love for us in his Word and Christ's teachings and how we respond to his love, mercy, and forgiveness. We will see how God's love inspired us to care and show love for others.

How do we live what we believe?

Unit Song:
"I Send You Out," John Angotti

Unit Prayer

Leader: Saint Ignatius of Loyola taught that God's reason for creating us is to "draw forth from us a response of love and service" here on Earth. He also believed that all of creation exists for us to know God better, and to help us to love and serve him. Let us listen to stories of people among us who have used God's creation to better know, love, and serve him.

Let us listen to stories of missionary disciples among us.

Leader: O God, when we look at our own face, we see your beauty. We praise you for your wonderful works.

All: We praise you for your wonderful works.

Leader: O God, we see you in the faces of everyone you have created.

All: We praise you for your wonderful works.

Leader: O God, you show us how much you love us by the gift of your creation.

All: We praise you for your wonderful works.

Leader: We praise you and show our love for you when we serve each other and care for all your creation.

All: We praise you for your wonderful works.

End the Unit Prayer by singing the unit song.

Missionary Discipleship

When were you asked to be of service to someone else? What did you do? How did you feel? Was there a time when someone served you?

How do we know God loves us?

God created us in his image, with free will and a soul. God's grace helps us use our free will to choose what is good and right, and to show respect and care for others and creation. Natural law, engraved on our hearts, expresses the dignity of every person.

Meditation

Before all else be free persons! Freedom means . . . knowing how to [choose] behaviors that make us grow. . . . it will make you persons with a backbone, who know how to face life, [and live as] courageous and patient persons.

Pope Francis, June 7, 2013

We are created in God's image, with free will and a soul.

God freely chose to enter into a relationship with humanity. And when he did, he created us in his image and likeness. We are his most wondrous creation, because he willed it to be so. He created us with a body and a spiritual **soul**, with an intellect, and with **free will**.

Each of us is on a journey toward God and eternal happiness. From the moment of our conception, God breathed his life into us, giving us a spiritual soul. Our soul is what makes us fully human. It is the part of us that will never die.

Faith Words

soul see p. 295

free will see p. 293

How do I know free will?

God also created each of us with an intellect and free will. These gifts mean we can freely choose to cooperate with God's action in our lives and God's plan for us. God invites us to become his adopted children, and he gives us the grace that helps us respond to this invitation. There is nothing we can do on our own to deserve this grace. God's grace is a gift he gives to us.

The life of a Christian disciple involves freely choosing to receive the holiness of God and participating in divine life. Sometimes we stray from the path and take detours on our journey to God. We freely choose not to cooperate with God's plan. God always takes the first step to bring us back to him.

Jesus' sacrifice on the Cross will forever have the power to draw us back to God the Father and to Jesus. In the sacraments Jesus gave to the Church, we are cleansed from our sins and reconciled with God. Sacraments make us sharers in God's life and love and work.

Did You Know?

There are many ways to be happy.

Activity

Having free will means we can choose to do what God wants us to do. Without free will, we would be unable to choose for ourselves. As disciples, we can always choose the path to journey with God. God accompanies us on our spiritual journey to holiness.

Write a story about a young person having trouble in freely choosing to cooperate with God's plan. Perhaps, the young person is being bullied by peers to not choose freely for him or herself. Write the title of your story below. How does your main character exercise free will?

____

____

____

____

____

____

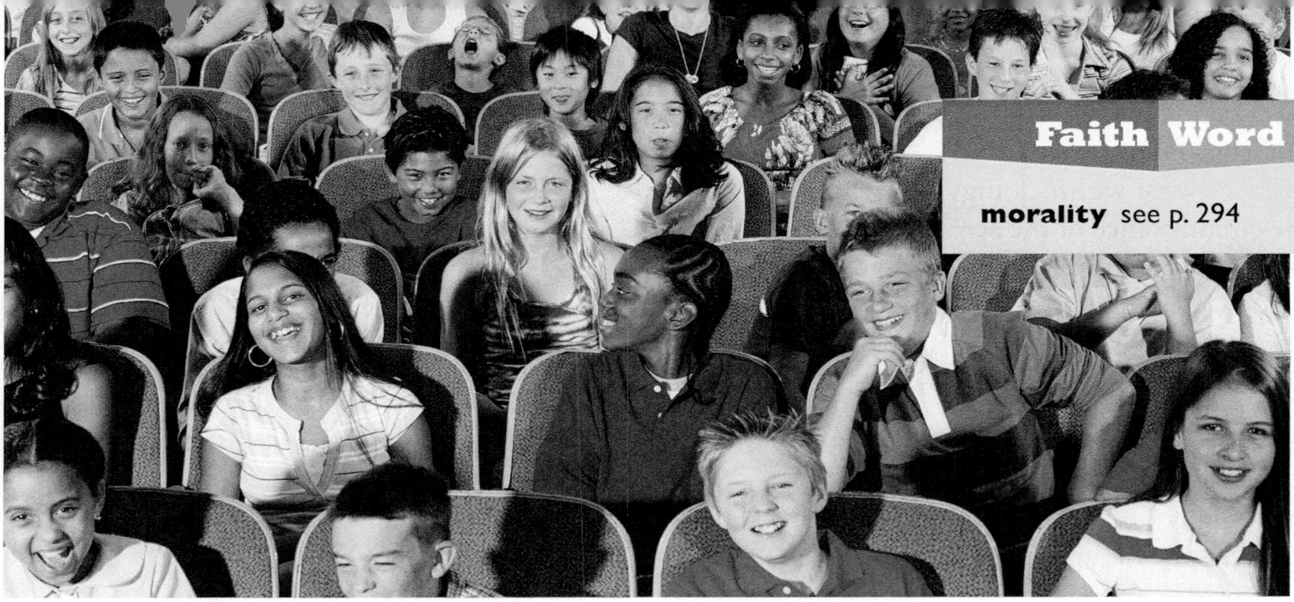

Faith Word

morality see p. 294

Prayer

Meditation

God's grace helps us respect and care for others and ourselves.

What do you see when you look in a mirror? You see a person created in the image and likeness of God. Now imagine looking in the same mirror and seeing not your face but the faces of the people in your life–family members, classmates, friends, neighbors. Use your imagination to see the faces of people from all walks of life–young, old, different nationalities, races, and ethnicities, from all over the world. These people, too, are created in the image and likeness of God.

The Church teaches that each of these people is "another self." This means that in a certain sense we see ourselves in other people, people created in the image and likeness of God, people whom God calls to be one with him. We see people whom God is calling to live forever in happiness with him, just like us.

When we see ourselves in other people, when we stand in their shoes, we recognize that we all have a fundamental right to dignity. Every person is deserving of respect and care.

Morality is the goodness or evil of our actions. A moral life is lived according to the teaching of Jesus and the Church. Every moral choice or act we make consists of three elements: the *objective* (the object, or what we do), the *intention* (the goal, or why we do the act), and the *situation or circumstance* in which we perform the action (such as where, when, with whom, and how).

What Makes Us Catholic?

God gave all of us human dignity. The Catholic Church teaches us to respect each other's minds, hearts, and bodies. We do this when we speak up for those who are being treated unkindly. Youth groups in some parishes in the United States have formed anti-bullying programs. They spread the word about showing respect for everyone. All Catholic young people are encouraged to stand up for what is right for themselves and for others. We are called to work together to stop bullying and other injustices.

A moral choice is one in which the object of what we are doing and the circumstance of the act are good. The intention behind our actions, why we do the act, must be good as well.

However, a good intention never makes a bad or evil action right or good. Some acts are always evil and morally wrong. The end never justifies the means.

In addition, the situation or circumstance within which we make a moral choice can either increase or decrease the goodness of an act. The act, the intention, and the circumstance all have to be good in order to have a morally good act.

Let us look at an example. Ryan is sitting in class during a test. He did not study for this test because he had to take care of his younger sibling. Ryan copies a classmate's answers.

Although Ryan's *intentions* were good (He wanted to pass the test.) and his *circumstances* had made it difficult for him to study (He had to take care of his sister.), the *act* of cheating is wrong.

The choices we make every day show whether or not we respect and care for ourselves and others. Our actions demonstrate whether or not we truly understand that every person is our neighbor, our brother or sister, in Jesus Christ.

God's grace, poured out on us most especially in the sacraments, helps us to seek the good in each other and ourselves. God's grace helps us respect and care for others and ourselves.

Activity

We are all created in the image of God. One way we honor this is through the Golden Rule: Do to others what you would have them do to you. On the Golden Rule chart, write one thing that you do for others that you would like them to do for you, using the letters as a guide.

G	
O	
L	
D	
E	
N	
R	
U	
L	
E	

Prayer

Meditation

Free will is the God-given gift and ability to make choices.

God created us as rational beings, each with a soul and intellect, and each with the dignity of being able to choose and control our own actions. The *Catechism of the Catholic Church* tells us that we have the freedom "to act or not to act, to do this or that" (*CCC*, 1731).

"You made me do it!" We have all heard and even said this at one time or another. The fact is, our voluntary actions, or actions that another person is not forcing us to do, are our own responsibility. They are not the responsibility of any other person or group.

Sometimes we do not know what the right thing to do is. We might act without knowing that what we are doing is not right. Or there are situations when a person might be acting out of duress, or fear. These situations are examples of why it's so important to understand that we have no right to take away another person's freedom.

All people have the right to exercise their freedom. We respect the God-given gift of freedom in everyone. This respect is what we owe each other as people created in the image of God, with human dignity. We should also note that freedom does not mean people have a right to say or do anything they want. Such actions would show a total disregard for the needs, rights, and freedom of others.

One Church, Many Cultures

Freedom to find opportunities to work and live is a human right. Catholics who are migrants leave their home countries to earn a living so they can support their families. In Ireland, the Catholic Church welcomes migrants from around the world, including Eastern Europe. Migrants from Poland, for example, participate in one of the many Masses celebrated in the Polish language. Some Irish Catholics who are not Polish also attend these Masses. They wish to enjoy the different cultural experience, including Polish music.

This gift of freedom, of free will, is an amazing and awesome power God has given us. The choices we make in exercising free will shape our lives. This freedom is a tremendous force for good in the world when we direct it toward God, toward happiness with him.

There is always the possibility of choosing between good and evil. When we choose the good, we grow toward the life with God that God desires for us. The more we choose and do what is good, the freer we become. When we choose evil, we sin by failing to love.

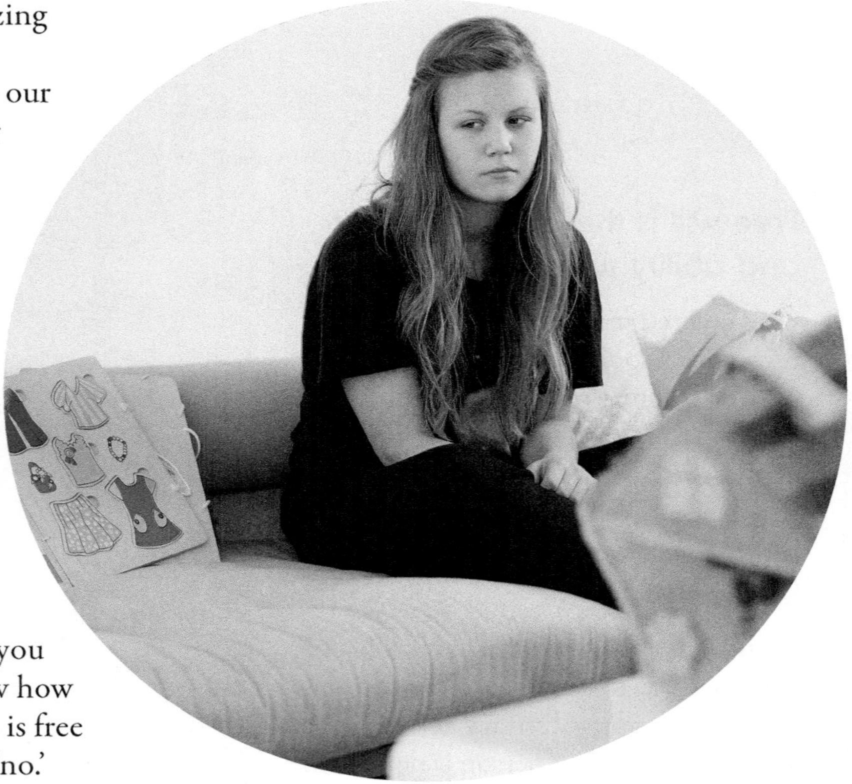

Pope Francis explains it this way:

"Many people will say to you that freedom means doing whatever you want. But here you have to be able to say no. If you do not know how to say 'no', you are not free. The person who is free . . . is able to say 'yes' and knows how to say 'no.' Freedom is not the ability simply to do what I want. This makes us self-centered and aloof, and it prevents us from being open and sincere friends; it is not true to say 'it is good enough if it serves me.'" No, this is not true. Instead, freedom is the gift of being able to choose the good: this is true freedom.

By God's grace, we use our free will to choose what is good and right, even when it is difficult for us to do so. The Holy Spirit, working within us, guides us in choosing what is good and just. Most especially, we grow in the proper use of God's gift of free will through participation in the sacraments.

Activity

How do you feel about these sentences?

"Someone took my only pencil, so it is okay for me to take one from someone who has extras. I do not need to tell anyone I took it because no one will notice."

"My friend hurt my feelings, so I should do the same to her. She needs to know how it feels. If I hurt her, it is her own fault."

"Some students in my class have been bullying another student. I am afraid they will bully me if I say something, so I keep quiet."

Knowing that God has made all of us in his image, how can you change these words so that everyone's rights are respected?

Prayer

Meditation

Faith Word

natural law see p. 294

Natural law expresses the dignity of every person.

Have you ever wondered where your sense of right and wrong comes from? Every day, we encounter situations about which we can say, "That just isn't right!" Or, on the other hand, we can also say "that *is* the right thing to do." Consider a time in which you see a friend being bullied. You might think, "That's not right!" And, with courage, you might do what you know *is* right–standing up for him. From where does this sense of right and wrong come? It comes from God.

God's plan is written on the hearts of every human. Something within each of us directs us to naturally seek God and to follow a path where we choose what is good for us and for others.

The Church calls this awareness, which is a moral sense and voice of reason within each of us, the **natural law**. We have this awareness of what is good and true because we are created in God's image. We have the use of reason and common sense. Natural law helps us discover the way to true happiness. At the same time, it helps us recognize that which turns us away from God, that which is evil. Natural law expresses the dignity of the human person. It is the guide for how we live as God's images in the world. It is the basis for our fundamental rights and duties as people.

The writing of Saint Thomas Aquinas is at the source of much of the Church's teaching about natural law. In his book *Summa Theologiae*, Aquinas said that "good is to be done and pursued, and evil is to be avoided." God designed us with a desire for the things that are best for us. These are called the Basic Goods:

Life. Life is a basic good, and *staying* alive is a good thing. Humans share this good with all creatures. It is the survival instinct, or self-preservation.

Reproduction. Once we have taken steps to ensure our own lives, we make more life, or reproduce, to ensure the survival of the species.

Educate one's offspring. We ensure the existence of the human race by teaching our children how to make their way in the world.

Activity

Below are some basic good attitudes. Write some ways you can apply the Golden Rule to each.

Seek God	**Avoid offense**
Naturally social	**Shun ignorance**

The Galilee landscape–where Jesus' disciples heard the Sermon on the Mount–as it appears today in Israel.

Seek God. This is a good that humans alone share. We have a desire to seek God, whether we've been exposed to him or not.

Naturally social. We are meant to live in community. We desire love and acceptance. We naturally seek ways to live peacefully in the world.

Avoid offense. We avoid doing things that hurt members of the community. We use our intellect and reason to avoid hurting others.

Shun ignorance. We have a natural curiosity to explore our world, to learn, and to grow in knowledge. We have an inclination to seek out what is true.

We can see from these Basic Goods of the natural law that it doesn't matter what religion we are. Natural law applies to all of us and expresses the dignity of every person.

God's plan was fulfilled in Christ, who said to his disciples: "Do to others whatever you would have them do to you. This is the law and the prophets" (Matthew 7:12).

Like the disciples, we look to Christ, who calls us to live by this Golden Rule, a New Law that perfects the Old Law established in the Ten Commandments. In the Sermon on the Mount, Jesus teaches us about the New Law: love our enemies, be peacemakers, live humbly, pray, trust in God. The grace of the Holy Spirit urges us to act out of love. The Sermon on the Mount teaches us what to do, and the sacraments give us the grace to do it.

Partners in Faith

Saint Thomas Aquinas

Saint Thomas Aquinas is one of the greatest theologians and philosophers of the Church. Thomas was a Dominican priest. His work *Summa Theologiae* is still studied at universities and seminaries today. One of his greatest contributions is his explanation of natural law. Near the end of his life, he experienced a mystical vision that caused him to stop writing and spend more time in prayer.

Learn more about the life of Saint Thomas Aquinas.

Good is to be done and evil to be avoided.

Prayer

Meditation

Faith Words			
soul	**free will**	**morality**	**natural law**

Show What You Know

1. What do we call an awareness of the voice of reason and a moral sense within us that moves us to seek God and make the right choices?

2. What term describes how we determine the goodness or evil of what we do or how we behave in situations?

3. When we talk about the invisible spiritual reality that makes each of us human and that will never die, what are we describing?

Live Your Faith

- When have you used *your* free will to show that you are following *God's* will for you?

- What tools do you have to determine the morality of an action, a decision, or a choice?

How do I stay on the path that leads to God?

Mini-Task

We have the ability to choose to follow Christ or to stray from his teachings. Developing a strong moral compass means that we know right from wrong and that we exercise our freedom and choose to do good. A compass always guides the way. Read the following situation. Then, fill in the compass below with choices that show movement toward Christ (north), away from Christ (south), or decisions that are somewhere in between (east and west).

A friend wants to attend a concert. His parents have told him he cannot go. He asks you to pretend that he is spending the night at your house, while he actually goes to the concert. What are some choices and decisions you can make?

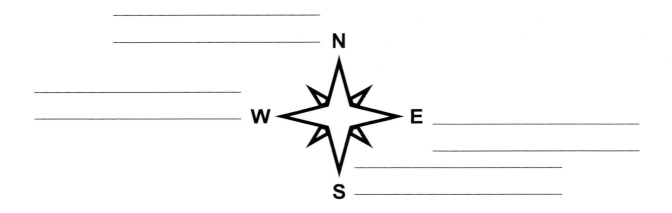

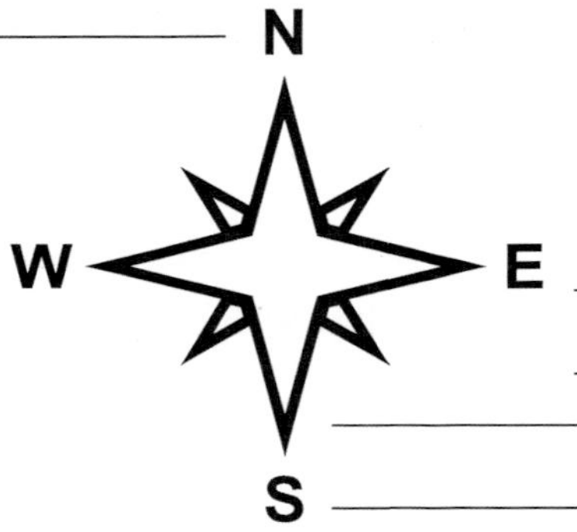

Want to do more? Go to your Portfolio to continue this activity.

At Home

Every person in your family was created in the image and likeness of God. Share with each other how you see the image of God in each of your family members.

How do we respond to God's love?

Lesson 12

God has placed the desire for happiness in every human heart. As we come to know who God is and seek happiness with him, we use an informed conscience to make good choices. We are guided by God, Scripture, and Church teaching. The divine grace of the sacraments strengthens us to live a virtuous life, and to work for peace, justice, and the common good.

Thanksgiving

Above all, let your love for one another be intense, because love covers a multitude of sins.
1 Peter 4:8

What leads me to God?

God has placed the desire for happiness in every human heart.

Saint Thomas Aquinas said simply, "God alone satisfies" (see *Catechism of the Catholic Church*, 1718). God's divine image is present in each of us. God created us out of love and for love. For this purpose, he created us with a longing for him, with a law written on our hearts and minds that guides us in discovering how to love as he loves.

God's plan for us, from the moment of conception, is that we share eternal beatitude, or happiness with God forever. Through our belief in Jesus Christ, we become sons and daughters of God, and we have new life in the Holy Spirit. The Holy Spirit makes present the action of God's grace in our lives especially through the sacraments. God's Spirit directs us toward love of God and love of neighbor. We seek and love what is true and good. We advance toward the glory of heaven where God has always intended us to be.

The Beatitudes (see Matthew 5:3–12), which are at the heart of Jesus' teachings, reveal the goal of human existence: to share in God's life and beatitude, or happiness forever. They provide a path for us to follow. God invites us to follow this path that leads to the Kingdom of God.

Activity

Think about a time when you got something you really wanted, but you were not as happy about it as you thought you would be. Share your experience with a friend. Now talk about a time when you felt God's love and how that made you feel. Share your feelings with a larger group.

Did You Know?

All people long for happiness.

Prayer

Thanksgiving

Faith Word

conscience see p. 293

An informed conscience is guided by God, human reason, and Church teachings.

Every person is called to follow the law that God has imprinted on our hearts. This is the law that encourages us to do good and avoid evil. Our **conscience**, which is our ability to know the difference between good and evil, and right and wrong, guides us in following this law. This gift from God helps us to make decisions and to judge our decisions and actions.

Every day we face situations in which we can either choose to do good or choose to do bad, or evil. We can make choices that reflect God's love and law, or we can make choices that don't. Educating our conscience about what is right and what is wrong is a lifelong task. An informed, well-educated conscience helps us make good choices about our words and actions.

God guides us in hearing the voice of our conscience to make life-giving choices. God created us with the ability to follow his plan for us. God also created us with the ability to reason. Reason guides our conscience to make the right judgments. With the gift of reason, we have the ability to recognize whether or not a concrete action is good and true, or bad. We also turn to the teachings of the Church, both in Sacred Scripture and Sacred Tradition, to inform our conscience in all that is true and good.

When we examine our conscience, such as when we celebrate the Sacrament of Penance and Reconciliation, we do so in light of God's truth, reason, and Church teaching. We determine whether the choices we have made showed love for God, ourselves, and others. We ask the Holy Spirit to help us judge the goodness of our thoughts, words, and actions.

Activity

Over the next several days, use each of these words in the list below as a personal "word of the day" to drive your actions for that day. Write down the things you do each day in journal entries.

Day 1: generosity
Day 2: compassion and forgiveness
Day 3: humility
Day 4: justice
Day 5: mercy
Day 6: honesty and integrity
Day 7: peacemaking
Day 8: courage

The Beatitudes, which Jesus taught us in the Sermon on the Mount, provide a path for us to follow. We can use them as an examination of conscience, including to prepare to celebrate the Sacrament of Penance. The Beatitudes help us examine our lives in light of Christian virtues. Read the Beatitudes in Matthew 5:3–10 and consider what they mean in your life.

The Beatitudes and Me

Matthew 5:3: How do I practice **generosity**?

- Do I recognize the gifts God has given me and share them?
- Do I serve others and think about their needs?

Matthew 5:4: How do I practice **compassion** and **forgiveness**?

- Do I say "I'm sorry" when I've hurt someone?
- Do I show compassion and comfort to those who are sick or sorrowful?

Matthew 5:5: How do I practice **humility**?

- Do I do my best to use the gifts God has given me to the best of my ability rather than trying to impress others?
- Do I admit my mistakes and learn from them?

Matthew 5:6: How do I practice **justice**?

- Do I give others what is due to them, and do I work for peace?

Matthew 5:7: How do I practice **mercy**?

- Do I forgive and treat others with compassion?

Matthew 5:8: How do I practice **honesty** and **integrity**?

- Am I trustworthy and truthful?

Matthew 5:9: How do I practice **peacemaking**?

- Do I focus on finding peaceful solutions to conflict?

Matthew 5:10: How do I practice **courage**?

- Do I respectfully stand up for what I believe and resist peer pressure?
- Do I trust that God is with me and that I can always count on him?

Prayer

Thanksgiving

Faith Word

virtue see p. 295

The divine grace of the sacraments strengthens us to live a virtuous life.

Good habits are a good thing. Good habits can help us be happy, healthy, and holy people. The Church recognizes the value in having good habits. Good spiritual habits called **virtues** help us to act according to God's love for us. People who are virtuous make these habits or virtues a part of their lives. People who are virtuous are people who *practice* or live the virtues in their concrete actions. They are in the habit of choosing and doing good.

What is the point of living a virtuous life? *The Catechism of the Catholic Church* tells us that living a virtuous life "allows a person not only to perform good acts, but to give the best of himself" (*CCC*, 1803).

Every day, Christ calls us to follow him and to live by his teachings. Every day, we have the opportunity to act as Jesus' disciples. The choices that we make show whether or not we follow Jesus' example. Sometimes we do not even realize that we are making a choice. We show love and respect because we are in the habit of doing it. We are living a life of virtue.

Activity

Imagine you and a partner are helping to lead a group of children receiving the Sacraments of Reconciliation and Eucharist for the first time. Work with your partner to create a game that children can play to help them understand one of the virtues celebrated in these two sacraments. Use this space to plan and write down your ideas.

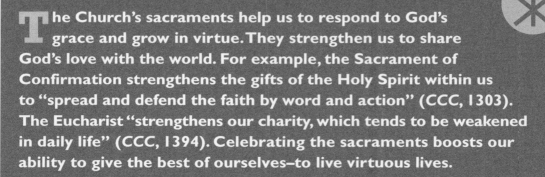

What Makes Us Catholic?

The Church's sacraments help us to respond to God's grace and grow in virtue. They strengthen us to share God's love with the world. For example, the Sacrament of Confirmation strengthens the gifts of the Holy Spirit within us to "spread and defend the faith by word and action" (*CCC*, 1303). The Eucharist "strengthens our charity, which tends to be weakened in daily life" (*CCC*, 1394). Celebrating the sacraments boosts our ability to give the best of ourselves–to live virtuous lives.

God's grace, which we receive in the sacraments, helps us to live virtuous lives. For example, in the Sacrament of Baptism, we celebrate the gift and virtue of faith. Faith in God guides us all throughout our lives: "Behold, I am with you always, until the end of the age" (Matthew 28:20).

We also celebrate the virtue of forgiveness. We are cleansed of Original Sin and personal sin. And we are joined to Christ and his Church—the powerful virtue of unity brings us strength to live as disciples of Jesus.

The Sacraments and the Virtues	
Baptism	faith, hope
Confirmation	faith, hope, courage, prudence
Eucharist	faith, hope, gratitude, love
Penance and Reconciliation	forgiveness, honesty, justice, generosity, humility
Anointing of the Sick	compassion, trust, fortitude, patience
Holy Orders	humility, service, reverence, temperance
Matrimony	unity, love, patience, respect, trust

One Church, Many Cultures

Theological Virtues guide catholics to carry out Christ's mission. For example, the Sant'Egidio community extends the hand of friendship to people everywhere, especially people in need. The community was founded by a high school student named Andrea Riccardi, in 1968. It has spread to over seventy countries. Sant'Egidio members dedicate themselves to a life of service and prayer and bringing peace to the world.

Prayer

Thanksgiving

Faith Words

Cardinal Virtues see p. 293

Theological Virtues see p. 295

The virtues lead us to work for peace, justice, and the common good.

The moral or **Cardinal Virtues** are habits that come about by our own efforts. The Cardinal Virtues are the virtues of prudence, justice, fortitude, and temperance.

Prudence	helps us to use reason to find the true good in every situation.
Justice	helps us to respect other people and give them what is rightfully theirs.
Temperance	helps us to use earthly goods in moderation.
Fortitude	helps us to use strength or courage to use good judgment and behavior during difficult or challenging times.

Although these virtues rest on the **Theological Virtues** of faith, hope, and charity (which are God's gifts), and they are brought to life by those virtues, we have to work to acquire the Cardinal Virtues and work to keep them! We have to learn about them, practice them, and keep practicing them.

The Cardinal Virtues guide the way we think, feel, and behave. They lead us to live a good life. They result from our making the decision, over and over again, to live by God's law.

While it does take a lot of our own effort to develop these virtues, we are not left on our own to struggle. For one thing, when we receive the Gifts of the Holy Spirit they also help us live virtuous lives. These seven gifts–wisdom, understanding, counsel, fortitude, knowledge, piety, and fear of the Lord–perfect the virtues. Most especially, God's divine grace–available to us in the sacraments–helps us develop these virtues and Gifts of the Spirit so that they grow in us, over time.

Our vocation, or calling from God, is "to show forth the image of God and to be transformed into the image of the Father's only Son" (*CCC*, 1877). This is our vocation as individuals, and it is our vocation as a human community. So what does it mean for how we are to live?

Activity

Write another word for each of the virtues. List one way that you can work on each of these virtues in the next week.

Prudence **Temperance**

Justice **Fortitude**

____

____

____

First, we cannot love God and hate our neighbor. It just is not possible. We need to live with each other, in mutual love and service. In this way, we develop our potential and respond to God's call to be his image in the world. **Society** is a group of people bound together by a principle of unity that goes beyond any one individual. A society works for the common good, a state of being in which the good of all people is valued more than the good of a few. A society has a spiritual purpose–to fulfill the human vocation.

Faith Words

society see p. 295

solidarity see p. 295

Society must promote the exercise of virtue. One of these virtues is **solidarity**. The Christian is called to consider members of society as people with rights, responsibilities, and fundamental human dignity, and also to recognize them as the living images of God. This has a profound impact on our actions, not only in the smaller societies of our families and neighborhoods, but also in the world. Pope Saint John Paul II reminds us that we are called to love our enemies "with the same love with which the Lord loves him or her" (*Sollicitudo Rei Socialis*–Social Concern, 1987). Every person has worth in God's eyes, and we are made for communion with each other and to share in the life of the Blessed Trinity.

Our actions of solidarity are actions that work for peace, justice, and the common good. These actions are not optional. They are what is expected of us as humans and as Christians. They are sign posts along the way toward salvation and the fulfillment of our vocation to show the image of God.

Partners in Faith

Saint Madeleine Sophie Barat

Saint Madeleine's brother taught her Latin, Greek, science, history, and literature in a time when few girls were educated. She believed that education was a matter of social justice and the common good. Madeleine also made up her mind that both boys and girls should be educated. She founded many schools throughout Europe.

Learn more about the life of Saint Madeleine Sophie Barat.

Even if you have fallen a thousand times in one day, but in the evening you stand up again, you may sing of victory.

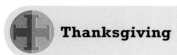

Thanksgiving

Faith Words

conscience virtue Cardinal Virtues
Theological Virtues society solidarity

Show What You Know

Circle the correct answer.

1. Which term means a group of people bound together by a principle of unity that goes beyond any one individual, with a spiritual purpose to fulfill the human vocation?
   a. society
   b. solidarity
   c. sacristy

2. What is a good habit that helps us act according to God's love for us?
   a. vice
   b. virtue
   c. viaticum

3. What word describes our ability to know the difference between good and evil, right and wrong?
   a. consciousness
   b. contrition
   c. conscience

4. What are the Theological Virtues?
   a. justice, fortitude, and fear of the Lord
   b. faith, hope, and love
   c. temperance, modesty, and piety

Live Your Faith

- How do you show solidarity with others?

____

____

- Which of the Cardinal Virtues gives you the most strength?

____

____

____

Lesson 12
Portfolio

How do virtues help me respond to God's love?

Mini-Task

The Cardinal Virtues help us to live a happy, holy life. Prudence, justice, temperance and fortitude guide our relationships with friends and family in real life as well as in the digital world.

Being a good digital citizen means using what you see and read online in a positive way. It means using the Internet to learn about and share what is good, interesting, and helpful, not to create a negative space.

What does being a good digital citizen mean to you? Talk about it with your group. Using the four Cardinal Virtues, plan a design of your own Digital Citizenship poster. Using words and art, give examples for how the virtues will guide your online choices and interactions.

Want to do more? Go to your Portfolio to continue this activity.

At Home

Talk with your family about what a society based on God's law and love for all people would look like. What can your family contribute to that society?

How does God teach us to love?

The Ten Commandments and Church law guide us in knowing, loving, and serving God. The commandments strengthen our relationship with God and guide us to live in truth and love. God's grace helps us keep God's laws. The precepts of the Church strengthen our bond with God and his Church.

Petition

Teach me, LORD, your way
that I may walk in your truth,
single-hearted and revering your name.

Psalm 86:11

God's grace helps us to keep God's laws.

We all are familiar with rules. Our families have them, our teachers have them, and our communities have them. Rules guide our actions. They tell us what is acceptable and what is not. Have you ever had a hard time following the rules? Sometimes it's difficult, and sometimes we just don't want to.

> Behold, the days are coming, says the Lord,
> when I will conclude a new covenant
> with the house of Israel and the house of
> Judah. . . .
>
> I will put my laws in their minds
> and I will write them upon their hearts.
>
> I will be their God,
> and they shall be my people.
>
> Hebrews 8:8, 10

Who is the ultimate authority for what is right, and good, and true? God is. Each of us is called to live in happiness with God. This is God's desire for us, and the desire of every human heart. However, wounded by sin, we sometimes lose our way. We are a people who stand in need of God's saving grace. The moral law–revealed by God in the Ten Commandments and fulfilled by Christ in the New Law, or Law of the Gospel–shows us the way to achieve eternal beatitude, happiness with God.

The New Law, or Law of the Gospel, is the work of Jesus Christ. It is the grace of the Holy Spirit given to us through faith in Christ. In the Sermon on the Mount (see Matthew 5–7), Christ taught us a way of living, a law of love for God, self, and neighbor. Saint Augustine tells us that Christ's law of love gives us "the perfect way of the Christian life . . . This sermon contains . . . all the precepts needed to shape one's life" (see the *Catechism of the Catholic Church*, 1966). We discover the qualities and actions of people blessed by God. Through the sacraments, God gives us the grace to follow the New Law and live as beatitude people.

What do God's laws mean to me?

Did You Know?

Laws are about listening.

Prayer

Petition

The Ten Commandments strengthen our relationship with God.

God's purpose in giving us the Ten Commandments was to teach us how to live in right relationship with him. We grow closer to God when we follow them. The commandments strengthen our relationship with him. God gives us the grace we need to follow his commandments.

In the First Commandment, God said,

> I am the LORD your God, who brought you out of the land of Egypt, out of the house of slavery. You shall not have other gods beside me.
>
> Exodus 20:2–3

We are called to manifest, or show forth to the world, the one, true God in whose image we are created. We celebrate the presence of God in the sacraments, and most especially in the Sacrament of the Eucharist. Sacramentals, such as sacred objects and images, draw our attention to the one, true God. They help us honor God and deepen our relationship with him.

In the Second Commandment, God said,

> You shall not invoke the name of the LORD, your God, in vain. For the LORD will not leave unpunished anyone who invokes his name in vain.
>
> Exodus 20:7

Activity

The name of God is holy. That's why we should not use God's name in anger or surprise. Using God's name is against the Second Commandment. Role-play with a friend what you could say to someone who was using God's name in vain. On the lines below, write what you could say to someone who believes that using God's name and using a bad word are the same thing.

____

____

____

Respect for God's name is an expression of respect for God himself. The name of God is holy. The Church begins her prayers and liturgy with the Sign of the Cross: "in the name of the Father and of the Son and of the Holy Spirit. Amen." (*CCC*, 2157). In the Sacrament of Baptism, we are baptized "in the name of the Father, and of the Son, and of the Holy Spirit."

In the Third Commandment, God said,

> Remember the sabbath day–keep it holy. Six days you may labor and do all your work, but the seventh day is a sabbath of the LORD your God. You shall not do any work, . . . For in six days the LORD made the heavens and the earth, the sea and all that is in them; but on the seventh day he rested. That is why the LORD has blessed the sabbath day and made it holy.
>
> Exodus 20:8–11

Faith Words

Chosen People see p. 293

Paschal Mystery see p. 294

God's **Chosen People** were the Israelites, whom God chose to be his people, and he would be their God. For them, the Sabbath was to be a day for the Lord, holy, and set apart to praise God, his work of creation, and his saving action in their lives. Sunday, the Lord's Day, is the Christian fulfillment of the Sabbath. Sunday Mass is at the heart of our Catholic celebration of the Lord's Day. We celebrate the **Paschal Mystery**, the Passion, Death, Resurrection and Ascension of Jesus, and we worship and adore God, present in the most profound way in the Eucharist. The Lord's Day is so important to our own lives and the life of the Church, the Church instructs us to participate in Mass on Sundays and on Holy Days of Obligation. Sunday is a holy day, a day of joy and grace.

God calls us to adore him, and only him. Adoration of God is an action of worship, an acknowledgment of God as Creator and Savior, the Lord and Master of everything that exists. Without God, we cannot exist. We adore and bless God in the Church's liturgy, most especially on Sunday, the Lord's Day.

What Makes Us Catholic?

To trace the roots of the Catholic faith, we look to our Old Testament ancestors in faith, the Chosen People. The tradition of the Jewish Sabbath continues in our celebration of Sunday as the Lord's Day. In the evening Mass on Holy Thursday, we read the story of the Passover meal celebrated when God led the Israelites out of Egypt. It was during a Passover meal that Jesus celebrated the Eucharist with his disciples. Our celebration of Pentecost is also connected to a Jewish feast, called Shavuot, which occurs forty days after Passover. The Holy Spirit came upon Jesus' Apostles during the festival of Shavuot in Jerusalem, and the Church's public ministry began.

Prayer

Petition

The Ten Commandments guide us to live in truth and love.

Jesus had a special gift of helping his followers focus on what was most important. He had summarized God's laws after being asked this question: "Teacher, which commandment in the law is the greatest?" (Matthew 22:36)

> You shall love the Lord, your God, with all your heart, with all your soul, and with all your mind. This is the greatest and the first commandment. The second is like it: You shall love your neighbor as yourself.
>
> Matthew 22:37–39

Take a closer look at Jesus' response, above. It was not enough for him to simply say, "You shall love the Lord, your God." Why? Jesus wanted to make sure his followers understood that loving God involves the *whole* person: our heart, our soul, and our mind.

And even that was not enough. Jesus goes on to connect the first and greatest commandment (love of God) to love of neighbor. The connection between the two commandments, love of God and love of neighbor, was a familiar one for those followers of Jesus who were already striving to live the Ten Commandments.

1 Corinthians 13:4-8 (Love is ...)

One Church, Many Cultures

Sacramentals can help us focus our attention on God and his love for us. In Uganda, Catholics celebrate their faith in special ways using sacramentals that include holy water and religious images. At the shrine of Our Lady Queen of Peace at Kiwamirembe, Catholics use sacramentals in their devotions. Statues on the mountain at the shrine depict different Mysteries of the Rosary and the Stations of the Cross. Ugandan Catholics also pray the Rosary in hopes of peace in their country.

Activity

Jesus wants us to love God with our hearts, souls, and minds. When you think about how you love God, which of these is easy for you to do? Which is more challenging and why?

I love God ...	This is easier for me because:	This is harder for me because:
with all of my heart		
with all of my soul		
with all of my mind		

The Ten Commandments are a "how-to" guide for right relationships. Take a closer look at how the Fifth through Tenth Commandments can guide us in our love of neighbor.

Fifth Commandment: "You shall not kill" (Exodus 20:13).

- Respect all life from the very beginning of life to the end of life.
- Protect people who are poor and vulnerable.
- Speak well of others; avoid killing through words of scandal and gossip.

Sixth Commandment: "You shall not commit adultery" (Exodus 20:14).

- Practice modesty, which means respecting your body and the bodies of others.
- Practice chastity, which means expressing friendship and love in appropriate ways.

Seventh Commandment: "You shall not steal" (Exodus 20:15).

- Treat people with justice and mercy.
- Do not cheat, steal, or take things that do not belong to you.

Eighth Commandment: "You shall not bear false witness against your neighbor" (Exodus 20:16).

- Be honest; do not lie.
- Respect the reputation and good name of others.
- Say you are sorry.

Ninth Commandment: "You shall not covet your neighbor's wife" (Exodus 20:17).

- Honor the love between husband and wife.
- Keep your own heart pure. Act with love.
- Be faithful and trustworthy.
- Practice the virtue of temperance, or moderation.

Tenth Commandment: "You shall not covet your neighbor's house . . . or anything that belongs to your neighbor" (Exodus 20:17).

- Be grateful for God's gifts; don't be jealous of others' gifts.
- Be a good steward of God's gifts; use the gifts of creation wisely.
- Share your material gifts and talents for the benefit of others.

Activity

The Tenth Commandment tells us to be a good steward of God's gifts. This means taking care of the things we have, but it also means taking care of God's creation–the Earth. Next week, think of something you can do to take care of creation each day. Keep track of all the things you accomplished.

Faith Word

precepts of the Church see p. 294

Prayer

Petition

The precepts of the Church strengthen our bond with God and his Church.

Christians fulfill their vocations in the Church, in communion with all the baptized. We receive the Word of God and the New Law of Christ: love of God and love of neighbor. In the liturgy and sacraments, the grace of Christ enlightens and nourishes the Christian life. The moral life, striving for right relationship with God and others, find its source and summit in the Eucharist.

The pope and bishops have established some laws to help us know and fulfill our responsibilities as members of the Church. The **precepts of the Church** are positive laws that present the minimum of what a Catholic should do in order to grow in love of God and neighbor. These laws remind us that we are called to grow in holiness and serve the Church. They help us to know and fulfill our responsibilities as members of the Church and to unite us as followers of Jesus Christ. They guide our behavior and teach us how we should act as members of the Church.

It is helpful to think of the precepts as rules or principles intended as a guide for behavior. They teach us how we should act as members of the Church. These precepts also make sure that the Church grows in love for God and neighbor.

1. You shall attend Mass on Sundays and Holy Days of Obligation and rest from servile work.
2. You shall confess your sins at least once a year.
3. You shall receive the Sacrament of the Eucharist at least during the Easter season.
4. You shall observe the days of fasting and abstinence by the Church.
5. You shall help to provide for the needs of the Church.

The precepts of the Church guide us in how we should act as members of the Church. We also have a duty as citizens to work within our civic communities to contribute to the good of society in a spirit of truth, justice, solidarity, and freedom.

Take another look at the precepts of the Church. Remember that each of them is intended to help us grow in love of God and love of neighbor. Why do you think the Church choose these particular precepts or rules? How would you describe to a friend who is not Catholic the rationale behind the Church's teaching? How does each of the five precepts help us grow in love of God and love of neighbor?

Activity

Work together as a class to develop some precepts for your classroom. The goal of your precepts should be to help everyone grow in love of God and neighbor.

Partners in Faith

Saint Rose of Lima

Saint Rose wanted to show her love for God. She spent many hours in prayer and decided never to marry. For her, the commandments were a way of life. She did penance and fasted every day. She also did needlework and grew flowers to support her family.

Learn more about the life of Saint Rose of Lima.

There is no other ladder by which to reach heaven than by the Cross.

Prayer

Petition

Faith Words

Chosen People **Paschal Mystery**
precepts of the Church

Show What You Know

In your own words, write definitions for the terms.

Paschal Mystery

____

____

____

____

precepts of the Church

____

____

____

____

Chosen People

____

____

____

____

Live Your Faith

- Which precept of the Church do you find easiest to follow?

____

____

- How would you explain the Paschal Mystery to someone who was not Catholic?

____

____

____

How do I live in God's love?

Mini-Task

Choose one of the commandments or one of the precepts of the Church from this lesson. Write it below.

____

____

What does this law tell us about God's love?

____

____

____

How does following this law show love for God?

____

____

____

How does this law lead to happiness?

____

____

____

What would the effect be of not having this law?

____

____

____

Want to do more? Go to your Portfolio to continue this activity.

At Home

How can your family commit to following the first three commandments more closely?

What turns us away from God's love?

God loves us, and God wants us to return his love. Sin sometimes stands in the way of our loving God and others. Original Sin created in us an inclination toward sin. Sin goes against our human reason and God's love. It damages our relationship with God. Committing sins repeatedly leads to vices, or capital sins, yet God always loves us and forgives us. His grace helps us return to the path of holiness.

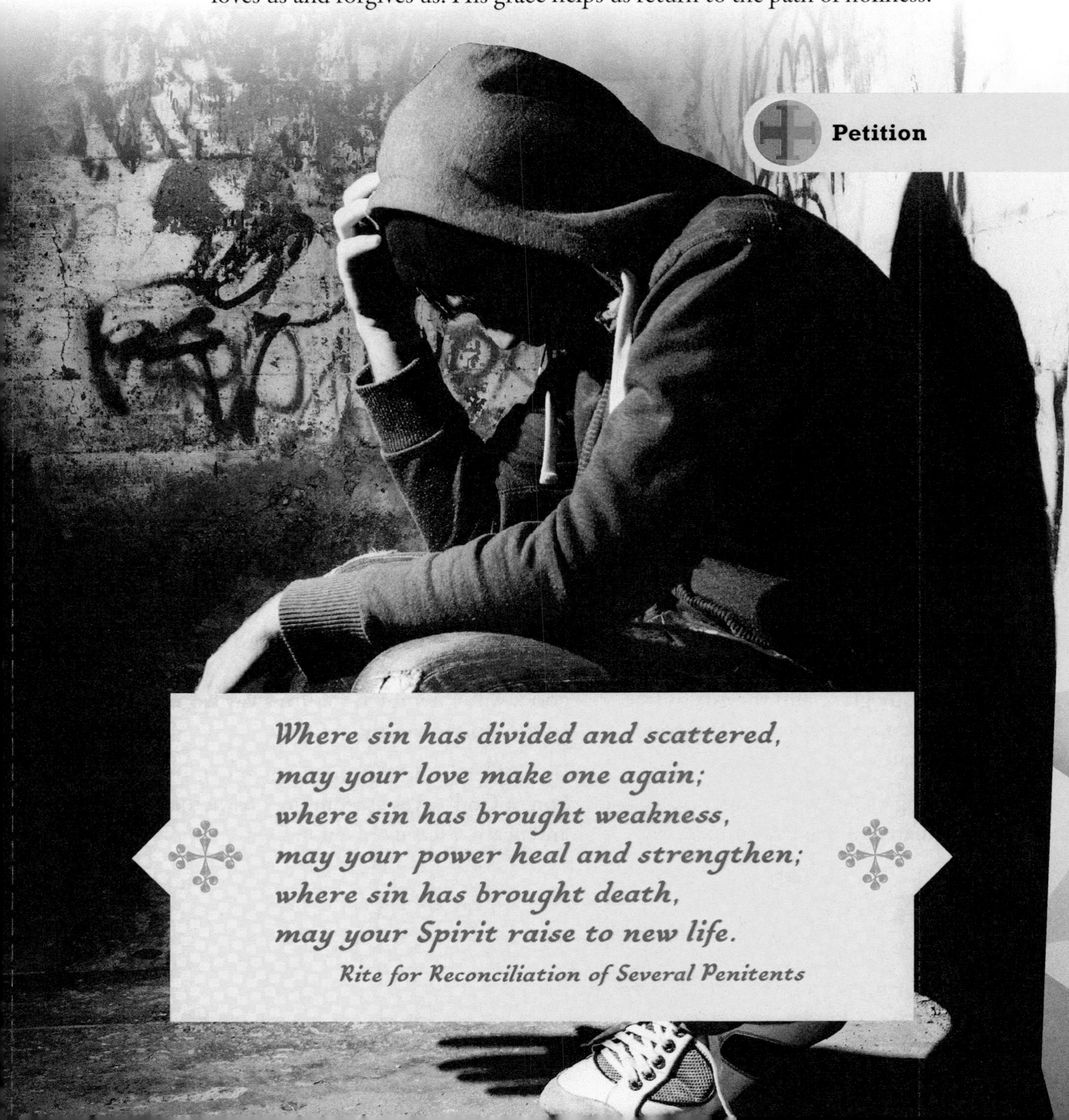

Petition

Where sin has divided and scattered,
may your love make one again;
where sin has brought weakness,
may your power heal and strengthen;
where sin has brought death,
may your Spirit raise to new life.

Rite for Reconciliation of Several Penitents

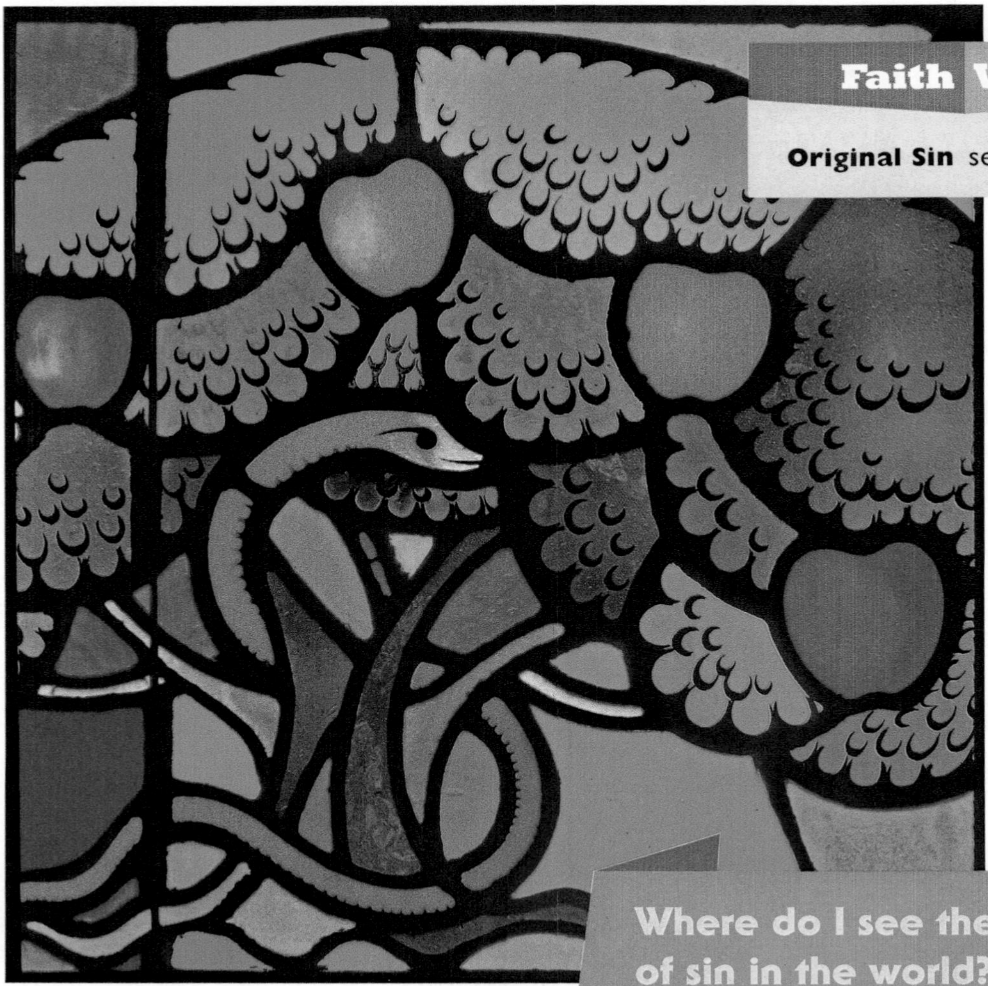

Faith Word

Original Sin see p. 294

Where do I see the effects of sin in the world?

Original Sin created in us an inclination to sin.

Life in the Holy Spirit is God's dream for us. This is a life of divine love and human solidarity. God created us in his image and likeness to share in his divine life. God created us to know him, to be close to him, and to share in his love forever. With the gift of reason, we are able to understand God's plan and the natural law which he imprinted on our hearts. With God's grace and the gift of free will, we are able to choose what is true and good. This is how God created us.

At the very beginning of our human history, however, the first man and woman turned away from God and disobeyed him. Because of their sin, called **Original Sin**, they lost their closeness with God. Ignorance, suffering, and death entered the world.

Because of Original Sin, human beings suffer. We are all born with Original Sin and are affected by it throughout our lives. While we still want what is good, we are tempted to turn away from God and commit personal sin.

By his Death and Resurrection, Jesus Christ–the Son of God–saves us from sin. His victory over sin and death offers us salvation.

Did You Know?

It is reasonable to seek out the good.

Prayer

Petition

Faith Word

sin see p. 295

Sin goes against our human reason and God's love.

People choose from a variety of operating systems when buying a computer, smart phone, tablet, or gaming system. The operating system, or OS, supports the device's basic functions. It is the most important program that runs the device.

Humans are not computers, but we can use the analogy to understand something about ourselves: God created us with an awesome "operating system." We are hardwired to love. God created us with all the software and hardware necessary to seek and love all that is true and good. He created us in his image–with a soul, with the ability to reason, and with free will.

Sin, however, is like the malware or virus that infects our operating system and causes it to malfunction. And like a virus, sin spreads beyond ourselves. Sin is an offense against God. When we sin, we turn our hearts away from God's love and choose that which we know is wrong. The choices we make weaken God's life in us. Sin is a thought, word, deed, or omission against God's law. Every sin weakens our friendship with God and others.

Activity

Has anyone ever said something about you that was not true? People who do not know you might have believed it. Your reputation might have been hurt by one untrue comment. Work in groups to have a panel discussion about a time when someone might have said or shared something that hurt another person. Have the rest of your group ask questions about what could have been done differently. Write the questions from your group on the lines below.

____

____

____

____

____

All people are created in God's image and share the same human dignity. This makes us one human community, and sin affects that community.

Sin can lead to unjust situations and conditions in society. Some results of sin in society are prejudice, poverty, homelessness, crime, and violence. The Church speaks out against social sin, and we work to stop things in society that allow unjust behaviors or conditions to exist. The Church encourages all people to turn to God and to live lives of love and respect.

Part of being reconciled with the Church is admitting that we have not lived as God calls us to live. During Mass, the whole assembly confesses that we have sinned. A prayer we often pray at Mass, called the *Confiteor*, begins:

"I confess to almighty God and to you, my brothers and sisters."

In this prayer we ask all the members of the Church to pray for us and our forgiveness. The *Confiteor* prepares us to receive Eucharist, as through this prayer God forgives all sins that are not mortal.

Activity

Work in small groups for each of the following issues. First, learn how these issues affect people in society. Share what you learn with your class. Learn what organizations in your area are doing to help, and find out how you can get involved. In the space next to each "issue" write an idea you can do as a class to help.

Prejudice	
Poverty	
Homelessness	
Crime	
Violence	

Faith Word

mortal sin see p. 294

Prayer

Petition

Sin damages our relationship with God.

When Pope Francis visited the Saint Magdalene of Canossa parish in Rome in 2017, a young girl named Sara asked him, "What scares you?" Pope Francis answered her: "What frightens me? I'm frightened when a person is bad; the wickedness of people." He told the children that the "seeds of wickedness" lie within each human being. What is really frightening, the pope shared, is the harm that people cause by choosing to sin.

At Mass that day, Pope Francis described sin as "a slap" to God's face. Sin is a failure to love God and our neighbor. Sometimes people turn completely away from God's love. They commit very serious sin that breaks their friendship with God. This sin is called **mortal sin**. Those who commit mortal sin must freely choose to do something that they know is seriously wrong. However, God never stops loving people who sin seriously. The Holy Spirit calls them to conversion, to turn back to God.

What Makes Us Catholic?

We all have fears. Fear is a real thing and can get in the way of our faith if we give in to it. In Scripture, God often tells us not to be afraid. We are to trust in God and in his love for us. This human fear is different from the "fear of the Lord." This is one of the gifts of the Holy Spirit. It fills us with wonder and awe of God, who created us out of love. It also means putting ourselves in God's hands. Having the "fear of the Lord" helps us love and *honor* God.

Faith Word

venial sin see p. 295

Less serious sin that weakens our friendship with God is called **venial sin**. Even though venial sins do not turn us completely away from God, they still hurt others, ourselves, and the Church. If we keep repeating them, they can lead us further away from God and the Church. However, God offers us forgiveness when we think or do things that harm our friendship with him or with others.

We restore our relationship with God in the Sacrament of Penance and Reconciliation. "The face of Jesus," Pope Francis said at the same Mass in 2017, "encourages us to ask forgiveness for our sins and not to sin so much. It encourages us most of all to trust because if he has made himself sin and has taken on our sins, he is always ready to forgive us. We just need to ask him."

Act of Contrition

One Church, Many Cultures

We can see the "face" of Jesus through the eyes of many artists. They often portray Jesus as part of their own culture. The different faces of Jesus remind us that Jesus came to save all people. Artists in Europe often painted Jesus as fair-skinned with light hair, while we know Jesus would have had darker features and hair. Asian and African Christian artists often show Jesus, the Holy Family, and early Christians with features similar to theirs. Seeing different images of Jesus helps us relate to Jesus in a way that is meaningful to us. It helps us to recognize Jesus in ourselves, and it can inspire the way we share Jesus' love and follow his teachings.

Prayer

Petition

Faith Words

vice see p. 295

capital sins see p. 293

Committing sins repeatedly leads to vices, or capital sins.

Over time, people develop habits. Our habits can be either good habits or bad habits. The more often we do something, such as brush our teeth every morning, say grace before meals, bite our fingernails, or miss Mass on Sunday, the more likely we are to continue doing it.

Committing sin over and over again can become a habit. It reproduces itself and clouds our judgment between what is good and evil. Committing the same sin over and over leads to **vices**, or capital sins. **Capital sins** are the source of all sins. They are habits that incline a person to sin.

Activity

The more we do something, the easier it is to do it. That thing becomes a habit. This is true for both good and bad things. Fill in the chart with some things you could do every day to create a good habit of prayer. Share with a friend the first thing you are going to do this week.

The Seven Capital Sins	I could . . .
Pride: improper appreciation of one's own worth	
Greed: a sin of excess; desire for earthly goods and power	
Gluttony: eating or drinking too much	
Lust: impure desires of a sexual nature	
Sloth: laziness	
Envy: jealousy; distress over the good fortune of someone else	
Anger: desire for vengeance, rage, or wrath	

Because of the effects of Original Sin, we are susceptible to the seven vices. God's grace helps us stay on the path to holiness, especially through the Sacraments of Eucharist and Penance and Reconciliation, by keeping the commandments and by practicing the virtues.

We can practice seven virtues to confront or counter the seven vices.

Seven Virtues

Humility helps us overcome Pride.

Generosity helps us overcome Greed.

Abstinence or self-restraint helps us overcome Gluttony.

Chastity, or decency, helps us overcome Lust.

Diligence, or dedication, helps us overcome Sloth.

Kindness helps us overcome Envy.

Patience helps us overcome Anger.

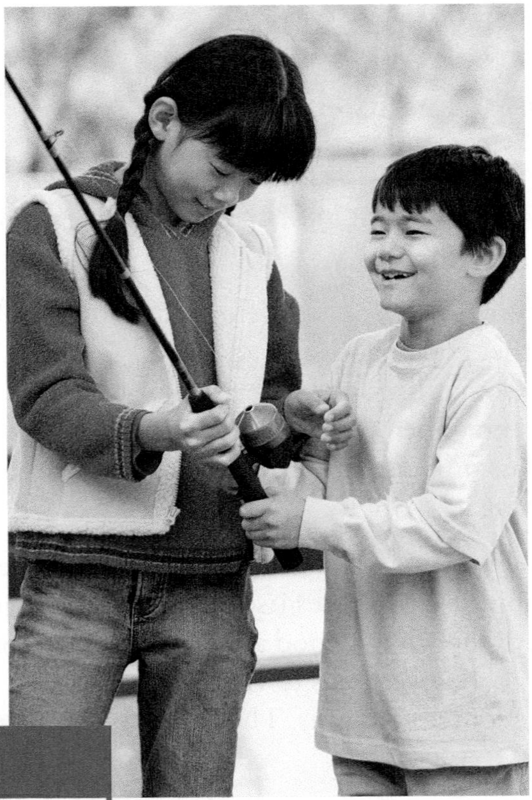

Activity

Looking at the list of Seven Virtues above. Notice how each one confronts or counters a vice? Do any of these vices give you trouble? Compose a prayer in private, asking God to strengthen you in the particular virtue that counters this vice.

Partners in Faith

Saint Magdalene of Canossa

As a teenager, Saint Magdalene of Canossa wanted to be a nun. That was not God's will for her life at the time. Instead, she used her family's fortune to help the poor. Later in her life, she founded a religious order that cared for poor children and worked in hospitals. Today, her sisters work all around the world.

Learn more about the life of Saint Magdalene of Canossa.

There is no greater act of charity than that of working together so that all may love God.

Prayer

Petition

Faith Words		
Original Sin	sin	mortal sin
venial sin	vice	capital sins

Show What You Know

Read the statements. Circle whether the statement is True or False. Correct any false statements you find.

1. Capital sins are the seven "deadly" sins.

   True | False

   ____

   ____

2. Mortal sin damages but does not break our friendship with God.

   True | False

   ____

   ____

3. Venial sin is the first sin that weakened human nature and brought ignorance, suffering, and death into the world; we all suffer from its effects.

   True | False

   ____

   ____

Live Your Faith

- Sin is like a virus. How do you keep the virus of sin from affecting your personal "operating system"?

____

____

____

- What good habits help you avoid the bad habits that can lead to vices?

____

____

____

Why is forgiveness important when I turn away from God?

Mini-Task

Sin harms our relationship with others and with God. While God is always ready to forgive us when we have a contrite heart, it is important to reflect on our actions and ask forgiveness. This is the first step in the Sacrament of Reconciliation. It is also the first step when we seek forgiveness from another person. In the space below, plan a personal narrative about an experience of asking someone for forgiveness.

Forgiveness

What happened?

____

From whom did you need to ask forgiveness, and why?

____

____

How did you ask for forgiveness?

____

Did the person forgive you?

____

How did it feel to ask to be forgiven?

____

____

Think about and discuss with a partner your answers to the question: How does it feel to forgive others?

Want to do more? Go to your Portfolio to continue this activity.

At Home

With others in your family, talk about how you can help each other make good choices and resist sin. This week, try to encourage another person in your family who is making good choices.

What turns us toward God's love?

God helps us turn away from sin toward his love. Through God's grace, we share in the life of the Trinity. The Holy Spirit fills our hearts with sanctifying grace. Through Baptism and faith, we are restored to holiness and receive the gift of justification.

Lectio* and *Visio Divina

Therefore, since we have been justified by faith, we have peace with God through our Lord Jesus Christ.

Romans 5:1

God helps us turn away from sin and toward his love.

Jesus told the following parable to help us understand what it means to be sorry for our actions and to turn back to God. He explained that a son once asked his father to give him the share of the family's estate that would belong to him. The father did so, but the son soon wasted the money his father had given him. He chose to live a sinful life. The son soon found out that there were consequences to his choice. Jesus said,

"Coming to his senses he thought, 'How many of my father's hired workers have more than enough food to eat, but here am I, dying from hunger. I shall get up and go to my father and I shall say to him, "Father, I have sinned against heaven and against you. I no longer deserve to be called your son; treat me as you would treat one of your hired workers."' So he got up and went back to his father. While he was still a long way off, his father caught sight of him, and was filled with compassion. He ran to his son, embraced him and kissed him. His son said to him, 'Father, I have sinned against heaven and against you; I no longer deserve to be called your son.' But his father ordered his servants, 'Quickly bring the finest robe and put it on him; put a ring on his finger and sandals on his feet. Take the fattened calf and slaughter it. Then let us celebrate with a feast, because this son of mine was dead, and has come to life again; he was lost, and has been found.'"

Luke 15:12–24

God is like the forgiving father in this story. He welcomes us back when we have sinned and rejoices when we decide to turn back to him.

God constantly calls us to **conversion**. Conversion is a turning to God with all one's heart. If we trust God, he will show us how to change and grow into the people he wants us to be. Conversion happens again and again. It leads us to live our lives according to God's great love for us. God the Holy Spirit gives us this desire to change and grow.

Faith Word

conversion see p. 293

When have I experienced God's forgiveness?

Activity

Write about a modern-day Prodigal Son or Daughter. What did the person do to turn from God? What did the person's parent do when the son or daughter returned? Be sure to include a conclusion which shows that both God and the parent forgave the person. Now share it with a partner. What parts of your stories are alike? What parts are different?

Prayer

Lectio and *Visio Divina*

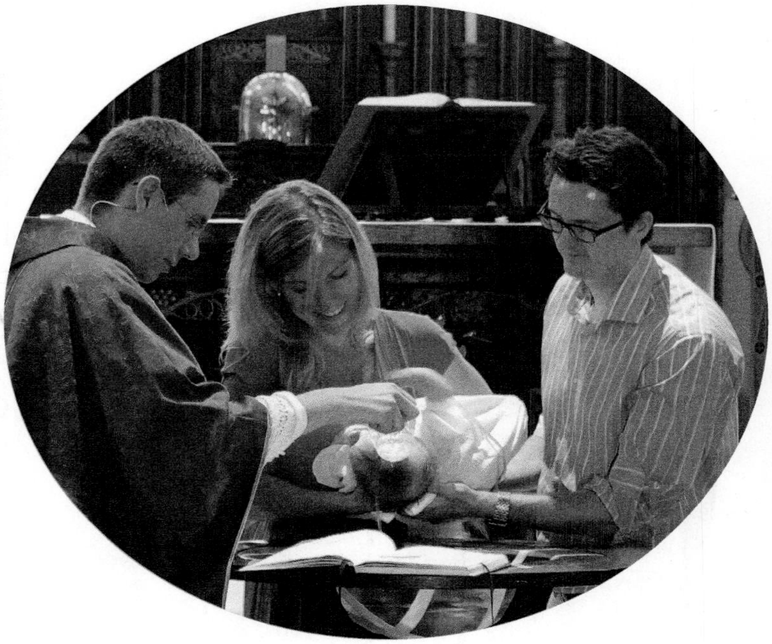

Grace makes us part of the life of the Trinity.

When we turn away from sin and back to God, we experience the work of God's love within us. This is God's grace, which is God's life that he shares with us. It is the free and undeserved help that God gives us to respond to his call. It is our participation in the life of God.

God's love was revealed to us in Jesus Christ and given to us by the Holy Spirit. Through our Baptism, we are born to new life. Through the power of the Holy Spirit, we take part in Christ's Passion and Resurrection. We become members of the Body of Christ, the Church.

By Baptism, grace makes us part of the life of the Trinity. We become adopted children of God, sharers in the life of Jesus Christ, and members of God's family.

One Church, Many Cultures

Through Baptism, we become children of God. As members of God's family, we are called to care for his gifts and for each other. Water is one of the most important of God's gifts. In many cultures, it symbolizes new life and growth. Access to clean water is a human right that the Church promotes and works for, around the world. Organizations like Catholic Relief Services work with local populations to build wells and improve their water systems. They help people receive the clean water they need, especially for drinking. In this way, the Church works to care for all God's people wherever they live.

Activity

List five acts of kindness you can perform this week that will help you walk as a child of Christ.

____

____

____

____

____

Did You Know?

Small changes can add up.

As baptized Christians and sharers in the gift of God's grace, we show the light of Christ and flame of faith to the world. At the presentation of a lighted candle during the Sacrament of Baptism, the celebrant tells the parents and godparents of a child:

"This child of yours has been enlightened by Christ. He (she) is to walk always as a child of the light. May he (she) keep the flame of faith alive in his (her) heart. When the Lord comes, may he (she) go out to meet him with all the saints in the heavenly kingdom."

Rite of Baptism, 100

Reflect on ways you "walk as a child of the light" and "keep the flame of faith alive" in your heart."

Activity

God's love is the greatest gift we can receive. Write a rap or a poem expressing your thanks for being an adopted child of God. Draft your rap or poem here.

Share your composition with two or three friends. Turn your combined work into a short presentation for the rest of the group.

Prayer

Lectio* and *Visio Divina

The Holy Spirit fills our hearts with sanctifying grace.

Faith Word

sanctifying grace
see p. 295

What do you normally do when you receive a gift? You open it! Most of us don't tuck gifts away on a closet shelf wrapped, and forget about them. We remove the wrapping, thank the giver, and usually appreciate and use the gifts.

A powerful, life-giving gift that a person can receive does not come wrapped and tied with a bow. In fact, it is invisible to the eye. This gift is God's grace. Grace is the help God gives us to know and love God as his adopted children. Grace is invisible, but it is essential to a life of holiness. The grace God gives us helps us to be holy.

Sanctifying grace is the gift of sharing in God's life. We receive the gift of sanctifying grace in Baptism and in the other sacraments. It is God's divine life within us that makes us his children. This grace helps us to trust and believe in God. It strengthens us to live as Jesus did.

The Holy Spirit fills our souls with this grace, healing our souls and making them holy. Sanctifying grace enables us to live with God. It empowers us to know and love God.

Pope Francis talks about grace

We ought never to lose hope. God overwhelms us with his grace, if we keep asking.

And with the grace of Baptism and of Eucharistic Communion I can become an instrument of God's mercy, of that beautiful mercy of God.

The Eucharist is essential for us: it is Christ who wishes to enter our lives and fill us with his grace.

What Makes Us Catholic?

In the sacraments, we receive sanctifying grace, the gift of God's own life and friendship. To help us stay on the right path, we can ask for God's help. Through *actual grace*, God gives us the support we need along the way. Actual grace helps us avoid making wrong choices and can also help us to do good. The *Catechism of the Catholic Church* tells us that "God has freely chosen to associate man with the work of his grace" (*CCC*, 2008). God's grace works in us and brings us closer to our Father.

Faith Word

justification see p. 293

Prayer

Lectio* and *Visio Divina

Through Baptism and faith in Jesus Christ, we receive the gift of justification.

We receive another amazing gift through our Baptism and our faith in Jesus Christ. This is the gift of justification. **Justification** by faith means that we are forgiven for our sins, renewed, and returned to the goodness and holiness for which God first created us. We are justified–freed from our sins and reconciled to God–through the power of the Holy Spirit. We become friends of God.

At Baptism, we are freed from sin and united with Christ and the Church. We become members of Christ who is Priest, Prophet, and King.

> God the Father of our Lord Jesus Christ has freed you from sin, given you a new birth by water and the Holy Spirit, and welcomed you into his holy people. He now anoints you with the chrism of salvation. As Christ was anointed Priest, Prophet, and King, so may you live always as a member of his body, sharing everlasting life.
>
> Rite of Baptism, 98

Activity

Think of a time you and a friend or close family member were apart from each other. What, if anything, brought you back together? How did it feel to be reunited? If you have not been reconciled, what can you do to make that happen?

____

____

____

Knowing how much God loves you, how do you think God feels when you are reconciled to God?

There is nothing we can do on our own to claim or deserve justification. Justification is an action of God. Through Baptism and faith in Jesus Christ, God's mercy and grace makes it possible for us to be cleansed of our sins, reconciled to God, and sharers in eternal life with God.

> The righteousness of God has been manifested apart from the law, wthough testified to by the law and the prophets, the righteousness of God through faith in Jesus Christ for all who believe. . . . All have sinned and are deprived of the glory of God. They are justified freely by his grace through the redemption in Christ Jesus, whom God set forth . . . to prove his righteousness in the present time, that he might be righteous and justify the one who has faith in Jesus.
>
> Romans 3:21–26

Christ the Saviour **by Guido Reni (1575–1642).**

Partners in Faith

Saint Anselm

Saint Anselm was the Archbishop of Canterbury. He is famous for defending the faith with reasonable arguments. He said that faith and understanding had to go together. Without faith, it is impossible to understand God. But without reason, not even faith is possible.

Learn more about the life of Saint Anselm.

I do not seek to understand that I may believe, but believe that I might understand.

Prayer

Lectio* and *Visio Divina

Faith Words

conversion	sanctifying grace	justification

Show What You Know

Circle the correct answer to complete the sentences.

1. ________________ is the action of God by which we are freed from sin and reconciled to God.

   a. Justification
   b. Sanctification
   c. Confirmation

2. A turning to God with all one's heart is called ________________.

   a. complication
   b. contrition
   c. conversion

3. ________________ is the gift of sharing in God's life.

   a. Sacramental grace
   b. Sanctifying grace
   c. Actual grace

Live Your Faith

- Justification is an action of God. In what other ways is God acting in you?

____

____

____

____

- The Holy Spirit gives us the desire to change and grow. How have you grown in your faith this year?

____

____

____

____

How do I share in God's life?

Mini-Task

The Parable of the Prodigal Son has a lot to teach us about God's love and forgiveness. The father represents God in the parable. He welcomes his lost son back with open arms. What about the brother in this story?

Read the Parable of the Prodigal Son in the Gospel of Luke 15:11–32. While you are reading, imagine yourself as the brother who stays with his father.

Why are you angry? Can you find it in your heart to forgive your lost sibling? In the space below, express your feelings in a letter to your sibling.

Want to do more? Go to your Portfolio to continue this activity.

At Home

As a family, talk about ways you can answer God's call to conversion. Make a list of ways your family can change and grow in God's love. With God's divine life in us through the gift of sanctifying grace, compose a family prayer answering God's call. Place the prayer on everyone's phone as a reminder to pray.

The Faith Prayed

In this unit you will learn about prayer and different ways we show our faith through forms of Christian spirituality. We will see how the saints are models for our prayer lives and how we are part of the Communion of Saints.

Unit 4

How do we become what we believe?

Unit Song:
"Here I Am, Lord," Dan Schutte

Unit Prayer

Leader: Saint Ignatius of Loyola wanted us to "Go forth and set the world on fire" with our faith. In order to be a disciple of Christ, we must become what we believe. Spreading the faith that is in our hearts is how we can set the world on fire. We believe that celebrating with our parish community at Mass helps us to become better followers of Jesus—to be his disciples.

Listen to the stories of missionary disciples among us, helping to "set the world on fire."

Leader: Let us pray the Sign of the Cross:
In the name of the Father,
and of the Son,
and of the Holy Spirit. Amen.

O Lord, we gather at Mass with all your disciples to learn about your love and to praise your name. Help us to "go forth and set the world on fire."

All: Go forth and set the world on fire.

Leader: O Lord, you feed us with your Word in the Scriptures at Mass. Teach us to "go forth and set the world on fire."

All: Go forth and set the world on fire.

Leader: Lord Jesus, you feed us with your Body and your Blood in Holy Communion. Feed us to "go forth and set the world on fire."

All: Go forth and set the world on fire.

End the Unit Prayer by singing the unit song.

Missionary Discipleship

When have you acted as Christ wanted? What did you do? Was it easy or hard? Has someone reached out to you when you felt alone, or when it was hard to do what Christ asked?

What is prayer?

When we pray, we raise our hearts and minds to God. We encounter God in prayer, especially in the sacraments. Prayer is a mystery in which we speak and listen to God. We address our prayers to God the Father, in Christ's name.

Lectio* and *Visio Divina

Prayer surges from the heart. It is a look toward heaven. It is a cry of love that embraces both suffering and joy.

Based on the words of Saint Thérèse of Lisieux

Prayer is raising our hearts and minds to God.

What do you think are the keys to developing a good friendship with someone? You might name things such as: talking to the person, getting to know him, listening to her, making time for each other. These elements serve to build a strong relationship.

Prayer is a two-way relationship between God and us. When we pray, we raise our hearts and minds to God. Prayer includes many of the same characteristics of good friendships: talking, listening, making time, and sometimes just being quiet together. The first prayers we pray are those taught to us by others, usually in our families. These are prayers our parents pray for and with us, such as nighttime prayers or blessings before meals.

Faith Word

prayer see p. 294

We memorize these first prayers, but as we grow, prayer becomes something much deeper than simply reciting from memory. We begin to use our own words to express to God the longings of our minds and hearts. We also listen. We tune in to God's continual, abiding presence with us.

Something amazing happens when we invite God into our lives in prayer. Over time we begin to recognize God's mysterious movement in our lives. Our friendship with God deepens. We hear his gentle words of love.

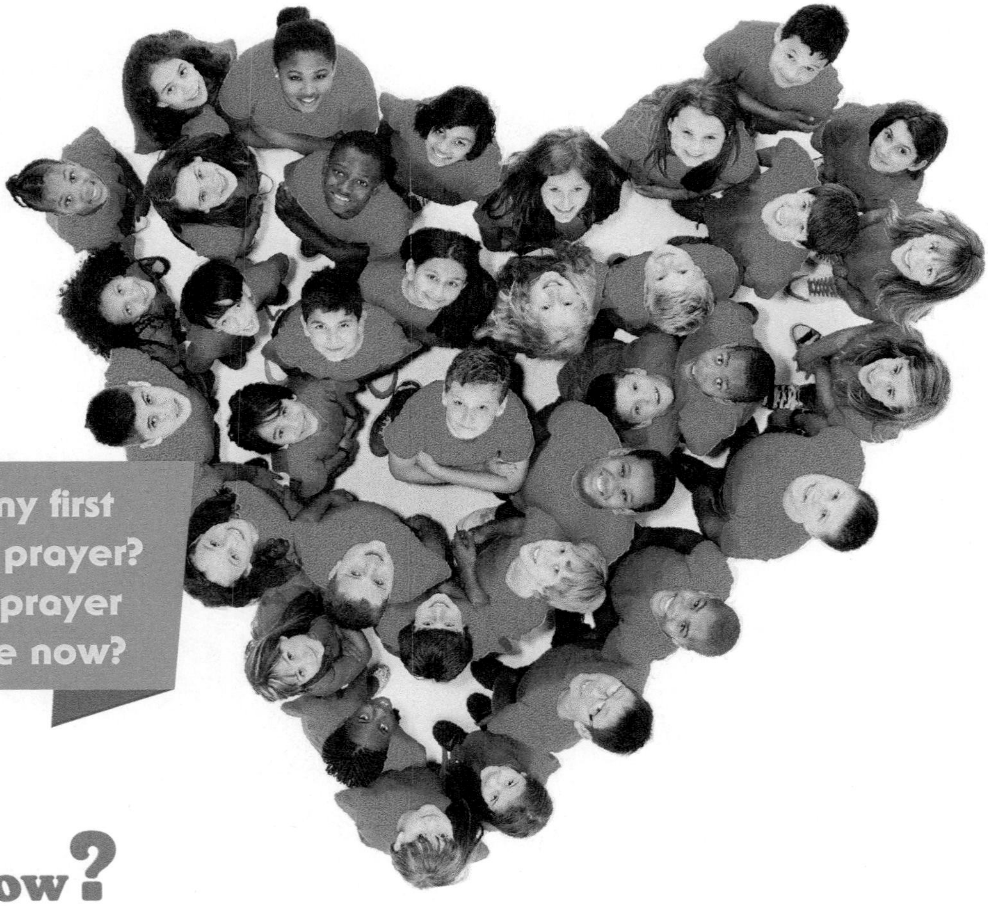

What was my first memory of prayer? What does prayer mean to me now?

Did You Know?

Family prayer builds relationships.

Prayer

Lectio* and *Visio Divina

Prayer brings God's people closer to him.

Why do we pray? Remember that God's desire is for us to know him and to love him. It is for this purpose that God created us.

> He made from one the whole human race to dwell on the entire surface of the earth, and he fixed the ordered seasons and the boundaries of their regions, so that people might seek God, . . . though indeed he is not far from any one of us.
>
> Acts of the Apostles 17:26–27

The deepest desire in our hearts is to seek and know God. This is why we pray. Prayer brings us closer to God.

Prayer is first and foremost the action of God who calls us into an encounter with him. He invites us into a living relationship with him and his people, with Jesus Christ, and with the Holy Spirit. Our first step in prayer is to respond to God's call.

Both personal prayer and **communal prayer**–prayer we pray together as a community–help us to feel and remember God's presence. Some of our most meaningful experiences of prayer are within the community of the Church.

Faith Word

communal prayer
see p. 293

Communal prayer has been a part of the Church since her very beginning. The first disciples encountered God in their communal prayer life and especially in the breaking of the bread, or Eucharist.

One Church, Many Cultures

Communal prayer is an important part of the Catholic Church in Uganda. The Bukalongo shrine welcomes thousands of people from all religions for special New Year's Eve prayers and celebrations. The shrine also participates in *Essangalo*, its overnight communal prayer, held once a month, rain or shine. Prayer begins late in the evening, continues all night, and ends with a dawn Mass. *Essangalo* means "happiness" in several Ugandan dialects, and Church members call it a "happy vigil."

Recall the two disciples who were walking to Emmaus. They were sad about Jesus' Death and had heard about the empty tomb. As they were talking, a stranger joined them. The disciples did not recognize him as the Risen Jesus. They told the stranger about the Death of Jesus and the empty tomb.

As they walked, Jesus taught them about Scripture. The disciples invited Jesus to have dinner with them. At this meal Jesus took bread and blessed it. He then broke the bread and gave it to them.

The disciples recognized Jesus. Imagine how close to him they must have felt in that moment of profound prayer! They returned to Jerusalem to tell others how Jesus "was made known to them in the breaking of the bread" (Luke 24:35).

Prayer and celebration of the Eucharist continued to bring God's people closer to him:

"They devoted themselves to the teaching of the apostles and to the communal life, to the breaking of the bread and to the prayers. . . . Every day they devoted themselves to meeting together . . . and to breaking bread in their homes . . . And every day the Lord added to their number those who were being saved" (Acts of the Apostles 2:42, 46, 47).

We, too, encounter God in prayer when we celebrate the sacraments. We pray with the Church when we celebrate the Sacrament of the Eucharist at Mass. We join a community of believers and together raise our hearts and minds to God through God's Word, through songs of praise and prayers of petition, and in thanksgiving for Jesus' gift of himself to us in Holy Communion.

What Makes Us Catholic?

Prayer leads us to Jesus, our light and our hope. The Apostles at the Last Supper experienced this when Jesus instituted the Eucharist. Jesus prayed and broke bread with the disciples in Emmaus, too. The words Jesus prayed brought the gift of Jesus himself to us. Pope Benedict XVI called our participation in the Eucharist "the highest point in all our prayer." When we receive the Eucharist, we "experience in an extraordinary manner the prayer that Jesus prayed, . . . that the transforming power of Christ's death and Resurrection may act within us." And Jesus continues to pray for us in the Eucharist. This is a prayer of love.

Activity

Read the story of the disciples on the road to Emmaus. With two friends, create a short skit that retells the story in your own words. Have one person play Jesus and the other two play the disciples. If there is time, switch roles so that each person gets to portray Jesus.

Prayer

Lectio and *Visio Divina*

Prayer is a mystery in which we speak and listen to God.

There is hardly a page in the Gospels that in some way doesn't reveal Jesus as a person of prayer–speaking and listening to God, his Father. Jesus is a model for how we can speak and listen to God.

Jesus taught us to pray with patience and complete trust in God. He prayed in many ways. He thanked God the Father for his blessings and asked God to be with him. He prayed for the needs of others and forgave sinners in the name of his Father.

One of the most beautiful examples of the mystery and power of prayer in the Gospels is the Transfiguration of Jesus. We read that Jesus takes Peter, John, and James up the mountain to pray. In the Gospel of Luke, the mountain is a regular place of prayer (see Luke 6:12 and 22:39–41). In this prayerful encounter, Jesus gives his Apostles a glimpse of his divine glory. The Church celebrates this event every year on the Feast of the Transfiguration.

[Jesus] took Peter, John, and James and went up the mountain to pray. While he was praying his face changed in appearance and his clothing became dazzling white. And behold, two men were conversing with him, Moses and Elijah. . . . Peter and his companions had been overcome by sleep, but becoming fully awake, they saw his glory and the two men standing with him. . . . Then from the cloud came a voice that said, 'This is my chosen Son; listen to him.' After the voice had spoken, Jesus was found alone. They fell silent and did not at that time tell anyone what they had seen.

Luke 9:28–36

Activity

Look for the following words as you read the story of the Transfiguration. When you have checked off all the words, write your favorite word on the whiteboard. Explain to the group why it is your favorite.

- ☐ **mountain**
- ☐ **white**
- ☐ **sleep**
- ☐ **awake**
- ☐ **glory**
- ☐ **cloud**
- ☐ **Son**
- ☐ **listen**
- ☐ **voice**
- ☐ **silent**

Mount Tabor in Galilee, Israel is the site of the Transfiguration of Jesus.

In the fifteenth century, Thomas à Kempis (learn about him on page 182) wrote the following, which he titled "Of God Speaking Within You":

"Make room for Christ, then, and place him at the center of your life. . . . He will care for you, and he will provide for you faithfully in everything. . . . Let your highest thoughts be with the Most High and your prayer be directed to Christ without ceasing. . . . A genuinely spiritual person who is free from a troubled heart, can turn himself to God at any time, rise above himself, and rest joyfully in the Lord."

The Imitation of Christ,
Book Two, Chapter 1

Activity

Reflect on these questions, and then write down your ideas:

How can I make room for Christ? How can I place him at the center of my life? What can I keep doing, stop doing, or start doing to hear God speaking within me?

Keep Doing	Stop Doing	Start Doing

Prayer

Lectio and *Visio Divina*

We address our prayers to God our Father, in Christ's name.

Listen carefully the next time you are at Mass. Listen to the prayers the priest prays, as well as your responses. You will notice something similar among them. You will recognize that they all follow a familiar pattern. First, they address God our Father. Next, they call on God for a need, or a blessing. Sometimes they refer to a specific person, such as a saint, or the Blessed Mother, and the prayer asks that we might have the courage to follow that person's example.

Here is a prayer you might hear during the celebration of the Rite of Marriage. Notice the prayer's pattern: it addresses God and calls on God to bless the couple to be married. The prayer then asks that the married couple will be given the strength of devoted servants to bear witness to their love for each other. The prayer ends in the name of Christ, God's Son.

O God, who consecrated the bond of Marriage
by so great a mystery
that in the wedding covenant you foreshadowed
the Sacrament of Christ and his Church; . . .

Look now with favor on these your servants,
joined together in Marriage,
who ask to be strengthened by your blessing. . . .

may these your servants
hold fast to the faith and keep your
commandments; . . .
may they bear true witness to Christ before all; . . .

And grant that,
reaching at last together the fullness of years
for which they hope,
they may come to the life of the blessed
in the Kingdom of Heaven.
Through Christ our Lord.

Order of Matrimony, 74

Activity

Using the pattern above, compose your own prayer.

1. Speak to God as a Father.

____

____

2. Call on God for a need or a blessing in your life.

____

____

3. Mention a specific person, such as a saint or Mary, and ask for help in following that person's example. You might refer to a specific quality or an event in his or her life.

____

____

4. End your prayer in Jesus' name.

____

____

This is a prayer you would hear at Mass on the Feast of Saint Francis of Assisi:

"O God, by whose gift Saint Francis was conformed to Christ in poverty and humility, grant that, by walking in Francis' footsteps, we may follow your Son, and, through joyful charity, come to be united with you. Through our Lord Jesus Christ, your Son, who lives and reigns with you in the unity of the Holy Spirit, one God, for ever and ever."

Roman Missal, Feast of Saint Francis

Notice that this prayer begins "O God, . . ." and that it ends "Through our Lord Jesus Christ, your Son . . ." The prayers of the Church, when she celebrates the sacraments and the liturgy, are always addressed first to God, the Father.

And as you can see from the prayer's ending, we pray to God the Father through–or in the name of–Jesus. Jesus, as truly human as we are human, is the way by which the Holy Spirit teaches us to pray to God the Father. Jesus is our connection point to God in prayer.

How we address our prayers to God in the Mass
"Almighty ever-living God . . . Through our Lord Jesus Christ, your Son . . ."
"O God . . . Through our Lord Jesus Christ, your Son . . ."
"Grant, we pray, almighty God . . . Through our Lord Jesus Christ, your Son . . ."
"Grant, O merciful God . . . Through Christ our Lord . . ."
"O God, you have taught us. . . . Through our Lord Jesus Christ, your Son . . ."

Partners in Faith

Thomas à Kempis

Thomas à Kempis' book *Imitation of Christ* is still popular 500 years after it was written. Saint Thomas More said it was one book every Christian should read. Thomas à Kempis wrote a great deal about prayer and devotion, but he also copied the Bible by hand four times! He served as a priest in the Netherlands.

Learn more about the life of Thomas à Kempis.

Do not ever be idle. Instead be either reading, praying, or doing something for the good of others.

Lectio and Visio Divina

Portfolio

Faith Words

prayer **communal prayer**

Show What You Know

Complete the sentences.

1. ____________________ taught us to pray with patience and complete trust in God.
2. ____________________ is raising our minds and hearts to God.
3. When we pray as a community, we participate in ____________________ prayer.
4. Our first step in prayer is to respond to God's ____________________.

Live Your Faith

- How would you explain, to someone who had never prayed before, how to raise your heart or your mind to God?

____

____

____

____

____

____

- What form of communal prayer do you enjoy? Whom would you like to invite to join you in communal prayer?

____

____

____

____

____

____

____

Lesson 16

Portfolio

How is prayer strengthening my relationship with God and others?

Mini-Task

In today's digital world, apps can help us keep track of daily responsibilities–like homework! They also give us information, entertain us through games and videos, and connect us to our friends and family.

In the space below, design and title your own prayer app. What would it do? How would it help connect you with God and your friends?

My Prayer App: ______________________

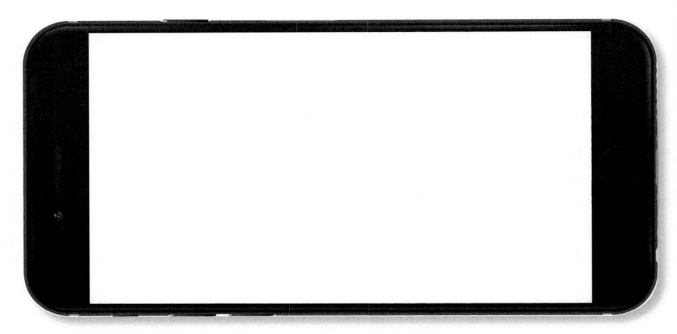

Want to do more? Go to your Portfolio to continue this activity.

At Home

In prayer, we deepen our friendship with God. Talk with your family members about their friendship with God. How do all of them feel that God is their friend? As a family, take time this week to speak and listen to God as your friend.

Why do we pray?

Prayer is an essential part of our Sacred Tradition. The Holy Spirit teaches the Church and her members to pray. We pray together in the liturgy and the sacraments. Prayer builds our trust in God. Prayer is at the heart of every Christian life.

Thanksgiving

Our prayer cannot be reduced to an hour on Sundays. It is important to have a daily relationship with the Lord.

Pope Francis

Prayer is essential in our Sacred Tradition.

One of the ways that we learn new things is with the help of a good teacher. But we have to want to learn. One of the most important things we will ever learn how to do is to pray. It is not enough to know what Sacred Scripture tells us about prayer. We have to learn *how* to pray. And for this, we look to the Sacred Tradition of the Church. There, our teacher, the Holy Spirit, teaches the Church to pray as a community.

The Holy Spirit is the living water within us that points us to Christ. Like drawing water to drink from a well, we can draw from the well of God's Word as a source for our prayer. We also draw from the well of the Church's sacraments as a source for our prayer. In the liturgy, Christ and the Holy Spirit are at work proclaiming, making present, and communicating the mystery of salvation. As people of faith, we bring prayerful hearts to the Church's celebration of the sacraments to seek the Lord, and to hear and keep his Word.

Over the centuries, many holy men and women have studied and reflected deeply on what prayer is and how to pray. They have shared with us the wealth of their knowledge and experience as people of prayer. They are a part of the Sacred Tradition of the Church through whom the Holy Spirit teaches us to pray.

How has the Church taught me how to pray?

Did You Know?

God's Word is a source of prayer.

Prayer

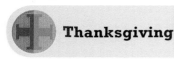

Thanksgiving

Faith Word

mindful see p. 294

Prayer builds our trust in God.

How do we get to the point where we can trust in the Lord with all our hearts, totally rely on him, and be **mindful** of him always?

In the Lord's Prayer, we pray to God our Father with the trust of children who look to their Father for everything that is good and beautiful. God our Father gives us everything that we need: "Give us this day our daily bread."

Notice that Jesus did not tell us to pray "Give *me* this day *my* daily bread." When we pray the Our Father, we are participating in the fulfillment of God's covenant promises to his people. When we gather as Church and pray "Give us this day, . . ." as we do in the Church's liturgy and sacraments, we pray to God, Father of *all*, for the needs of our brothers and sisters.

Our trust in God grows through our prayerful participation in the liturgy and sacraments of the Church. God responds to our prayer, most especially in the Eucharist, where we receive the nourishment of our "daily bread."

Activity

Saint Dominic said there were nine ways to pray with your body:

1. Bowing
2. Lying face down on the floor
3. Repeating "Have mercy on me, O God" while sitting or standing
4. Genuflecting
5. Standing with open hands before a crucifix
6. Standing with arms outstretched
7. Standing with arms raised above the head
8. Sitting and reading Scripture
9. Walking in silence

Choose one of these ways that you have *never* prayed before. Pray in that way this week. Tell a friend what it felt like to pray this way.

Trust in the LORD with all your heart,
on your own intelligence do not rely;
In all your ways be mindful of him,
and he will make straight your paths.

Proverbs 3:5–6

> *[Jesus said] I am the bread of life. . . . I am the living bread that came down from heaven; whoever eats this bread will live forever; and the bread that I will give is my flesh for the life of the world.*
>
> *John 6:48, 51*

In the Eucharist, the source and summit of the Church's life and prayer, God gives us the Bread of Life.

When we receive the Eucharist in Holy Communion, we receive the wondrous gift of God's grace in us. With this grace and the spiritual food that is the Body and Blood of Christ, we can love God and open our hearts to the needs of those around us, to those who hunger physically and spiritually. Our trust in God–who desires nothing less than to live in us–grows.

One Church, Many Cultures

Each culture has distinct customs and ways of living. Catholics may be able to keep some of their country's customs without changing the practice of their own faith. For example, there is a small but growing population of Catholics in Jordan. Most people in this Middle Eastern country practice Islam. Jordanian Catholics may keep the custom of fasting during the Muslim holiday of Ramadan. Catholics, however, are not expected to give up the wine that is transformed into the Blood of Christ at the Eucharist.

Prayer

Thanksgiving

The Church prays together in the liturgy and the sacraments.

Why do we pray? We do so because it is a necessity for us as Christians (see *Catechism of the Catholic Church*, 2757). It is impossible to be a disciple, or live the Christian life, without prayer. Prayer and living as a Christian are inseparable. Saint Paul tells us to "Pray without ceasing. In all circumstances give thanks, for this is the will of God for you in Christ Jesus" (1 Thessalonians 5:17–18).

Saint Paul would be happy to know that over the centuries, the Church has taken his words to heart. At any moment on any day, somewhere in the world, the Church is at prayer in the liturgy and sacraments.

Communal prayer, or praying as the Church, is an important dimension of our lives as people who pray. As members of the Body of Christ, the Church, we join together to pray together in the liturgy and sacraments.

The communal prayer of the Church includes the Liturgy of the Hours. Bishops, priests, deacons, men and women religious, and laypeople come together to pray the Liturgy of the Hours in the morning and evening, and at other times of the day. The Liturgy of the Hours includes songs and psalms, Scripture readings, the Lord's Prayer, and other readings and responses. The Church has prayed the Liturgy of the Hours for centuries. While it is a communal prayer, it can also be prayed alone.

What Makes Us Catholic?

The Liturgy of the Hours is the liturgical prayer of the Church. Early Christians gathered for prayer at certain times throughout the day. They recited the Psalms of the Old Testament and read from the New Testament. In later years, Church leaders and those in religious orders mainly prayed the Liturgy of the Hours. They used a special prayer book called the Breviary. Beginning in the 1970s, though, the bishops encouraged the whole Church to pray the Liturgy of the Hours. Even if we pray it alone, we know that others are praying, too. The Liturgy of the Hours is the prayer of the entire Church.

The Liturgy of the Hours is also known as the Divine Office, or the Work of God. According to the General Instruction of the Liturgy of the Hours, the five Hours of the Divine Office are as follows:

Office of Readings
The Office of Readings provides us with a wide selection of passages from Sacred Scripture for meditation. It also includes excerpts from spiritual writers.

Morning Prayer
Morning Prayer blesses and sanctifies, or makes holy, the morning hours. It sets our hearts on God at the start of the day.

Daytime Prayer
Daytime Prayer follows an ancient Christian tradition of praying private devotions at various times of the day, even in the middle of work.

Evening Prayer
The focus of Evening Prayer is thanksgiving. We give thanks for what the day has given us, or what we have done well during the day.

Night Prayer
Night Prayer ends the day and is said before bedtime, even if bedtime is after midnight! The theme of the psalms we pray during Night Prayer is confidence in the Lord.

Activity

Look through the Book of Psalms in the Bible. Choose a psalm to pray at each of the times below. Copy a few verses of the psalm here or on a separate sheet of paper. For the next three days, read and pray the psalm at the times below.

____

____

____

Daytime (before a test or another important activity)

____

____

____

Prayer

Thanksgiving

Prayer is at the heart of Christian life.

The *Catechism of the Catholic Church* tells us that "Prayer is the life of the new heart. It ought to animate us at every moment . . . ; prayer is a remembrance of God often awakened by the memory of the heart" (*CCC*, 2697). Saint Gregory of Nazianzus reminds us that "We must remember God more often than we draw breath."

Imagine a life of prayer so deep, so connected to God, that we "remember God more often than we draw breath." Prayer is at the heart of Christian life. Like breath, which is life, the heart is life. These are two profound images about the place of prayer in our lives.

Does this mean that we must be constantly falling to our knees in prayer on the sidewalk of life? No, but what it does mean is that we remember. This is the deep, meaningful kind of remembering where we consciously remember and acknowledge God's presence–in our history *and* right now. Then our lives do become a prayer offered to God. We become aware that God is present and connected to us as we move through and focus on the ordinary moments and tasks of our day. We can pray: "Here I am, God. I am here. And I know you are here, too."

Activity

God is always with us, but sometimes it can be hard to remember that fact during our busy days. Think about a time when you "remembered" that God was with you. Write it on the lines below. Tell a friend about what happened. If there is time, share your experiences with the entire group.

____

____

____

The most profound connection we have with God is at Mass, which is the fullest or most complete expression of the Church's communal prayer. At Mass we gather, listen to God's Word, and are nourished by the Real Presence, the Body and Blood of Christ.

During the Eucharistic Prayer, we remember the Paschal Mystery.

> Therefore, O Lord, as we now celebrate the memorial of our redemption, we remember Christ's Death and his descent to the realm of the dead, we proclaim his Resurrection and his Ascension to your right hand, and, as we await his coming in glory, we offer you his Body and Blood, the sacrifice acceptable to you which brings salvation to the whole world.
>
> *Roman Missal*, Eucharistic Prayer IV

We bring everything we are, have been, and will be to Mass. This prayer, the "source and summit" of the Church's life, nourishes us to go out and be bread for the world.

Activity

In your own words, write a short note to Jesus expressing how you feel about receiving him in the Eucharist. Speak from your heart.

Use your note to form a prayer to say as you prepare to receive Jesus in Holy Communion. After you have received Jesus, listen to what he is saying to you.

Partners in Faith

Saint Louise de Marillac

Saint Louise de Marillac felt that God wanted her to be a nun, but she was already married. While she was praying, God told Louise that there would be a time when she would be a nun. After her husband's death, she did become a nun. She spent the rest of her life working with the poor.

Learn more about the life of Saint Louise de Marillac.

I beg you for the love of God to show great tenderness to the poor.

Faith Word

mindful

Show What You Know

In your own words, write a definition for the term.

mindful

____

____

____

Fill in the blanks to complete the sentences.

1. Prayer is at the center of our Christian ____________________.
2. The ____________________ is the fullest or most complete expression of the Church's communal prayer.
3. The ____________________ teaches the Church to pray as a community.

Live Your Faith

- What kinds of prayers do you like to pray alone? What kinds of prayer do you like to pray as part of communal prayer?

____

____

____

____

____

- How can you be mindful of God in prayer and in your everyday life?

____

____

____

____

____

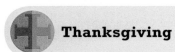

What are the ways I pray?

Mini-Task

Sing and Pray Twice

There are many ways to pray. In the activity on page 187, we read some of the ways Saint Dominic said we can pray with our bodies.

Another way to pray is with song. Saint Augustine said that when we sing, we pray twice.

Write your own song that expresses an aspect of prayer. You can set the words to music that you write or to the melody of another song that you like.

How does your prayer song inspire you? Write down your thoughts and share with the group.

____

____

____

____

____

____

____

____

____

Want to do more? Go to your Portfolio to continue this activity.

At Home

Have your family take a moment to remember God's presence during a time when you do not ordinarily pray. Quietly think or say, "Here we are, God. We are here. And we know that you are here, too." Ask family members to tell one way they know God is with them in prayer.

How do we pray?

Christians around the world pray in different ways, but everywhere around the world, people are praying with the Church all day long and all through the year. Our prayers bring us closer to God. The Church prays together in her liturgy, and certain prayers are spoken in the silence of our hearts.

Blessing

This is a prayer we must pray every day: "Holy Spirit, make my heart open to the Word of God, make my heart open to goodness, make my heart open to the beauty of God every day."

Pope Francis

Christians around the world pray in different ways.

Take a moment to think about this fact: On the other side of the planet, right now, Christians are at prayer. At any given moment in any given place, the Holy Spirit is at work in the Church, helping us remember all that Jesus taught. The Holy Spirit never stops teaching us how to pray.

All around the world, the members of the Church are praying the basic forms of prayer in ways that are unique to the needs and gifts of their own cultures.

- African American spirituals celebrate what Sister Thea Bowman called "our God, his goodness, his promise, our faith and hope, and our journey toward the promise."
- The Church in Asia praised and thanked God with songs and prayers reflective of their culture when Pope Francis beatified 124 Korean martyrs in Seoul, South Korea, in 2014.
- Some Hispanic Catholics make pilgrimages on their knees to the Basilica of Our Lady of Guadalupe in Mexico City.

Each culture brings its own expression to blessings, prayers of petition and intercession, and prayers of thanksgiving and praise.

Have I ever experienced prayer from a different culture?

Did You Know?

We can pray with music from our own culture.

Faith Word

intention see p. 293

Prayer

Blessing

Our regular prayers bring us closer to God.

Have you ever had to take a test that was very difficult? Maybe, you muttered the words (in your head because there's no talking during tests), "O God, help me!" If your heart was present to that unspoken prayer–if you really meant it–then God heard your prayer. The fact is, when we pray from our hearts, with words either spoken or not, God hears our prayers. And something is worth noting about the "O God, help me!" prayer: It is short! When we pray, the number of words does not matter. It is the **intention** behind the words that does.

The Church invites us to pray all the time. In fact, one of the best habits we could ever develop is to pray spoken and unspoken prayers at any moment during the day. Someone once described being with a friend who would stop in the middle of a conversation to say a short prayer for whatever or whomever they were talking about! We can pray about anything and anyone, all day long.

The Church prays every day in the Liturgy of the Hours and the celebration of Mass. The Church prays every week when her members gather for Sunday Mass. The Church prays throughout the year by celebrating the feasts and seasons of the Church's liturgical year.

Activity

In a small group, discuss the following:

The Mass and the Liturgy of the Hours are ways the Church calls people to prayer. Some churches also use bells before Mass begins or play the "Ave Maria" at certain times of day to remind people to pray. What are ways you could remind yourself to pray? When might you want to call others around you to prayer? How would you call them?

____

____

____

____

The *Angelus* is a Catholic devotion and daily prayer. The devotion began in the twelfth century as the reciting of three Hail Marys upon the ringing of the evening bell. It is still accompanied by the Angelus bell in places such as Vatican City, where the pope often shares a teaching to accompany the praying of the *Angelus*. The *Angelus* reminds us of the Annunciation and pays tribute to Mary, the Mother of God, and her role in the Incarnation.

Activity

The Church invites us to pray all the time. One way to begin to do this is to write a very short prayer that you can say at any moment. Your book suggests "O God, help me." Write your own prayer that you could say throughout the day.

____

____

____

The Angelus

V. The angel of the Lord declared unto Mary.

R. And she conceived of the Holy Spirit.
Hail Mary, . . .

V. Behold the handmaid of the Lord.

R. Be it done unto me according to thy word.
Hail Mary, . . .

V. And the Word was made flesh.

R. And dwelt among us.
Hail Mary, . . .

V. Pray for us, O holy Mother of God.

R. That we may be made worthy of the promises of Christ.

Let Us Pray

Pour forth, we beseech Thee O Lord,
Thy grace into our hearts;
that we to whom the Incarnation of Christ,
Thy Son, was made known
by the message of an angel,
may by his Passion and Cross be brought
to the glory of his Resurrection
through the same Christ our Lord.

Amen.

Prayer

Blessing

The Church prays together in her liturgy.

One of the wonderful things that happens at Baptism is that we become members of a community whose purpose is to love and serve God. This community is the Church. The Holy Spirit has, from the Church's beginning, provided her with everything necessary to love and serve God in the best way possible. One of these ways is through prayer.

The Church unites all of God's people in prayer. She invites us to pray on our own or with others, every day. The Church also invites us to participate in her liturgy, which is the public prayer and work of the whole Church. We can join with the Church in praying the Liturgy of the Hours, in participating at Mass, and in celebrating all the feasts commemorating the Blessed Mother and all the saints throughout the year.

When we are at Mass, we join together as the Body of Christ in prayers of forgiveness, petition, praise, and thanksgiving to God. We prayerfully listen and respond during the Liturgy of the Word and the Liturgy of the Eucharist.

Activity

Here is a partial list of prayer responses that we pray together as the assembly during Mass on Sunday. How many more can you add?

Responses

"And with your Spirit."

"Amen."

After the first and second Scripture readings: "Thanks be to God."

After the Gospel: "Praise to you, Lord Jesus Christ."

Prayer of the Faithful: "Lord, hear our prayer."

What Makes Us Catholic?

The Liturgy of the Hours always includes psalm prayers. These are beautiful and ancient prayers from the Book of Psalms in the Bible. When we say or sing the psalms, we are following Jesus' example of prayer. For the Liturgy of the Hours, the source of the
psalms is from a book called the Psalter. The Psalter arranges the psalms in a special order according to the time of day and the liturgical season. The psalms help us to praise God through the many seasons of the Catholic Church.

One of the responses that we pray every week during the Liturgy of the Word is during the Responsorial Psalm, which follows the first reading. The Responsorial Psalm is "an integral part of the Liturgy of the Word and . . . fosters meditation on the Word of God" (*General Instruction of the Roman Missal,* 61).

It is preferable that the Responsorial Psalm be sung, or at least the response be sung by the assembly. "If the Psalm cannot be sung, then it should be recited in a way that is particularly suited to fostering meditation on the Word of God" (*GIRM,* 61).

The next time you are at Mass, pay close attention to the Responsorial Psalm. In what way does the psalm and psalm response help make the Word of God meaningful for you?

Activity

In a small group, create a Responsorial Psalm prayer service. Together, select a chapter of the Psalms. Each person in the group can choose one verse from the chapter to read aloud. Then choose a different verse to be the psalm response for the entire group to say. Share your Responsorial Psalm with your class.

Fill in the psalm chapter, the verses, and the name of each person who will read them:

Psalm Chapter: ______________________________

Verse 1: ______________________________ Name: ______________________________

Verse 2: ______________________________ Name: ______________________________

Verse 3: ______________________________ Name: ______________________________

Verse 4: ______________________________ Name: ______________________________

Write out the psalm verse here for the group response:

____

____

Prayer

Blessing

Faith Words

meditation see p. 294

contemplation see p. 293

Certain prayers are spoken in the silence of our hearts.

In the Christian tradition, there are three major forms of prayer: vocal prayer, meditation, and contemplation. **Meditation** and **contemplation** are forms of silent prayer. This is prayer spoken in the silence of our hearts.

Meditation is a quest, maybe even an adventure, to seek to understand the why and how of being a disciple of Christ (see *Catechism of the Catholic Church*, 2705). We can meditate on what we read (such as Sacred Scripture), on what we hear, or on what our senses experience in God's creation. When we meditate, we use our thoughts, imagination, creativity, emotions, and desires. Meditation is prayerful reflection guided by the Holy Spirit that takes us into the heart of Jesus.

Contemplation is being with Jesus. Saint Teresa of Ávila described it as a conversation with a close friend. In contemplative prayer, our mind is quieter, or less active, than when we meditate.
We simply sit in the presence of God, sharing time with him. All of our attention is fixed on God.

Activity

You can learn how to meditate or contemplate through practice. Start by sitting in a comfortable position. Fold your hands on your lap. Close your eyes. Now imagine that Jesus is in front of you. Imagine what he is saying to you. For a few minutes, think about what he is telling you. Then open your eyes and write down what came to mind.

One Church, Many Cultures

Catholics brought Christianity to Korea more than two hundred years ago. In recent years, the Catholic Church in South Korea has grown rapidly. While small compared to the total population, the number of Catholics has nearly doubled in the past ten years. More and more Korean young people are considering the priesthood and religious vocations. Pope Francis visited South Korea in 2014. He celebrated Mass at Myeongdong Cathedral in Seoul and honored Korean martyrs. Catholics gathered to join their prayers to those of the martyrs.

The celebration of Mass is an example of how, when we gather for the liturgy and pray together as a Church, we pray both aloud and silently. We are very familiar with the spoken prayers of the Mass, but what about the times of quiet and silence?

One such moment of silence happens when we first enter the church. We kneel and pray before Mass to prepare ourselves to celebrate the Eucharist. Another time of silence occurs after we listen to God's Word in the Liturgy of the Word. First we respond vocally, "Praise to you, Lord Jesus Christ." Then we meditate on what we have heard, especially in the quiet moments after the homily.

The most profound time of silence is during the Liturgy of the Eucharist, when we receive Jesus in Holy Communion. Jesus becomes a part of us. We kneel in silence just being with Jesus. This is a prayer of contemplation. In this moment of prayer, spoken in the silence of our hearts, we are as close to Jesus as we can be.

Partners in Faith

Saint Andrew Kim Taegŏn

The Korean martyrs are 124 Christians who were killed for their faith in the eighteenth century. Christianity was not allowed in Korea at the time, and Christians had to practice in secret. Saint Andrew Kim Taegŏn, the patron saint of Korea, was the first Korean-born Catholic priest. His parents were converts, and he was raised a Catholic. His father was also killed for being a Christian.

Learn more about the life of Saint Andrew Kim Taegŏn.

God cares for the least hair of our heads.

Prayer

Blessing

Faith Words

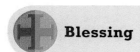

intention **meditation** **contemplation**

Show What You Know

Match the terms to the correct definitions.

1. contemplation
2. intention
3. meditation

wordless silent prayer in which we seek to understand the why and how of being a Christian

wordless silent prayer in which we focus entirely on God and his presence with us

the aim of our prayers or plan for them

Live Your Faith

- Which kind of prayer is easier for you to pray, meditation or contemplation? Why?

- What is your prayer intention this week?

Portfolio

How do I integrate prayer into daily life?

Mini-Task

There are many types of prayer. Praying with Scripture in a reflective manner is called *lectio divina*. We also pray while meditating on sacred art through *visio divina*, and reflecting upon and meditating to music are called *audio divina*. On the lines below, write the song title and lyrics of a song you know that inspires you to reflect.

Share the information about your song with a partner. If you can, listen to the song that inspires your partner.

Want to do more? Go to your Portfolio to continue this activity.

At Home

Your family is praying with your Church family all over the world. Have each of your family members voice an intention for the whole family. Pray on these intentions together silently for a few minutes.

What helps us to pray?

When we gather to pray with the Church at Eucharist, we are united as a family in Christ with all believers. We are united with the Communion of Saints with whom we join to offer prayer and praise. The family is our first community of prayer. Our faith helps us pray when it is hard to do so.

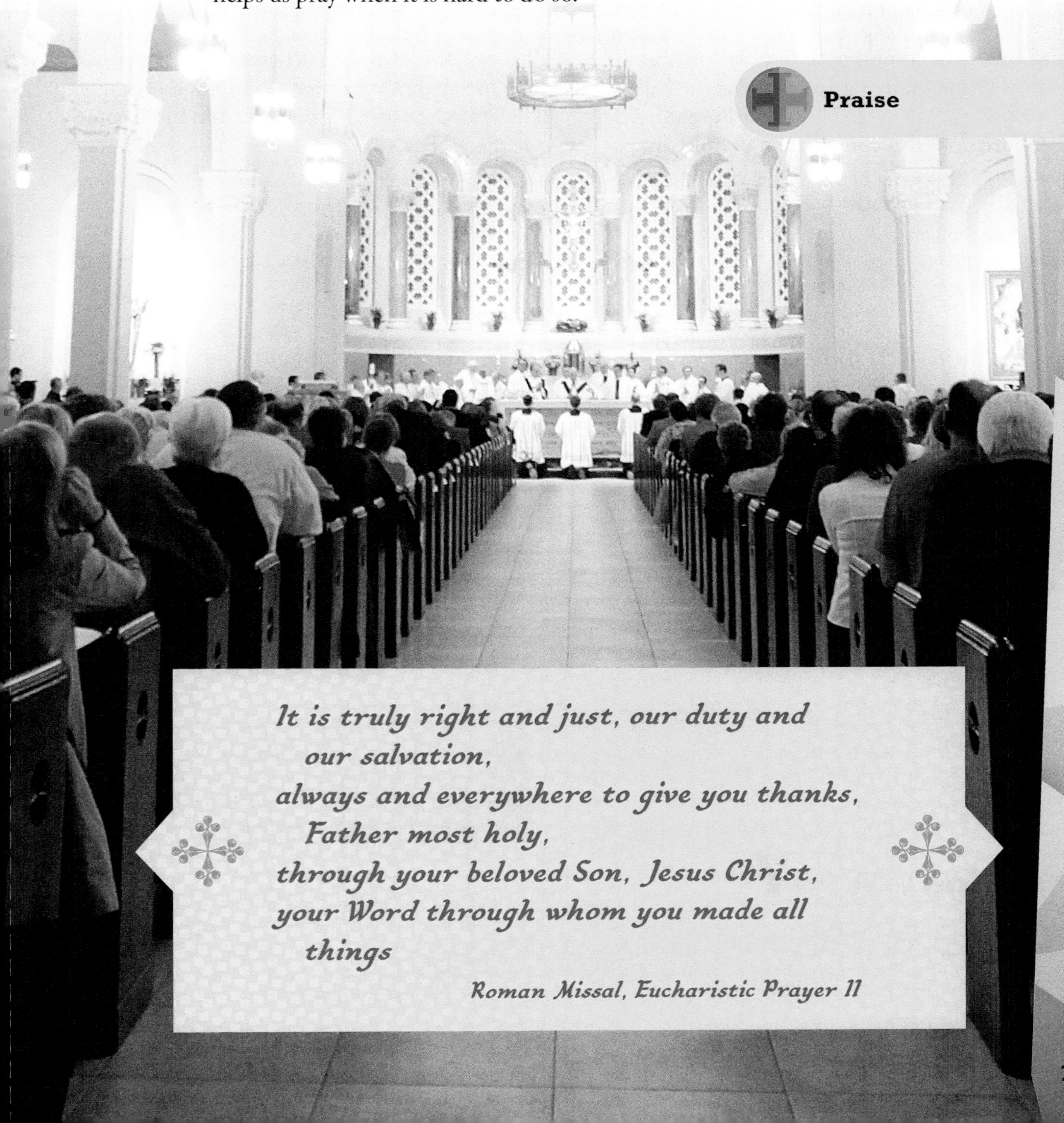

Praise

It is truly right and just, our duty and
our salvation,
always and everywhere to give you thanks,
Father most holy,
through your beloved Son, Jesus Christ,
your Word through whom you made all
things

Roman Missal, Eucharistic Prayer II

The Communion of Saints is united at prayer in the Eucharist.

"I believe in the Communion of Saints" (Nicene Creed).

We profess belief in the **Communion of Saints** every time we recite the Nicene Creed at Mass. The English word "saint" can translate in Latin into two words: *sancti* ("holy people") and *sancta* ("holy things"). Knowing these meanings helps us realize that this is the Church: It is the communion of holy people and holy things.

The Church is a communion of holy, faithful people (1) who are living and (2) who have died but are alive with God in heaven or Purgatory. The Church is also a communion of holy things. These holy things refer to the sacraments, particularly the Eucharist.

Faith Word

Communion of Saints
see p. 293

To profess that we are a part of the Communion of Saints means two things: We are connected to all faithful people living now and those who have died, and we are united as the one Body of Christ through "holy things," especially the Eucharist.

When we celebrate the Eucharist, the Church asks God's mercy for the entire Communion of Saints–all believers, those living on earth and those who have died. Next time you are at Mass, remember that the entire Communion of Saints is there, praising and thanking God with you!

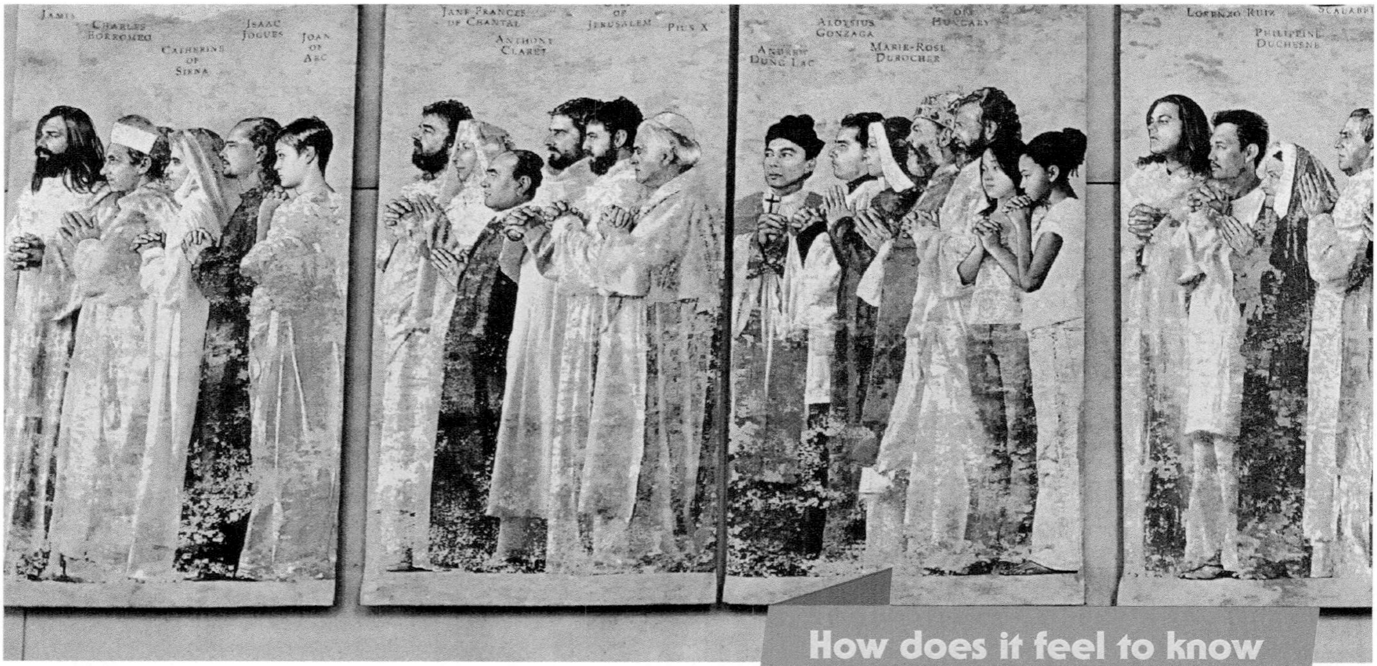

How does it feel to know that I am connected to the Communion of Saints?

Did You Know?

The Eucharist feeds the Church.

Christ and the Samaritan Woman at the Well **by Annibale Carracci (1560-1609).**

> Jesus said to her, 'Give me a drink.' . . . The Samaritan woman said to him, 'How can you, a Jew, ask me, a Samaritan woman, for a drink?' (For Jews use nothing in common with Samaritans.) Jesus answered and said to her, 'If you knew the gift of God and who is saying to you, "Give me a drink," you would have asked him and he would have given you living water.' [The woman] said to him, 'Sir, you do not even have a bucket and the well is deep; where then can you get this living water? Are you greater than our father Jacob, who gave us this well and drank from it himself with his children and his flocks?' Jesus answered and said to her, 'Everyone who drinks this water will be thirsty again; but whoever drinks the water I shall give will never thirst; the water I shall give will become in him a spring of water welling up to eternal life.'
>
> John 4:7–14

Prayer

Praise

The Church's liturgy offers prayer and praise.

When we want water to drink, or to bathe, or to wash our clothes, we turn on the faucet. We probably do not think a lot about the source of the water that flows out of the tap. Millions of people around the world draw their water from wells. When a well runs dry, the people's physical well-being is threatened, because water is necessary for life.

The *Catechism of the Catholic Church* uses the image of a well to teach us about prayer. The Church tells us that "the Holy Spirit is the *living water* that wells up to eternal life in the heart at prayer" (*CCC*, 2652). Christ is the source of this living water.

As Jesus told the Samaritan woman at the well, this living water is necessary for our spiritual health. We read about this encounter in the Gospel of John. Remember that it was unheard of for a Jewish man to approach a Samaritan, let alone a Samaritan woman, and engage her in conversation.

The story begins with Jesus traveling from Judea to Galilee by way of Samaria. He is likely hot and tired and thirsty. At around noon, he comes upon Jacob's well and sits down. A Samaritan woman approaches to draw water.

Of course the woman wants some of this kind of water! She says to Jesus, "Sir, give me this water, so that I may not be thirsty or have to keep coming here to draw water" (John 4:15).

Activity

How would you summarize the story of Jesus and the Samaritan woman in one phrase or sentence?

____

What does this passage say to you about how you can pray to God?

____

What does it tell you about who speaks first in our prayer?

____

Share your thoughts with a partner. Together, present your ideas to the class.

As the talk continues, Jesus, with great love and tenderness, encourages the woman to recognize the truth about herself: "He told me everything I have done" (John 4:39). Jesus reveals himself to her: "I am he, the one who is speaking with you" (John 4:26). The woman, amazed, runs into town to share the news about the Messiah.

The Samaritans then invited Jesus to stay in their town, and he did for two days. Because of the woman's witness and the teaching of Jesus, many of the Samaritans in that town began to believe in him: "We know that this is truly the savior of the world" (John 4:42). Jesus is truly the living water for all people, everywhere.

One of the Church's spiritual wells that enables us to drink of the Holy Spirit is the liturgy. When the Church gathers to celebrate liturgy, "the mission of Christ and of the Holy Spirit proclaims, makes present, and communicates the mystery of salvation, which is continued in the heart that prays" (*CCC*, 2655). When we pray during the Church's liturgy, we pray with the Church. We make the Church's prayer a part of ourselves. Liturgy is the prayer of the Church, and it is always prayed in communion with the Blessed Trinity.

The Church's liturgy is a source of prayer from which we can draw the "living water" of God's Spirit. We offer prayer and praise to God in the liturgy.

Activity

The Holy Spirit is the living water. We can draw this living water from the liturgy. Work with a partner to write what these statements mean. Use your explanation to teach another pair about the relationship between the Holy Spirit and the liturgy.

One Church, Many Cultures

It is important for a community to have access to clean, safe water. Catholic World Mission (CWM) works around the globe to share the Word of God and help people who live in poverty. In Ghana, CWM is working with local people to build water wells in the village schools, medical clinics, and other public buildings. Before the wells were built, people sometimes had to walk several miles every day to find clean water. Now the children and their families can focus on their schoolwork or jobs.

Prayer

Praise

The family is our first school of prayer.

For most of us, the first place we meet Jesus is in our families. We don't often think of our families as a school, but in a real sense, our families are a school of prayer, our *first* school of prayer, because we first learn to pray in our families.

Our homes are meant to be a community of prayer, where we learn Christian virtues and how to love one another. Our homes are communities of grace, where God is present. We pray together at home in many ways–grace before and after meals, blessings to greet the day and to end the day, special prayers for special events and occasions in our lives, and family prayers, rituals, and traditions throughout the Church's liturgical year, such as Advent, Christmas, Lent, and Easter.

We pray together with our families at church, too. It is with our families that we first learn to pray with the Church in her liturgies. The celebration of the Sacraments of Christian Initiation are big moments in the lives of Catholic families. We gather to celebrate Baptisms, First Eucharist, and Confirmation. We attend Sunday Mass every week with our families. All of these are ways that the family prays together. These experiences of praying, both at home and with the Church community in her liturgies, contribute to what makes a family holy.

Activity

Your classroom is a Christian community. Below, write down some of your favorite classroom prayer experiences from this year. Why were they special to you? Are there any ways you might adapt these prayers for your own personal use, either on your own or with your family?

My favorite prayer experience was when we:

____

I liked it because:

____

Here's how I might use it on my own or with my family:

____

Here is a prayer you can pray together with your family, for your family.

Prayer for Families
We bless your name, O Lord,
for sending your own incarnate Son,
to become part of a family,
so that, as he lived its life,
he would experience its worries and its joys.

We ask you, Lord,
to protect and watch over this family,
so that in the strength of your grace
its members may enjoy prosperity,
possess the priceless gift of your peace,
and, as the Church alive in the home,
bear witness in this world to your glory.

We ask this through Christ our Lord.
Amen.

from *Catholic Household Blessings and Prayers*

What Makes Us Catholic?

There are many ways Catholic families can participate in worldwide prayer. Every January, for example, the Church celebrates a World Day of Peace. With the pope, we pray that peace will reign in our hearts. Prayer events may have a specific theme, such as the World Day of Prayer for the Care of Creation started by Pope Francis. Other worldwide opportunities for prayer include World Day of the Poor and World Youth Day. Even if an event is held in a faraway place, we can still join in the prayer celebration. Your parish may hold a special service on these days. Or, you may join your family in prayer at home.

Prayer

Praise

Our faith supports our prayers.

As people of faith, one of the things that we can know with certainty is that God is always there when we pray, even when it does not seem that he is. It is not uncommon to struggle in one's prayer life. That struggle is also not something to worry about. One of the main difficulties we can have in the practice of prayer is distraction. So many things in life compete for our time and attention. At other times, our prayer seems dry and empty. It might seem as if God is not listening, or not even there.

Sometimes when we pray, we might feel alone, afraid, or full of doubt. We might feel bored or even tempted to stop praying altogether. Prayer might just seem ordinary. These experiences can happen when we pray alone, with others, and even during Mass. In all of these experiences, God is very much present with us.

Activity

Think about the ways we are distracted when we are trying to pray. Check off any of these ways that have distracted you. Then tell how you were able to put your focus back on God.

Distraction	Has this happened to you?	What did you do?
Too much noise around.		
Someone interrupted.		
I get bored.		
I do not know what to pray for or about.		
I feel ashamed or unready to talk to God.		

An angel appears to Jesus in this painting *Agony in the Garden* by El Greco, 1590.

Jesus' prayer to his Father in the Garden of Gethsemane the night before his Passion can teach us to persevere in prayer through the most difficult struggles in life. Tradition calls this prayer the "priestly" prayer of Jesus. In this prayer, everything comes together in Christ (see John 17). It is the longest prayer of Jesus we find in the Gospel. He knows what the next day will bring–his Passion and Death. Yet Christ did not run away from the suffering and the Cross that were waiting for him. He did not run away from God. His was the prayer of pure faith. He persevered in prayer.

With faith, nourished with the Bread of Life, we can persevere in prayer, too. At Mass, the memorial of Christ's Passover, Christ himself, the eternal High Priest, offers the Eucharistic sacrifice. Our participation in this Holy Sacrifice unites us to Christ and nourishes us with the strength we need to live faithfully.

Partners in Faith

Saints Felicity and Perpetua

Saints Felicity and Perpetua are among those listed in Eucharist Prayer I of the Mass. Perpetua was a Roman noblewoman and young mother. Felicity was a slave. Together, they were imprisoned and put to death for being Christians. Their story is one of the earliest accounts of martyrs in the Church. It is said to be Perpetua's actual diary written while she was in prison.

Learn more about the lives of Saints Felicity and Perpetua.

I was inspired by the Spirit not to ask for any other favor but simply the perseverance of the flesh.

Faith Word

Communion of Saints

Show What You Know

In your own words, give a short explanation for each term. Compare your responses with a partner.

Communion of Saints

perseverance in prayer

the liturgy as "living water"

Live Your Faith

- How can you draw from the living water in your prayer life?

- What could you say to someone who feels too distracted to pray?

Who helps me to pray?

Mini-Task

The Communion of Saints reminds us that we are always connected to our brothers and sisters in faith. The Litany of the Saints is a prayer for the intercession of the saints. It includes a list or "litany" of many canonized saints and martyrs.

In the space below, write your own Litany of the Saints. Include saints and any friends or family members who have died in Christ.

My Litany of the Saints

All you holy men and women, pray for us.

Saint ______________________ and Saint ______________________

Pray for us.

Saint ______________________ and Saint ______________________

Pray for us.

Saint ______________________ and Saint ______________________

Pray for us.

Saint ______________________ and Saint ______________________

Pray for us.

All you holy men and women, pray for us!

Amen.

Want to do more? Go to your Portfolio to continue this activity.

At Home

Who are some saints that are important in your family's life? In your family prayers at night or at meals, ask those saints to pray for you. The next time your family is at Mass, remember that you are joined to the Communion of Saints in prayer.

Why is the Lord's Prayer called the perfect prayer?

The Lord's Prayer expresses the Church's hope in God. Through it, we are united with God and his Son, Jesus. When we pray the Lord's Prayer, we glorify God and show our trust that God hears us.

Meditation

God thirsts for us so that we may thirst for him. Prayer is an encounter between God's thirst and our own.

Saint Augustine

The Lord's Prayer expresses the Church's hope in God.

Have you ever wondered why nearly every time the Church gathers to pray, we pray the Lord's Prayer? This is because the Lord's Prayer, or the Our Father, is the perfect prayer.

Since the time of the first Christians, the Lord's Prayer has been the prayer of the Church. In fact, the first Christian communities prayed it three times a day. The Church has prayed it ever since, usually as a part of her liturgy. It is prayed in the Liturgy of the Hours, during the celebration of certain sacraments, and especially the Eucharist.

Have you ever wondered why we pray the Lord's Prayer at every Mass? Or, why we pray it when we do during Mass? The Lord's Prayer is placed within the Sacrament of the Eucharist. We pray it after the Eucharistic Prayer and before Holy Communion. We pray it *after* the Eucharistic Prayer because it sums up all of our prayers of petition and intercession that we have just prayed. We pray it *before* Holy Communion because it is our prayer of expectation that the Lord will come again. We express our hope in the fulfillment of God's Kingdom.

When do I pray the Lord's Prayer?

Did You Know?

The first Apostles prayed the Lord's Prayer.

Prayer

Meditation

We are united with God and his Son through the Lord's Prayer.

Sometimes we use the phrase "They're really close" to describe a friendship or relationship between two people. There are many passages in the Gospels that reveal how close the relationship is between God the Father and his Son, Jesus. For example:

"All things have been handed over to me by my Father. No one knows the Son except the Father, and no one knows the Father except the Son and anyone to whom the Son wishes to reveal him."

Matthew 11:27

"I am the true vine, and my Father is the vine grower."

John 15:1

"As the Father loves me, so I also love you. Remain in my love. If you keep my commandments, you will remain in my love, just as I have kept my Father's commandments and remain in his love."

John 15:9–10

"Everything that the Father has is mine. . . ."

John 16:15

One Church, Many Cultures

In Scripture we find many references to vineyards, vines, grapes, and wine. Jesus even uses this imagery when he calls himself the "true vine." We are Jesus' disciples, the branches of the true vine. These images may also come to mind when we think of the Eucharist. The wine consecrated at Mass is made from grapes, a gift of the earth. Some monastic communities in Europe and the Americas have built grape vineyards. The monks pray, work the land, and make the wine. We offer the gift of wine at every celebration of the Mass. Once consecrated, it becomes the gift of Jesus' Blood in the Eucharist.

Activity

There are two versions of the Lord's Prayer in the Gospels. Work in small groups to read Matthew 6:9–13 and Luke 11:2–4. Then answer the questions.

1. How are the two versions alike?

____

____

____

2. What are some of their differences?

____

____

____

Which version is closest to the prayer you know by heart? Share with your reasons with your group.

The oil painting *The Solitude of Christ*, 1918, by Maurice Denis shows Jesus praying to his Father.

When Jesus taught his disciples how to pray, saying "Our Father. . . ," he invited them into a new, close relationship with God. Through his Death and Resurrection, Jesus has made it possible for us to share in the life of God. He called us his brothers and sisters (see Matthew 12:48–50). He revealed God as his Father and as our Father. Through Christ, we are the adopted children of God:

"In love he destined us for adoption to himself through Jesus Christ, in accord with the favor of his will, for the praise of the glory of his grace that he granted us in the beloved" (Ephesians 1:4–6).

We pray "Our Father," not "Your Father" or "My Father." When we say *Our* Father, we proclaim the truth that through our Baptism, we are united to each other in communion with the Blessed Trinity. We express this unity in all of the celebrations of the sacraments, beginning with Baptism and Confirmation in which the handing on of the Lord's Prayer signifies new birth into the life of God. When we pray the Lord's Prayer, we are united with God and Jesus, his Son, and with each other through our Baptism.

What Makes Us Catholic?

The word *Father* is an important way to describe people in the Church. We call some early Church leaders and teachers our *Church Fathers*. Priests are called "Fathers" as well, for they guide and care for the people of their parish. The connection to family continues in the way some monks are called "Brothers" and some women religious are called "Sisters." Yet we all believe in and worship only one Father: God the Father. Praying the Lord's Prayer, or the Our Father, is one of the best ways to remind ourselves that God is Father of all.

We glorify God in the Lord's Prayer.

When the Church prays, she always addresses God the Father first. When Jesus teaches his disciples to pray, he makes it very clear that our prayer is all about God first. All glory and praise belongs to God, our Father. The Lord's Prayer focuses our minds and hearts on God first. When we pray the Lord's Prayer in the liturgy, in the celebration of the sacraments, and in our personal prayers and devotions, we glorify God.

In the first petition of the Lord's Prayer, "hallowed be thy name," we glorify God's name. The word "hallowed" means "holy." In the Lord's Prayer, we do more than just say that God's name is holy. We ask God to help us glorify him by glorifying his name. We pray for reverence and wonder at the awesomeness of God.

In the second petition, "thy kingdom come," we give glory to God, whose reign of peace, justice, and love has been fulfilled in the Death and Resurrection of Jesus. Jesus teaches us to pray for the coming of the **Kingdom of God** at the end of time. Our prayer also reminds us that we can be a part of God's Kingdom, in the here and now, by how we live. At Mass we experience the Kingdom of God in our midst in the Eucharist–Jesus himself is present. At the end of Mass, the priest sends us forth, saying, "Go in peace, glorifying the Lord by your life."

Faith Word

Kingdom of God
see p. 293

Activity

In the space below, draw a symbol to represent each of these lines of the Lord's Prayer.

Hallowed be thy name . . . Thy will be done . . . Forgive us our trespasses . . .

The third petition, "thy will be done," gives glory to God by reminding us that our lives aren't about what we want but what *God* wants. We unite our will with Jesus, who taught us to "love one another. As I have loved you, so you also should love one another" (John 13:34). To love and to be loved is to glorify God and to experience a taste of heaven. The Eucharist nourishes us to love with Jesus' love and to follow God's will.

***Saint Francis of Assisi* by Jusepe de Ribera, 1642.**

Saint Francis of Assisi wrote and prayed praises that paraphrased the Our Father. Here is a more modern version of Francis' praises, including the first three petitions of the Our Father:

Our Father, most holy, our Creator, Redeemer, and Comforter.

Who art in heaven, in the angels and in the saints lighting their way to knowledge, for you, O Lord, are light; burning with love, for you, O Lord, are Love; . . .

Hallowed be Thy Name: may your knowledge shine in us . . .

Thy kingdom come, that you might reign in us by grace and make us come to your Kingdom . . .

Thy will be done on earth as it is in heaven, that we might love you with our whole heart by always thinking of you; with our whole soul by always wanting to be with you; with our whole mind by pointing all our intentions to you and seeking your honor in all things and with all our strength . . .

Activity

Using Saint Francis' words as inspiration, write the first three petitions of the "Our Father" prayer in your own words.

Our Father: ______________________________

Who art in heaven: ______________________________

Hallowed be thy name: ______________________________

Thy kingdom come: ______________________________

Thy will be done on earth as it is in heaven:

____

We show our trust that God hears us in the Lord's Prayer.

In the last four petitions of the Lord's Prayer, we pray with trust that God listens to us and responds to our needs. We pray for the graces of nourishment, mercy, and strength to live as children of God.

Give us this day our daily bread . . .
In the Sacrament of the Eucharist, we receive the living bread, Jesus himself. We become what we receive. We ask God to give us everything we need to live as Christ's disciples.

And forgive us our trespasses as we forgive those who trespass against us . . .
We pray for forgiveness of our own sins, and we pray for hearts that are merciful so that we can forgive others. All of us are in need of forgiveness, and all of us need to forgive. Forgiveness is a two-way street. We celebrate God's mercy and the forgiveness of sins in the Sacrament of Penance and Reconciliation.

And lead us not into temptation . . .
The temptations that we face every day try to convince us that there is something better than God's way. In the Lord's Prayer, we ask God to lead us away from situations and choices that try to pull us away from his love. The Sacrament of Confirmation, with the graces and gifts of the Holy Spirit it confers, strengthens us to avoid temptation and follow Jesus more closely.

Activity

It is not hard to see evil in the world. Often, however, there is a temptation to blame God when bad things happen. Why do you think this is so? Share your thoughts with a partner.

Together, think of what you might say to people who want to blame God for evil. Share your answers with the class.

Here are the final four petitions of the Our Father as they might appear in a modern version of the praises of Saint Francis:

Give us this day, through memory and understanding and reverence for God's love for us and for those things Christ said, did, and suffered, for us,

our daily bread, your beloved Son, our Lord Jesus Christ.

And forgive us our trespasses, in your mercy . . . and through the intercession of the Blessed Virgin Mary and the saints.

As we forgive them that trespass against us, and whatever we do not fully forgive, O Lord, make us fully forgive, so that for your sake we may truly love our enemies . . .

And lead us not into temptation, hidden or visible temptation, or sudden temptations always around us.

But deliver us from evil, past, present, and to come. Amen.

But deliver us from evil . . .

Evil is real. The forces of evil work hard to distract us, to turn us away from God. But there is no power stronger than that of Jesus. In Jesus, God's love has overcome evil. Regular participation in the sacraments, especially the Sacrament of the Eucharist and the Sacrament of Penance and Reconciliation, helps us resist evil and live in God's love.

Partners in Faith

Saint John Neumann

Saint John Neumann arrived in America with the clothes on his back and one dollar. He had hoped to be ordained in his native Bohemia–part of what we now call the Czech Republic– but there were too many priests in that country. Three weeks after coming to America, John was ordained as a priest and began to work with German immigrants. Saint John helped found the first Catholic school system in the United States.

Learn more about the life of Saint John Neumann.

If it is your will, my Jesus, increase my sufferings, but hear my prayers!

Faith Word

Kingdom of God

Show What You Know

Choose the correct term to complete the sentences.

1. When we pray the ______________________________, we are united with God and Jesus, his Son, and with each other through our Baptism.

   Lord's Prayer | Baptismal Promises

2. God's reign of peace, justice, and love is called the ______________________________.

   Priesthood of God | Kingdom of God

3. In the last four ______________________________ of the Lord's Prayer, we pray with trust that God listens to us and responds to our needs.

   petitions | psalms

Live Your Faith

- What are you doing now to help build up the Kingdom of God?

____

____

____

____

____

____

- Why do we ask God to "lead us not into temptation"? What strength does God give you to avoid temptation?

____

____

____

____

____

____

How do I live out the Lord's Prayer?

Mini-Task

Bullying is a huge problem in our society. It is easy to say or share mean or degrading things, especially online when we may not face immediate consequences. How you treat others is a reflection of your character. The Lord's Prayer reminds us that we are called to be disciples of Jesus Christ.

On the lines below, write a pledge to be kind to your friends and classmates and to stand up for those who are bullied.

I Pledge to Be Kind . . .

____

____

____

____

____

____

I Pledge to Defend . . . .

____

____

____

____

____

____

Want to do more? Go to your Portfolio to continue this activity.

At Home

Pray the Our Father slowly together as a family. Ask each family member to share a word or phrase from the prayer that stood out to her or him.

Seasons and Feasts of the Church Year

In this unit you will learn about how the Church celebrates the Paschal Mystery of Christ through her feasts and seasons. We will see how Jesus Christ remains the central figure of the Church all year long.

Unit 5

Why and how do we celebrate the Church Year?

Unit Song:
"We Are Called," David Haas

Unit Prayer

Leader: Saint Ignatius of Loyola taught that it is more important that we show our love for God by the way we live, that our deeds mean more than our words. Let us listen to how Jesus' love is shown to us today.

Listen to the stories of missionary discipleship in our midst.

Let us pray:
Jesus, at Mass we are given all the tools that we need to be your disciples. It is there we are taught by your Word, fed by your Body and Blood, and sent to show the world that we love you by the way we live. Through each season of the Church year, we experience a different way to know of your love.

For Advent and Christmas, when we learn to wait for your coming and celebrate your birth in our hearts.

All: We bring your love to the world.

Leader: For Lent and Triduum, when we learn how to love by your Word, your life, and your Death and Resurrection.

All: We bring your love to the world.

Leader: For Easter, when the words of the prophets were fulfilled by your rising from the dead.

All: We bring your love to the world.

Leader: For Pentecost, when we are filled with the Holy Spirit, sending us forth to live as you have loved us.

All: We bring your love to the world.

Leader: For Ordinary Time, when we hear stories that teach us how to live your commands, showing the world in deed more than word of your love for us all.

All: We bring your love to the world.

Leader: Let us offer each other a sign of peace.

End the Unit Prayer by singing the song for this unit.

Missionary Discipleship

When have you been able to show someone how much God loves them? How did it feel? When has someone shown God's love to you? How did it feel?

How do we celebrate Jesus Christ?

Pray . . . that God may open a door to us for the word, to speak of the mystery of Christ.

Colossians 4:3

Gathering Prayer

Leader: The Church year guides our celebrations of Jesus through different seasons and feasts. Each season focuses on a differe nt aspect of the Paschal Mystery, yet all direct our focus toward the life, work, and love of Jesus Christ. We listen to the stories of all Christ did for us and learn from his example in all things.

We praise you, O God, for the life, work, and love of your Son, Jesus.

All: We praise you, O God, for the life, work, and love of your Son, Jesus.

Leader: In Advent, we prepare our hearts for the gift of Jesus Christ and the hope of his return in glory. We pray:

All: We praise you, O God, for the life, work, and love of your Son, Jesus.

Leader: At Christmas, we celebrate the infant King, Jesus, who was born for us and would die for us. We pray:

All: We praise you, O God, for the life, work, and love of your Son, Jesus.

Leader: During Lent, we ask Jesus Christ to help us turn our hearts back toward you, O God, and we give thanks for the gift of Christ's life and Death. We pray:

All: We praise you, O God, for the life, work, and love of your Son, Jesus.

Leader: The three holy days of the Easter Triduum bring us closer to God and makes us more aware of Jesus' sacrifice for us, as we remember Jesus' Passion, Death and Resurrection.

All: We praise you, O God, for the life, work, and love of your Son, Jesus.

Leader: In the joyful season of Easter, we celebrate that Christ is risen from the dead. His rising brings us hope that we, too, will live forever with God in heaven. Alleluia, Alleluia! We pray:

All: We praise you, O God, for the life, work, and love of your Son, Jesus.

Leader: All year, we learn from Jesus Christ and aim to live in his love, and to show that love to the world. We pray:

All: We praise you, O God, for the life, work, and love of your Son, Jesus.

Activity

Mind maps can help us understand ideas. In groups, create a mind map about one of the seasons of the liturgical year. Choose one season and write that season's name at the center of your map. Then, create your map by drawing lines from the center to other sections where you write words that come to mind when you think of that season. Circle the one word in your map that means the most to the entire group. Share your mind map with the other groups. Combine the seven words from all groups into one mind map to post at the front of the classroom.

Christ's Paschal Mystery inspires the Church's feasts and seasons.

The liturgical year is made up of different feasts and seasons. All the seasons are united, because each season reveals the one mystery of Christ.

The central point of the liturgical year is Christ's suffering, Death, Resurrection, and Ascension. This is called the Paschal Mystery. Every season circles around this central mystery and points to it.

There are signs that point to the Paschal Mystery in every season. During Ordinary Time, Jesus tells his followers to take up their crosses. During Lent, Jesus predicts his Passion, and the story of the Transfiguration is like a preview of the Resurrection. The *Paschal*, or Easter Triduum, the highest point of the year, remembers in a special way the life, Passion, Death and Resurrection of Jesus Christ.

Even during Christmas, we have signs of the Paschal Mystery. The aromatic spices brought by the Magi are used for burial. Yet the gold and frankincense they bring show that Jesus will be victorious as Lord and God.

The Paschal Mystery is what we celebrate in the Eucharist. The dying and rising of Jesus is made present to us in the Mass. We participate in it there. When we were baptized, we entered into this mystery. We died to sin and rose to a new life in Jesus. When we celebrate the Eucharist and receive Holy Communion, the Holy Spirit renews the life of God within us.

Sunday is the original feast day. It is the oldest observance in the Church calendar. Sunday is special because we believe that Jesus rose from the dead on the first day of the week. Therefore, every Sunday is considered a "little Easter." It is the day of light, the day of Eucharist.

Sacraments are celebrated on many days throughout the year, but the Catholic community always returns to the Eucharist on Sunday. It is our central, weekly celebration of the Paschal Mystery.

Did You Know?

Signs are everywhere.

Activity

Form small groups to discuss the Church's seasons and the Paschal Mystery. Have each person in your group choose one season of the liturgical year and describe that season's connection to the Paschal Mystery.

Church Year Prayer Ritual

"The Lord Has Done Great Things For Us,"
Jamie Cortez

Leader: In the name of the Father, and of the Son, and of the Holy Spirit, Amen.

The liturgical year is made up of the seasons of Advent, Christmas, Ordinary Time, Lent, Triduum, and Easter. We experience this calendar most clearly when we gather for Mass each week. Through the Liturgy of the Word and the Liturgy of the Eucharist, we encounter the living Christ in the Word of God and in the Body and Blood of Christ.

The Church teaches that we also encounter Christ in each other. One of the ways that we celebrate Christ alive in each other while at Mass is to pray and sing together.

In Advent, we ask Jesus to help us prepare a place in our hearts for his return and birth at Christmas. Prepare a place in our hearts, O Lord.

All: Prepare a place in our hearts, O Lord.

Reader 1: At Christmas, we celebrate the birth of our Lord, Jesus, alive in our hearts!

All: O Lord, help us to celebrate the birth of your Son with wonder and awe.

Reader 2: In Ordinary Time, we listen to Jesus teach us how to love one God and one another in his many parables. We ask him to help us listen to his Word with open hearts and minds.

All: O Lord, help us to listen to your Word with open hearts and minds.

Reader 3: In the season of Lent, we make time for Jesus by prayer, fasting and abstinence, and gifts of charity. We use this season to focus on Christ's love for us all and on our response to his call to love one another as God has loved us.

All: Help us to love one another as God has loved us.

Leader: The Liturgies of the Easter Triduum are Holy Thursday, Good Friday, and the Easter Vigil. These are the most powerful liturgies of the liturgical year. We first celebrate the Last Supper, when Jesus took bread and wine and gave us his Body and Blood. On Good Friday, we remember the death of Jesus on the Cross. At the Easter Vigil, we gather in darkness that is lifted by the risen Light of Christ, and we celebrate his love that can never be removed or darkened.

All: Let all creation lift its voice in praise!

Reader 1: During the joyful season of Easter, we celebrate Jesus' Resurrection from the dead. Christ came to die for us, and to rise from death, banishing all sin and darkness from our lives.

We are an Easter people, who no longer live in darkness and sin but live in the light of Easter!

All: Alleluia, Alleluia, Alleluia!

Reader 2: And, finally, on the great feast of Pentecost, we receive the Holy Spirit of God to go out into the world and spread the Good News of Christ. We celebrate the manifestation of the Church!

All: Come, Holy Spirit, and renew the face of the earth.

Reader 3: As we pass around this candle, let us ask God to help us live in the Light of his Son Jesus, throughout the liturgical year.

Pass around an unlit candle. When all have held the candle, pray.

Leader: The Light of Christ shines in us throughout the year. Amen, Alleluia!

All: Amen, Alleluia!

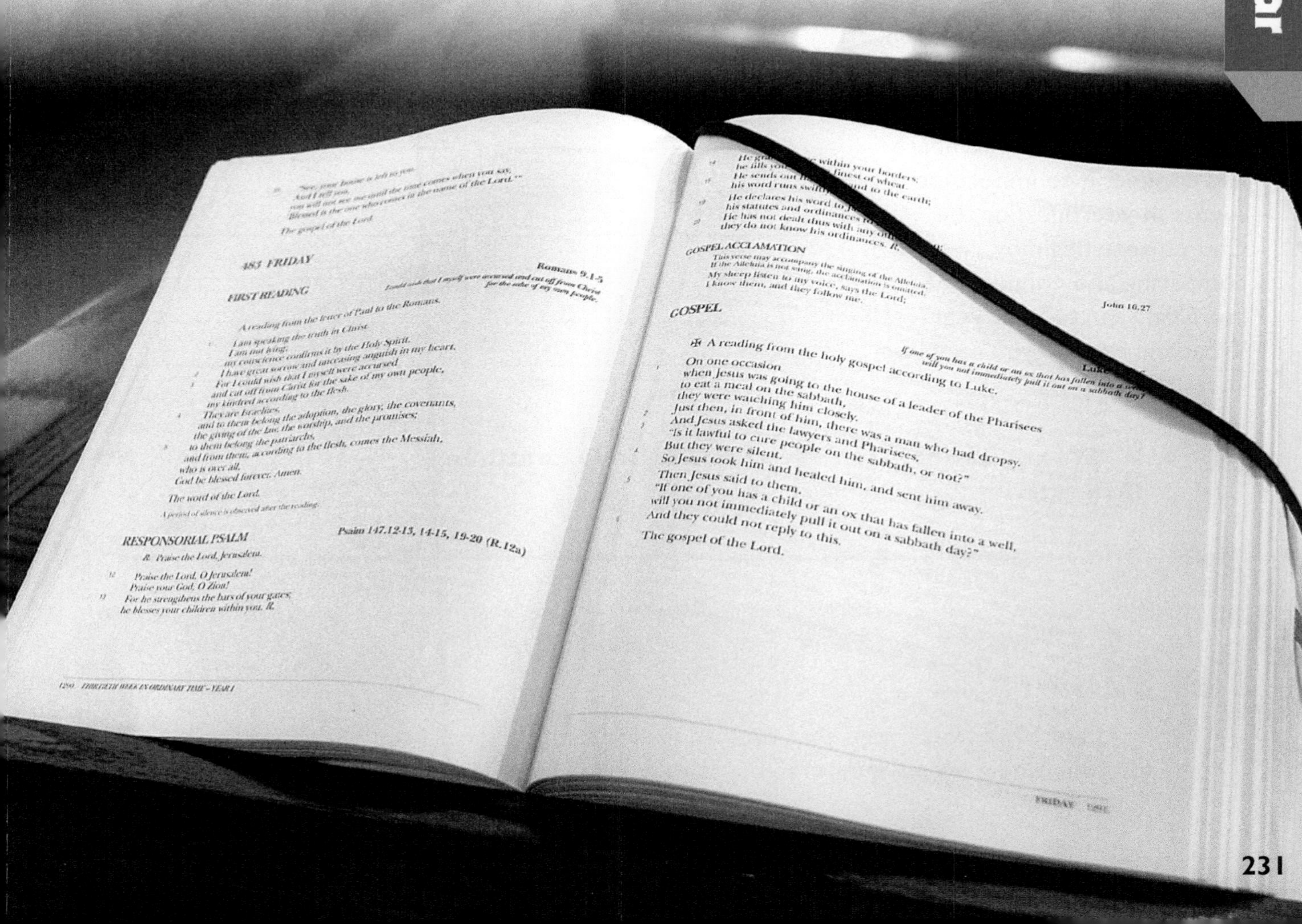

Portfolio

How is Christ a part of my life all year long?

Mini-Task

The seasons of the liturgical year help us remember and celebrate the events of the Paschal Mystery: the life, Passion, and Resurrection of Christ. Christ is the center of our life and Catholic faith. He is present in all of the Church's sacraments.

You will learn about seven seasons of the liturgical year. The Church celebrates the Seven Sacraments. In every season and in every sacrament, the Church celebrates and remembers Christ and his presence in the Church today.

As you learn and experience each season, you will compare and connect it to important events in your life. For the Church year, begin by comparing and connect the liturgical year to your year. What and how do you celebrate in each?

Compare and Contrast Chart Graphic Organizer

1. ____________________

2. ____________________

How are they alike?

____

____

____

____

How are they different?

____________	____________
____________	____________
____________	____________
____________	____________
____________	____________
____________	____________
____________	____________
____________	____________
____________	____________

Want to do more? Go to your Portfolio to continue this activity.

At Home

Together, brainstorm ways that you can make Sunday a special day of the week for your family, even if family members have different responsibilities on that day.

Why does Jesus come to save us?

Lesson 22

Advent

*Whoever is in Christ is a new creation:
the old things have passed away; behold,
new things have come.*

2 Corinthians 5:17

Gathering Prayer

Leader: Bless us this Advent as we wait in joyful hope for your coming to us. We celebrate this season by preparing our homes and our hearts. Each Sunday, another candle in the Advent wreath is lit. On the fourth Sunday of Advent, the four lights for each week give off your light.

We wait in joyful hope for your coming to us, Lord Jesus.

All: We wait in joyful hope for your coming to us, Lord Jesus.

Leader: "A voice proclaims:

In the wilderness prepare the way of the LORD!" (Isaiah 40:3).

All: We wait in joyful hope for your coming to us, Lord Jesus.

Leader: "Every valley shall be lifted up, every mountain and hill made low" (Isaiah 40:4).

All: We wait in joyful hope for your coming to us, Lord Jesus.

Leader: "Then the glory of the LORD shall be revealed, and all flesh shall see it together" (Isaiah 40:5).

All: We wait in joyful hope for your coming to us, Lord Jesus.

Leader: Lord Jesus, prepare in our hearts the path of your return.

All: We wait in joyful hope for your coming to us, Lord Jesus.

Activity

The Church does not celebrate Christmas until December 25. But many places in the world start celebrating the Christmas holidays on December 1, or earlier. As a class, discuss ways that you can take part in the holiday spirit while still keeping Advent as a time of penance and prayer.

Our hearts look forward to the coming of Christ.

In the Nicene Creed, we profess our faith. We say that we believe that Jesus "will come again in glory."

The season of Advent is that time of the year when we remember and celebrate the fact that Jesus Christ will come again in glory. No one knows the day or the hour when Christ will return. Therefore, we must be ready to meet him whenever he comes, our hearts filled with wonder, love, and praise.

Many people are fearful when they think about the end of the world. It will be a time of great turmoil and destruction. Yet believers can be confident that Christ will gather all who believe in him together and protect us from all harm. We need never be afraid.

We know that the world is not eternal. It had a beginning, and it will have an end. The story of creation assures us that God is the source of the world's beginning. The New Testament assures us that when Jesus comes again in glory, he will reign over all things. The end of time, as well as its beginning, is in the safe hands of our God.

Advent marks the beginning of the liturgical year. Yet the first Sunday of Advent emphasizes the coming of Jesus at the end of time. Does it not seem strange that at the beginning of a new liturgical year, the readings for Mass speak about the end of the world?

The liturgy reminds us every year that we are on a journey together. At the start of each new liturgical cycle, we look ahead to the ultimate goal of all that we celebrate in the year to come: the revelation of Jesus Christ. His birth in Bethlehem is good news, and so is his coming at the end of time.

Did You Know?

Jesus is here—be not afraid.

Activity

Advent means "coming." Ask two or three friends why Advent in the Church does not mean waiting for Christmas but waiting for the coming of Jesus. Summarize their answers and present your results to the class.

Readers Theater

Joseph's Dream

ROLES:
Narrator 1, Narrator 2, Narrator 3, Joseph, Angel

Joseph faces a difficult decision when he finds out that Mary is pregnant. An angel helps him to decide.

Narrator 1: This is an account of how Joseph became aware that Mary would give birth to Jesus. It was during the time when Joseph and Mary were betrothed.

Narrator 2: "Betrothed" was the first stage of marriage during the time of Joseph and Mary. It was like being engaged.

Narrator 3: Mary was found to be with child through the Holy Spirit. Joseph did not yet fully understand what this all meant.

Joseph: I love Mary and want to protect her. But when people find out that she is pregnant and we are not yet married, she will be shamed. It would be better for her if I leave.

Narrator 1: As he was thinking of all of this, he fell into a deep sleep.

Narrator 2: Suddenly, an angel of the Lord appeared to him in a dream!

Angel: "Joseph, son of David, do not be afraid to take Mary your wife into your home. For it is through the holy Spirit that this child has been conceived in her. She will bear a son and you are to name him Jesus, because he will save his people from their sins" (Matthew 1:20–21).

Narrator 3: When Joseph woke up, he did all the angel of the Lord told him to do.

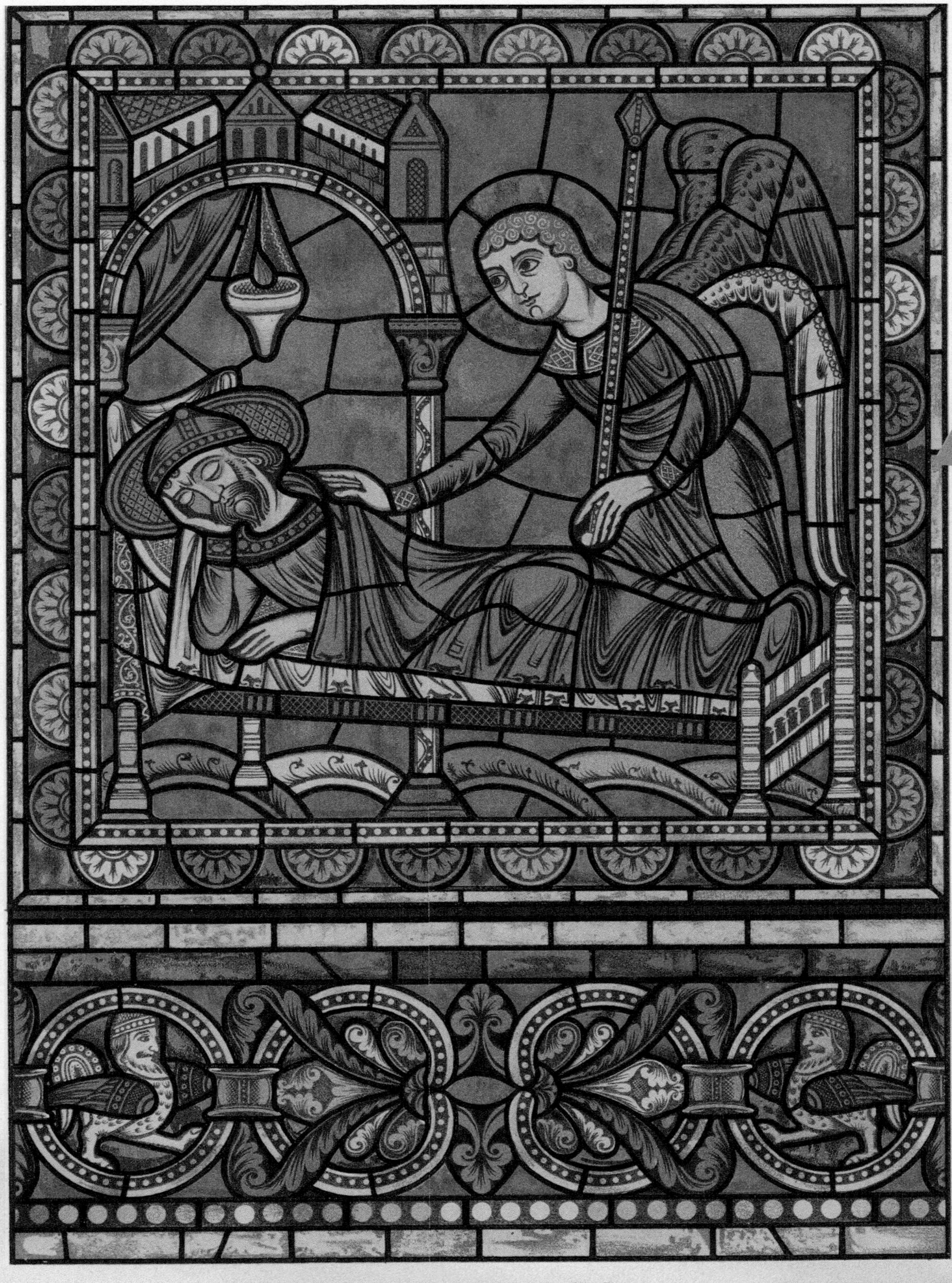

The Dream of Saint Joseph, 19th-Century lithograph by Emile Beau.

How do I look forward to the coming of Christ?

Mini-Task

Advent begins the liturgical year. During the season of Advent, we look forward to celebrating the birth of Jesus. It is fitting that the first season of the liturgical year helps us to remember the hope that Jesus would bring to God's people.

Compare and connect the meaning and experience of Advent to an event in your life.

Compare and Contrast Chart Graphic Organizer

1. ______________________

2. ______________________

How are they alike?

____

____

____

____

How are they different?

____

____

____

____

____

____

____

____

Want to do more? Go to your Portfolio to continue this activity.

At Home

Talk with your family about a family event or occasion you are looking forward to. Pray together that the beginning and end of this event or occasion will go well for your family.

How did the Son of God enter human history?

Christmas

And the Word became flesh . . .
and we saw his glory.

John 1:14

Gathering Prayer

Leader: This Christmas, let us celebrate the gift of Jesus, the gift of love. As we gather at Mass to sing carols and hymns of the season, let us offer prayers of thanksgiving to God for the gift of Jesus, his Son. God loved us so much that he became one of us. Through Jesus we have come to know the love of God the Father.

Jesus, Prince of Peace, we give glory to your name!

All: Jesus, Prince of Peace, we give glory to your name!

Leader: Lord Jesus, you are Word Made Flesh. We give glory to your name!

All: Jesus, Prince of Peace, we give glory to your name!

Leader: Christ Jesus, you are Wonder-Counselor. We give glory to your name!

All: Jesus, Prince of Peace, we give glory to your name!

Leader: Lord Jesus, you are Light from Light, true God from true God!

All: Jesus, Prince of Peace, we give glory to your name!

Leader: Christ Jesus, you were begotten, not made, one in being with the Father!

All: Jesus, Prince of Peace, we give glory to your name!

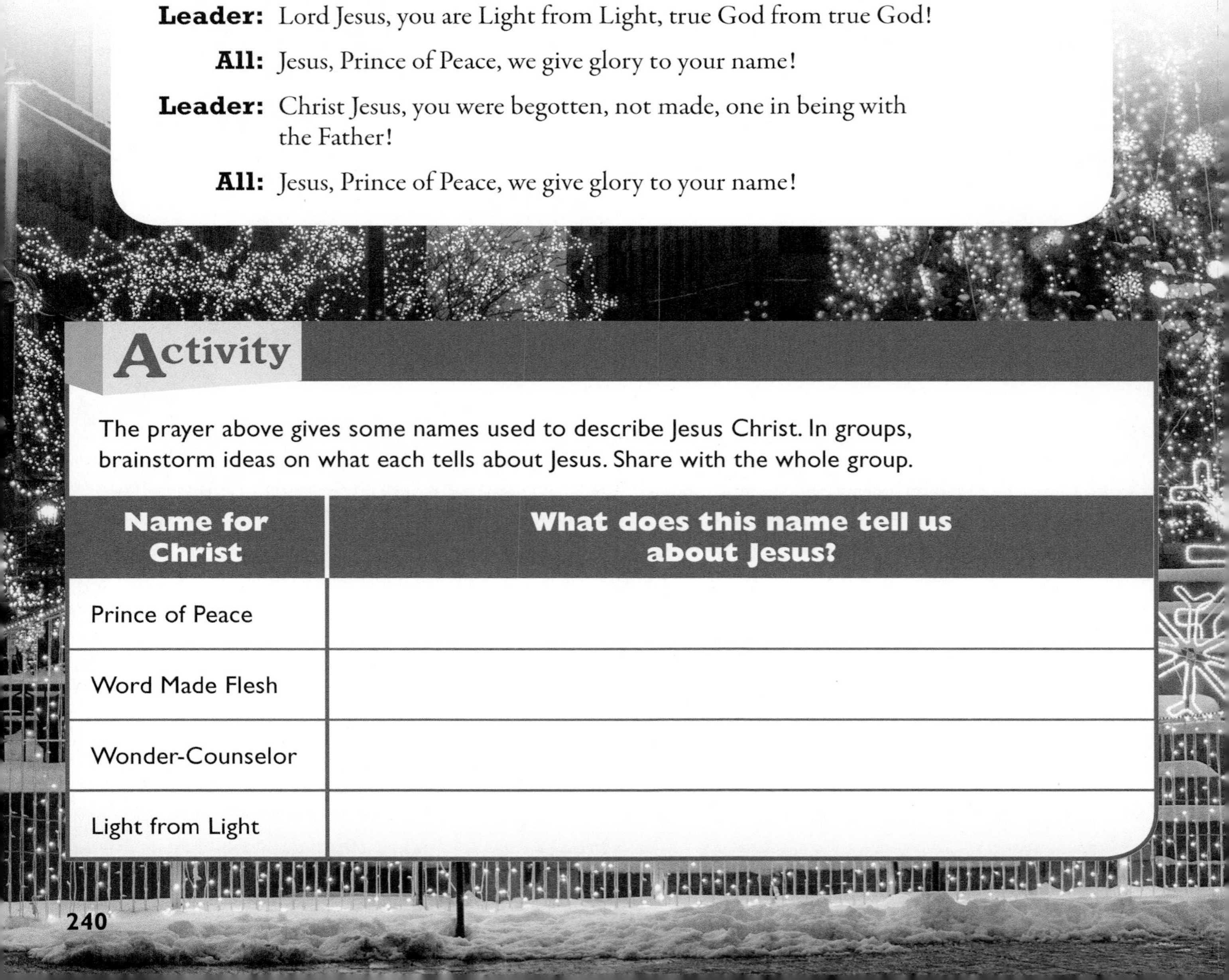

Activity

The prayer above gives some names used to describe Jesus Christ. In groups, brainstorm ideas on what each tells about Jesus. Share with the whole group.

Name for Christ	What does this name tell us about Jesus?
Prince of Peace	
Word Made Flesh	
Wonder-Counselor	
Light from Light	

The Incarnation strengthens Catholics in the belief that God works through the material world rather than remaining far apart from it. The physical world, although imperfect and full of suffering, can also be a medium for God's presence. By using material signs and symbols as well as words, the sacraments underline our faith in the Incarnation.

The Incarnation shows us that we must respect everyone. Because God's Son took on human flesh and dignified it by the Incarnation, we know that our own bodies and those of others are made in the image of God.

At Christmas we celebrate the Incarnation of the Son of God.

The Gospel according to John does not tell the story of Jesus' birth as it is told in the Gospels of Matthew or Luke. Instead, John offers a beautiful, poetic hymn to the Incarnation.

"In the beginning was the Word, and the Word was with God, and the Word was God," John writes (1:1). He goes on to talk about the Son of God as "light" coming into the world. Finally, he says:

"And the Word became flesh
and made his dwelling among us,
and we saw his glory,
the glory as of the Father's only Son,
full of grace and truth." John 1:14

This passage, which is the reading for the Mass During the Day on Christmas, tells us something very important about what we celebrate.

This Scripture reading shows that Christmas is, above all, the feast of the Incarnation. The Word was made flesh. God's Word, in an act of grace, became a human person. The Son of God, the Second Person of the Trinity, was present with God from the beginning—even before creation. Yet he took on human flesh in Jesus.

Did You Know?

God uses physical things to explain spiritual mysteries.

Activity

The word "Incarnation" comes from the Latin, meaning "to make flesh." It refers to Jesus' becoming a human. List three reasons why it is important to our faith that Jesus became a human person.

____

____

____

Using these reasons, write a brief poem, paragraph, or song to share with the group. If you write a song, you might want to use a Christmas carol for the melody.

Readers Theater

Shepherds at the Birth of Jesus

ROLES:
Narrator 1, Narrator 2, Narrator 3, Narrator 4, Shepherds (2 or 3), Heavenly Host, Angel

Glory to God in the highest.

Narrator 1: In those days a decree went out from Caesar Augustus declaring that the whole world should be enrolled.

Narrator 2: This meant that all family members had to travel to their own town to be counted.

Narrator 3: So Mary, who was with child, and her husband, Joseph, went up from the town of Nazareth to the city of David called Bethlehem.

Narrator 4: Joseph was of the house and family of David.

Narrator 1: While Mary and Joseph were there, the time came for Mary to have her child, and she gave birth to Jesus.

Narrator 2: She wrapped him in swaddling clothes and laid him in a manger, because there was no room for them to stay at the inn.

Narrator 3: At the same time, shepherds who lived in fields outside Bethlehem were keeping watch on their sheep all night. All was quiet.

Narrator 4: Then suddenly an angel appeared to them. The glory of God shone all around them! The shepherds were very afraid.

Shepherds: What is happening?

Angel: "Do not be afraid; for behold, I proclaim to you good news of great joy that will be for all the people. For today in the city of David a savior has been born for you who is Messiah and Lord. And this will be a sign for you: you will find an infant wrapped in swaddling clothes and lying in a manger" (Luke 2:10–12).

Heavenly Host: "Glory to God in the highest and on earth peace to those on whom his favor rests" (Luke 2:14).

Narrator 1: The shepherds were amazed.

Narrator 2: They hurried to see this baby whom the angels sang about.

Narrator 3: The shepherds went back to watching their sheep.

Narrator 4: But they wanted to tell everyone about the baby Jesus.

***The Adoration of the Shepherds*, 1534, by Lorenzo Lotto.**

How has my world been changed by the birth of Jesus?

Mini-Task

During the season of Christmas, we celebrate that God became man in the Incarnation of Christ. Christmas is a time of peace and joy. It can be a time of healing for families and groups of people, as we all celebrate the birth of Jesus.

Compare and connect the meaning and experience of Christmas to an event in your life. What and how do we celebrate in each?

Compare and Contrast Chart Graphic Organizer

1. ______________________ 2. ______________________

How are they alike?

____

How are they different?

______________________ ______________________

Want to do more? Go to your Portfolio to continue this activity.

At Home

Ask your family members to tell about some ways they see Jesus' presence in the world. Talk about ways you see his presence in each other.

How are we called to repentance today?

He restores my soul.
He guides me along right paths
for the sake of his name.

Psalm 23:3

Gathering Prayer

Leader: The season of Lent is a time for us to prepare our hearts for the celebration of Christ's rising from the dead at Easter. We take this time in Lent to pray and fast, and to experience conversion. God's presence in his holy Word feeds our minds with wisdom and knowledge. The Real Presence of Jesus in his Body and Blood fills us with his love and strength. We experience conversion as we celebrate the Sacrament of Penance and Reconciliation. We reflect on the choices we have made and turn our hearts back toward God.

Lord Jesus, help us to listen to your Word with the ears of our hearts, that we may turn our hearts to you and live as your light in the world.

Create in me a clean heart, O God.

All: Create in me a clean heart, O God.

Leader: Lord Jesus, your Real Presence in the Eucharist is the food that feeds and strengthens us. Your light in us will shine for all to see.

Create in me a clean heart, O God.

All: Create in me a clean heart, O God.

Leader: Lord Jesus, forgive us our sins and celebrate with us the conversion of our hearts in the Sacrament of Penance and Reconciliation. Guide us to live so that others may recognize you in everything we do.

Create in me a clean heart, O God.

All: Create in me a clean heart, O God.

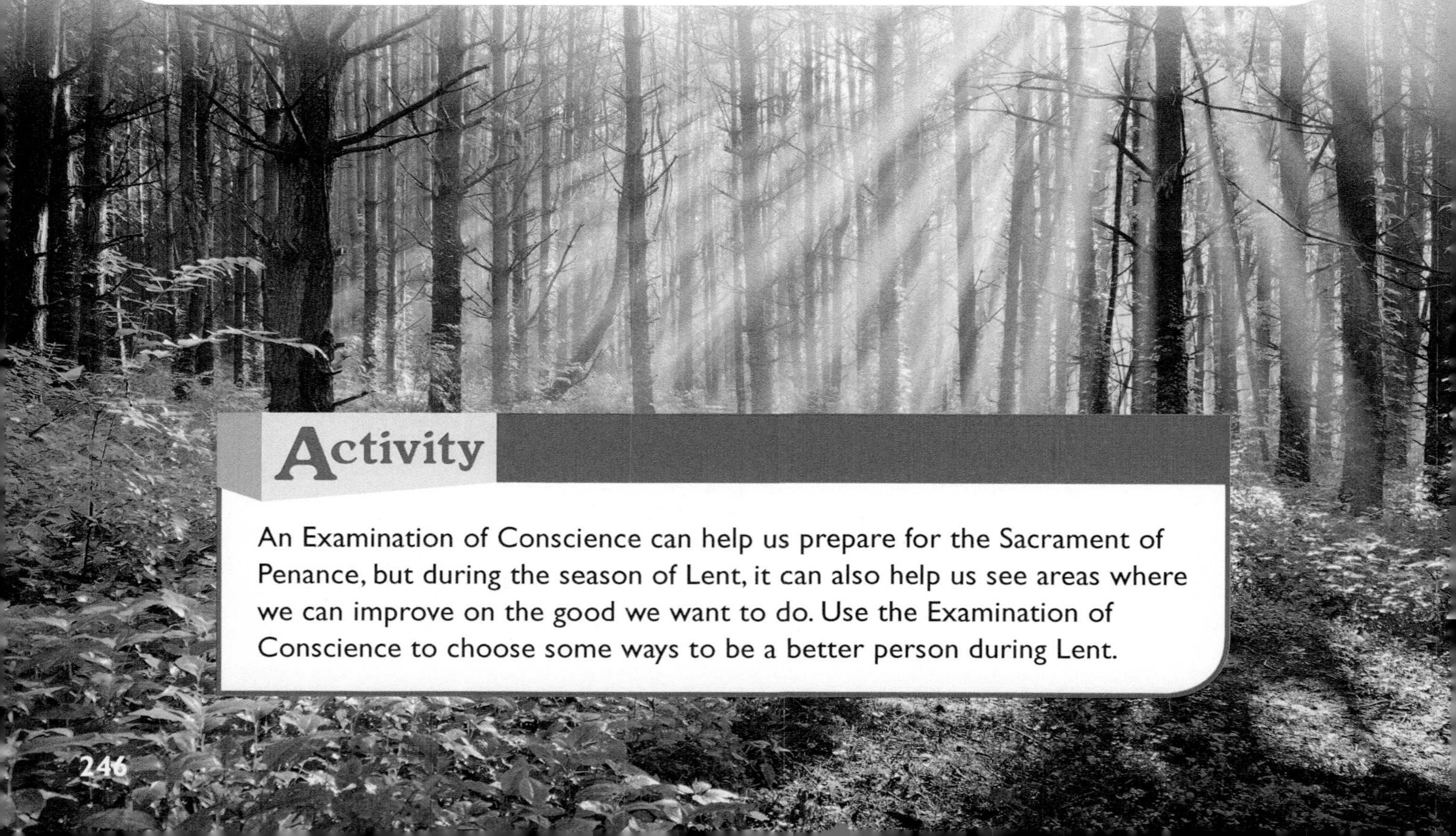

Activity

An Examination of Conscience can help us prepare for the Sacrament of Penance, but during the season of Lent, it can also help us see areas where we can improve on the good we want to do. Use the Examination of Conscience to choose some ways to be a better person during Lent.

Lent calls us to renewal.

Lent is a season in which we renew our faith. Just as Jesus went out into the desert and fasted for forty days to prepare for his mission, so we renew our call to faith each year during the forty days of Lent.

We renew our faith, first of all, by following the three disciplines of Lent: prayer, fasting, and almsgiving. Our prayer, both personal prayer and communal prayer, should be especially earnest at this time.

During Lent, Catholics fast according to the rules of the Church on two days: Ash Wednesday and Good Friday. We abstain from meat on Fridays. But we might also practice self-denial by fasting at other times or by voluntarily giving up something we enjoy. Almsgiving, which means giving to the poor, is something we should do in all seasons, but during Lent we should be especially generous.

The other way we renew our faith is through the Sacrament of Eucharist and the Sacrament of Penance and Reconciliation. The Eucharist is a sacrament that strengthens us in holiness. It cleanses us from our less serious sins and renews the life of God within us. Every time we say "Amen" when receiving Holy Communion, we are saying "Yes" to the life God has given us in Baptism. Eucharist commits us to live as followers of Jesus.

The Sacrament of Penance and Reconciliation is the other sacrament that renews our faith in a special way. By confessing our sins and receiving God's forgiveness through absolution, we are freed from our sins and strengthened to resist temptation.

In the liturgy of Easter, we will renew our baptismal promises. We promise to reject Satan, and we profess our faith. We take the whole season of Lent to prepare for this renewal at Easter so that our words will not be empty promises but a true expression of faith.

Did You Know?

Transformation happens.

Activity

English speakers refer to this season of the Church year as Lent, from the Old English word *lencten* for "springtime." Most of the rest of the world calls the season by different names. Latin-based languages use words that mean "fortieth," since the Lenten season is forty days long. Other languages use words that mean "fasting time" or "great fast." Think about what the Church remembers and does during Lent. As a group, talk about which name for this season makes the most sense to you given what happens during this time.

Lent Prayer Ritual

"Your Grace Is Enough,"
Matt Maher

Leader: In the name of the Father, and of the Son, and of the Holy Spirit. Amen.

The season of Lent is a time for us to prepare our hearts for Jesus' Death and Resurrection. The Sign of the Cross that we just made reminds us that we are a people who is loved by a God, who became one of us only to die and then rise from death. Just as Jesus died on the Cross, we carry the cross of Jesus in our own lives and are reminded that we are never alone, that Jesus is always with us when we are carrying our own crosses. As we pray, let us pass this cross among us.

Our eyes are always on you, O Lord.

All: Our eyes are always on you, O Lord.

Reader 1: In you, O Lord, we place all our trust and hope, because of your goodness.

All: Our eyes are always on you, O Lord.

Reader 2: Remember your love, O Lord, that you have shown from of old.

All: Our eyes are always on you, O Lord.

Reader 3: Do not let us down; protect us from our foes. Turn to me, O Lord.

All: Our eyes are always on you, O Lord.

Reader 1: What joy and peace is life in you; you alone give us joy and peace. You alone are Lord!

All: Our eyes are always on you, O Lord.

Reader 2: We now ask God to hear our own prayers as we take the cross of Jesus and pray.

Hold the cross and offer a brief prayer in your own words. Then, hand on the cross to the next person. After each prayer, all pray:

All: Our eyes are always on you.

Leader: O Lord, we ask you to hear our prayers and lift up the needs of everyone that we prayed for today.

Let us close with the Lord's Prayer. Our Father . . .

Portfolio

How do I renew my faith during Lent?

Mini-Task

Lent is a time to focus our thoughts on how we can better live as Christ's disciples. We perform acts of self-denial and renew our faith. We get ready to celebrate the wonders of Christ's Resurrection at Easter.

Compare and connect the meaning and experience of Lent and an event in your life. What and how do we celebrate in each?

Compare and Contrast Chart Graphic Organizer

1. ____________________

2. ____________________

How are they alike?

____
____
____
____

How are they different?

____
____
____
____
____
____
____
____

____
____
____
____
____
____
____
____

Want to do more? Go to your Portfolio to continue this activity.

At Home

As a family, talk about things we renew, like library or school ID cards, driver's licenses, and car registrations. Talk about how renewal is a fresh start. Have family members choose ways they can renew their faith this week.

Why did Jesus die on the Cross and rise again?

Triduum

Your light must shine before others, that they may see your good deeds and glorify your heavenly Father.

Matthew 5:16

Gathering Prayer

Leader: During Holy Week, Lent ends and we celebrate the Triduum: the life, Death and Resurrection of Jesus, believing that one day we too will be with God in heaven. Every knee shall bow at the name of Jesus! Glory and praise to you, Lord Jesus Christ.

All: Glory and praise to you, Lord Jesus Christ.

Leader: On Holy Thursday, we celebrate the gift of the Eucharist. Thank you, Jesus, for teaching us how to love God through the gift of the Eucharist. Glory and praise to you, Lord Jesus Christ.

All: Glory and praise to you, Lord Jesus Christ.

Leader: On Good Friday, we remember how much you have loved us by dying on the Cross. We know how much you suffered for us. Glory and praise to you, Lord Jesus Christ.

All: Glory and praise to you, Lord Jesus Christ.

Leader: Lord Jesus, just as you promised, you rose from the dead on Easter. Let us praise you by living as people of light–as Easter people.

All: Glory and praise to you, Lord Jesus Christ.

Leader: As we make the Sign of the Cross, help us remember how much Jesus loves us by giving his life for us on the Cross.

All: In the name of the Father, and the Son, and the Holy Spirit, Amen.

Glory and praise to you, Lord Jesus Christ.

Activity

Triduum comes from the Latin word meaning "three days." Another word that contains "tri" is *Trinity*. What role does each member of the Blessed Trinity play during the Triduum? Fill in the chart, and then discuss your thoughts with your group.

Father	
Son	
Holy Spirit	

The Triduum is the high point of the liturgical year.

The Triduum is celebrated over three days. It begins with the Mass of the Lord's Supper on Holy Thursday night. It continues with the Celebration of the Passion of the Lord on Good Friday. On Holy Saturday night, we celebrate the Easter Vigil, the greatest of all solemnities. The Triduum ends on Easter Sunday night.

The Triduum celebrates the Death and Resurrection of the Lord, which is the central mystery of the Christian faith. The Easter Vigil is the high point of the Triduum. We move from darkness into light and from Death to Resurrection.

The Easter Vigil is an occasion for celebrating the Sacraments of Initiation. This celebration shows the connection between the Resurrection of Jesus Christ and the new life given in the sacraments. The whole parish community renews their own Baptism.

The Paschal Candle is lit from the Easter fire at the Vigil. The candle symbolizes the Light of Christ. A candle lit from the Paschal Candle is given to each of the newly baptized. The white garment worn by the newly baptized symbolizes their new identity in Christ. Through Baptism, we pass from death to a life that never ends.

Did You Know?

There are sacred times and spaces.

Activity

Many Catholic churches have a candle or a special light that burns all the time, showing that Jesus is present. It is called the Tabernacle Light. During the Easter Triduum, that light is put out. It is not lit again until Easter Sunday. Why do you think the light is put out during the Triduum? Interview several members of your group to get their ideas as well. Is there one reason you all agree on?

Triduum Prayer Ritual

"I Will Have Faith In You,"
Sarah Hart

Leader: In the name of the Father, and of the Son, and of the Holy Spirit, Amen.

At the end of the season of Lent, we celebrate the Easter Triduum for three days, with only one liturgy that begins with Holy Thursday, a night of service by our Lord and the gift of Holy Communion. On Good Friday, the liturgy continues as we remember the Death of Jesus by listening to the story of his Passion and Crucifixion. On Holy Saturday, the liturgy continues as we begin in darkness, light the Easter Candle, listen to the *Exsultet*, and celebrate the Resurrection of Jesus. When we celebrate the Triduum, we celebrate Christ's passing from this world back to the Father.

Let us listen to a Scripture reading from the Gospel of John (13:3, 4, 12, 15).

Reader 1: "Fully aware that the Father had put everything into his power and that he had come from God and was returning to God, he rose from supper and took off his outer garments. He took a towel and tied it around his waist. . . . So when he had washed their feet [and] put his garments back on and reclined at table again, he said to them, "Do you realize what I have done for you? . . . I have given you a model to follow, so that as I have done for you, you should also do."

Leader: Let us take a few minutes to think about this reading.

Silent reflection.

Reader 2: What do you think it would have been like to have your feet washed by Jesus? Do you think that some of the Apostles were upset, or confused? How would you have felt?

Reader 3: At your Baptism, you were "commissioned" to go and live the Gospel, to wash each other's feet. Your parents, godparents, and friends were asked to renew their own baptismal promises. Let us come to the table now to renew our baptismal promises, by responding in a strong voice, "I do."

Leader: Do you believe in God, the Father almighty, Creator of heaven and earth?

All: I do.

Reader 1: Do you believe in Jesus Christ, his only Son, our Lord, who was born of the Virgin Mary,

Suffered death and was buried, rose again from the dead, and is seated at the right hand of the Father?

All: I do.

Reader 2: Do you believe in the Holy Spirit, the holy Catholic Church, the communion of saints, the forgiveness of sins, the resurrection of the body, and life everlasting?

All: I do.

Reader 3: Let us now ask God to hear our prayers:

We pray for the Church, that it washes the feet of others as Jesus did.

All: Lord, help us to love one another.

Reader 1: We pray for all on earth, that we treat each other as God's creation, made in his image and likeness.

All: Lord, help us to love one another.

Reader 2: We pray for our parish, that it be a light to the community that it is in, always living as Christ taught: "love one another as I have loved you."

All: Lord, help us to love one another.

Reader 3: We pray for our families, that we might live in the Light of Christ and celebrate his love in all we say and do.

All: Lord, help us to love one another.

Leader: We now pray for all of your own intentions . . .

All: *Say, "Lord, help us to love one another" after each spoken intention.*

Leader: Let us pray as Jesus taught us: Our Father, who art in heaven, . . .

Lesson 25
Portfolio

How do you pray during the Triduum?

Mini-Task

The three holy days of the Easter Triduum are a time to connect what we do in the Church now to how Jesus shared his love and life with his followers during the last days of his life on earth. We remember the gifts we receive from Christ in the sacraments. We get closer and closer to the miracle of Jesus' Resurrection at Easter.

Compare and connect the meaning and experience of the Triduum and an event in your life. What and how do we celebrate in each?

Compare and Contrast Chart Graphic Organizer

1. ____________________

2. ____________________

How are they alike?

____
____
____
____

How are they different?

____________________	____________________
____________________	____________________
____________________	____________________
____________________	____________________
____________________	____________________
____________________	____________________
____________________	____________________
____________________	____________________
____________________	____________________

Want to do more? Go to your Portfolio to continue this activity.

At Home

During your evening prayers tonight, turn off the lights in your home. Illuminate your prayer time with candles or small flashlights. Talk with your family about how the Light of Christ lights your way, every day.

How is the Risen Jesus present in his Church?

"Were not our hearts burning [within us] while he spoke to us on the way and opened the scriptures to us?"

Luke 24:32

Gathering Prayer

Leader: The song of Easter is "Alleluia!" Because we are a people of light, we are Easter people. "Alleluia" is our song. The song of Easter is meant to be sung loudly and lively throughout this joy-filled time of light, water, hope, and sacrament. As we gather each Sunday at Mass to celebrate the Risen Lord in song, word, meal, and in each other, we are nourished by the rituals of the Church this beautiful season.

Like flowers blooming in the spring, so does the love of God bloom in our hearts. Jesus lives, Alleluia, Alleluia!

All: Jesus lives, Alleluia, Alleluia!

Leader: Let us be the Light of Christ in the world.

All: Jesus lives, Alleluia, Alleluia!

Leader: Let us be a river of hope to all people.

All: Jesus lives, Alleluia, Alleluia!

Leader: Let us be the eyes and hands of Christ.

All: Jesus lives, Alleluia, Alleluia!

Leader: Jesus lives, Alleluia, Alleluia!

All: Jesus lives, Alleluia, Alleluia!

Activity

The disciples met Jesus on the road to Emmaus but did not recognize him at first. Jesus was a stranger to them. Imagine that you were one of the disciples who met Jesus on the way to Emmaus. Get into groups to discuss these questions:

How would you explain to the stranger what had happened to Jesus?

What would you say and do when Jesus broke the bread during your meal?

What would you tell other people about what you had seen?

Share your thoughts with the whole group.

Jesus is with us at Easter and always.

On the Third Sunday of Easter each year, the Gospel reading tells a story of how the Risen Jesus appeared to his followers and ate with them. The Gospel that is read in Year A, Luke 24:13–35, may be the most special of these stories.

This reading tells about two disciples who met a stranger on the road to Emmaus. They talked with him as they walked along. His words inspired them. He seemed to understand everything.

It was only when the stranger came to supper with them, broke the bread, and said the blessing that the disciples realized this was Jesus! The Gospel says, "their eyes were opened and they recognized him" (Luke 24:31). The disciples ran to tell everyone: Jesus is risen.

The Risen Jesus continues to make his presence known today in the Eucharist. When we share his Body and Blood, the Risen Jesus is truly present. The presence of Jesus in the Eucharist is a mystery. But through the power of the Holy Spirit, we know that Jesus is with us. The joy of Easter is part of every Eucharist.

Did You Know?

It is always the right time to know the Risen Jesus.

Easter

Activity

Work in groups to build a timeline of what happened on the first Easter. Write some of the things that happened, who was present, and what they did. Read Luke 24:1–49 for details. Use the list of events below to help you.

Cleopas and the other person go to the Apostles.

Jesus appears to his disciples.

Jesus breaks bread with Cleopas and another person.

Jesus rises from the dead.

Mary Magdalene, Joanna, and others go to the tomb.

Peter runs to the tomb.

The men tell the women Jesus had risen.

The women tell the Apostles.

On the Road to Emmaus

ROLES:
Narrator 1, Narrator 2, Narrator 3, Cleopas, Disciple, Jesus

Two disciples of Jesus have a most interesting encounter on the road to Emmaus.

Narrator 1: On the very same day that Peter ran to the tomb of Jesus and was amazed to find it empty, two of Jesus' disciples were walking to a village seven miles outside Jerusalem–a town called Emmaus.

Narrator 2: Both disciples were talking about the events that had occurred over the past several days. Jesus had been tried and convicted. He was made to carry a heavy cross to the place where he was crucified. Then he was buried in the tomb. A large rock was hauled in front to seal the tomb. And now the tomb was empty!

Narrator 3: Empty! The two men could not get over it. They talked about what might have happened. Had Jesus' body been stolen? How could the rock have been moved? It was so heavy. They debated all the facts. They did not pay much attention to the man who started walking alongside them.

Narrator 1: They did not recognize that the stranger was Jesus.

Jesus: "What are you discussing as you walk along?" (Luke 24:17)

Narrator 2: The two men stopped abruptly. They looked downward. Their faces looked so sad. One of the men, named Cleopas, answered the stranger.

Cleopas: "Are you the only visitor to Jerusalem who does not know of the things that have taken place there in these days?" (Luke 24:18)

Jesus: "What sort of things?" (Luke 24:19)

Disciple: "The things that happened to Jesus the Nazarene, who was a prophet mighty in deed and word before God and all the people." (Luke 24:19)

Narrator 2: The men continued to tell the stranger about the events of the last few days. They recounted the hope they had had that Jesus would be the one to redeem Israel. But it had been three days, and now Jesus was dead.

Narrator 3: But then the two men's faces changed expression. They talked about how some women from their group who had told them astounding news! The women were at Jesus' tomb early that very morning. They did not find his body! Instead, they had seen a vision of angels who announced Jesus was alive!

Narrator 2: Then the stranger, whom the two men still did not recognize as Jesus, spoke to them.

Jesus: "Oh, how foolish you are! How slow of heart to believe all that the prophets spoke! Was it not necessary that the Messiah should suffer these things and enter into his glory?" (Luke 24:25–26)

Narrator 3: Jesus continued to explain the scriptures to the two men. Presently, the village of Emmaus stood before them. The men thought the stranger was going on farther. The men urged him to stay with them, for night was approaching. So Jesus went and stayed with them.

Narrator 1: While Jesus was with the two men at table, he took bread, said the blessing, broke it, and gave it to them. Suddenly, the men's eyes were opened!

Cleopas and Disciple: You are Jesus!

Narrator 2: At that very moment, Jesus vanished.

Narrator 3: The two men were stunned. They looked at each other.

Cleopas and Disciple: "Were not our hearts burning [within us] while he spoke to us on the way and opened the scriptures to us?" (Luke 24:32)

Narrator 1: The two men hurried off into the night and walked all the way back to Jerusalem. They could not wait to tell the others what had happened to them. As they approached the others, they exclaimed to them.

Cleopas and Disciple: "The Lord has truly been raised!" (Luke 24:34)

Narrator 2: Then the two men told all about what happened on the road to Emmaus and how they had met the Risen Lord in the breaking of the bread.

Lesson 26

Portfolio

In what ways has Jesus revealed himself to you?

Mini-Task

Easter is a time of joy and celebration in the Church. We celebrate the Resurrection of Christ and sing the "Alleluia" again. We are reminded of Christ's presence in the sacraments and our lives every day.

Compare and connect the meaning and experience of Easter and an event in your life. What and how do we celebrate in each?

Compare and Contrast Chart Graphic Organizer

1. ______________________

2. ______________________

How are they alike?

____

How are they different?

______________________ | ______________________

Want to do more? Go to your Portfolio to continue this activity.

At Home

Share a meal tonight or tomorrow morning with Jesus. As a family, prepare a simple meal and choose a prayer or blessing to pray before you eat. Thank God for both the meal and his presence in your family's life.

Lesson 27

Who is the Holy Spirit?

Pentecost

But as for me, I am filled with power, with the spirit of the Lord.

Micah 3:8

Gathering Prayer

Leader: On the feast of Pentecost, the mission of the Church was created. Filled with the Holy Spirit, the disciples were sent out into the world as living witnesses to the love and message of Jesus, our Savior and King. We, too, are filled with the Holy Spirit and sent out into the world to share the love of Christ in us. We ask the Holy Spirit of God to guide us in our journey.

Lord send us your Spirit, let us be one in you.

All: Lord send us your Spirit, let us be one in you.

Leader: Lord, send us out, one by one, in your Spirit. Renew the face of the earth.

All: Lord send us your Spirit, let us be one in you.

Leader: Lord, we will bring the Spirit of your peace to the world.

All: Lord send us your Spirit, let us be one in you.

Leader: Lord, we will bring hope to all those needing your peace, hope, and love.

All: Lord send us your Spirit, let us be one in you.

Leader: Lord, your Spirit gives strength to be a light when there is darkness.

All: Lord send us your Spirit, let us be one in you.

Activity

The Holy Spirit is sometimes represented as a dove. Create a word cloud about the Holy Spirit inside the picture. Share your word cloud with a friend. If there is time, create a new word cloud together.

The gifts of the Holy Spirit are with us today.

On Pentecost Sunday, the Church celebrates the wonderful way in which the Holy Spirit fulfills the promises of Jesus and showers gifts on us.

Jesus promised that he would send the Holy Spirit. He called the Spirit the "Advocate," because the Holy Spirit is active on our behalf. The Spirit intercedes for and speaks to God on our behalf. In the struggle against temptation, the Holy Spirit is always fighting on our side.

Jesus also spoke about the Holy Spirit as the "Paraclete," or teacher, who would explain everything that Jesus did for our salvation. The Holy Spirit enlightens our minds, so that we can see what is good and what is evil.

Throughout Easter, the liturgy tells the story of how the Holy Spirit influenced the early Church. These stories offer us great examples of how the Spirit helps us on our way. The Gifts of the Spirit help us always to follow where the Holy Spirit leads. These gifts are: wisdom, understanding, knowledge, counsel, piety, fortitude, and fear of the Lord.

Pentecost summarizes and celebrates the whole Easter season that comes before it.

Did You Know?

The Holy Spirit has connections.

Activity

Jesus calls the Holy Spirit the "Advocate" and the "Paraclete." An advocate is a helper or someone who speaks on behalf of another. "Paraclete" is a word that means "teacher." Write about a time when you experienced the Holy Spirit helping or teaching you. You might also write a prayer asking the Holy Spirit to help or teach you now.

____

____

____

____

Readers Theater

Life in Community

ROLES:
Narrator 1, Narrator 2, Narrator 3, Onlooker 1, Onlooker 2, Peter

After Pentecost, amazing things began to happen to the early Christian community.

Narrator 1: The time had passed when the Church revealed herself at Pentecost.

Narrator 2: Many remembered the day in Jerusalem when the Apostles and Jesus' mother, Mary, were in one place together. All would never forget the sound of the heavenly noise that was like a strong driving wind.

Narrator 3: Others recalled that there were tongues of fire that rested on each of the Apostles and that they were filled with the Holy Spirit.

Onlooker 1: That was the day Jesus' followers came out of where they were staying. Outside, the crowd was enormous, what with this loud noise. There were devout Jews from every nation.

Onlooker 2: There also were Parthians, Medes, and Elamites, inhabitants of Mesopotamia, Judea and Cappadocia, Pontus and Asia, Phrygia and Pamphylia, Egypt and the districts of Libya near Cyrene, as well as travelers from Rome. There were both Jews and converts to Judaism, Cretans and Arabs. Just everyone from many nations were there.

Onlooker 1: Here we all were from different parts of the world, yet the Apostles were speaking to each group in its own language. We were astounded! "What does this mean?" (Acts of the Apostles 2:12)

Onlooker 2: Peter stood up and spoke.

Peter: "God raised this Jesus; of this we are all witnesses. . . . Therefore let the whole house of Israel know for certain that God has made him both Lord and Messiah, this Jesus whom you crucified" (Acts of the Apostles 2:32, 36)

Narrator 2: After Peter spoke, the crowd wanted to know what to do.

Peter: Repent and be baptized in the name of Jesus Christ.

Narrator 3: Thousands did. All received the Gifts of the Holy Spirit.

Narrator 1: But Pentecost did not end there. Those early followers of Jesus Christ lived out their newfound faith in the Risen Lord. What a wonderful time it was. They spent time learning the teachings of the Apostles and telling others about Jesus. They developed communities in which daily life was devoted to the breaking of the bread. They lived out a deeply felt prayer life.

Narrator 2: Many sold their property and gave away their possessions to share with the community. They ate their meals with joy, praising God in the highest. Soon, their neighbors and even strangers began admiring their sincerity and good will.

Onlookers 1 and 2: "And every day the Lord added to their number those who were being saved." (Acts of the Apostles 2:47)

Lesson 27

Portfolio

In what ways have you shared the Good News of Jesus Christ?

Mini-Task

Pentecost is a time to respond to the call of discipleship. We celebrate the Holy Spirit coming to the Apostles to strengthen and encourage them. We remember that we are called to the same mission they were given–to share the Good News of Christ to all the world.

Compare and connect the meaning and experience of Pentecost and an event in your life. What and how do we celebrate in each?

Compare and Contrast Chart Graphic Organizer

1. ____________________

2. ____________________

How are they alike?

____

How are they different?

____

Want to do more? Go to your Portfolio to continue this activity.

At Home

Talk with your family about teachers or advocates you have known who helped you. In your prayers, ask God to bless these people and their work.

How does Jesus invite us into God's Kingdom?

Whoever is joined to the LORD becomes one spirit with him.

1 Corinthians 6:17

Gathering Prayer

Leader: Throughout the Church year, we learn about and experience God's love in many ways. Ordinary Time occurs after Christmas and Easter. It is the longest season of the Church year. During this season, we hear the stories of the early Church and how the first followers of Jesus began to change the world. Let us thank and praise God for the season of Ordinary Time and for the example of Jesus and the first disciples.

We are grateful for your Son and those who first believed in him.

All: O God, we are grateful for your Son and those who first believed in him.

Leader: For the stories we hear of the early Church,
we are grateful for your Word in the Bible.

All: O God, we are grateful for your Word.

Leader: For the example of the disciples,
we are grateful for their courage and strength.

All: O God, we are grateful for their courage and strength.

Leader: For the opportunity that this season gives us to learn from Jesus' example again and again, we are grateful for Ordinary Time.

All: O God, we are grateful for Ordinary Time.

Activity

Ordinary Time occurs in January and February, and in July through November. On the calendar, write some things that happen in your life during Ordinary Time. Write how you can use those events to grow in holiness. For example, you might celebrate your birthday by taking food to a shelter for the homeless.

Mary and the saints show us how to be like Christ.

The season of Ordinary Time is a time for the Church to reflect on Christ's life and to grow in faithfulness to his teachings. Woven throughout the year is another calendar, the calendar of saints. The saints do not change our focus on Jesus, but they enrich it.

The saints offer us examples of holiness. They intercede for us before God. Devotion to the saints is part of the Church's life of prayer, which strengthens us in holiness.

Mary, the Mother of Jesus, is the most important saint. We celebrate her Immaculate Conception, her birth, and other events in her life, such as the Annunciation, the Visitation, and her Assumption into heaven. Several other days in the calendar honor Mary, too.

Aside from Mary, there is only one saint whose birth we celebrate, that of John the Baptist. Most other saints are celebrated on the anniversary of their death, which is considered their birthday into heaven.

We remember Mary and the saints in the Eucharistic Prayer at Mass. They join us in praising and thanking God for all that Christ has done.

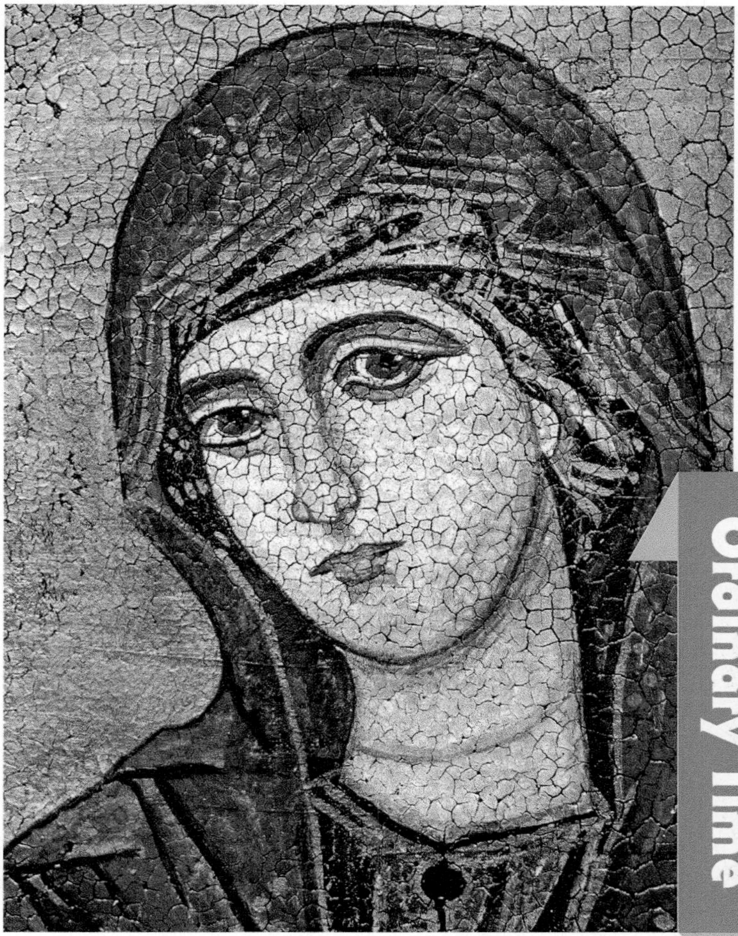

Did You Know?

Patron saints are special.

Activity

Saints are our role models. Have you ever thought about how you can be a role model, too? Think about ways you would like to be remembered for your faith. Maybe you enjoy singing or playing music in church. Maybe you love to compose prayers. On the lines below, write some ideas here about how you would like your faith to inspire others.

____

____

____

Ordinary Time Prayer Ritual

"We Are His People,"
Greg Walton

Leader: In the name of the Father, and of the Son, and of the Holy Spirit, Amen.

During the season of Ordinary Time, we follow in the footsteps of the early disciples. All who came to want to know more about Jesus would follow him as he went from town to town, teaching them about God's love for them and how to love God as Father.

He taught by using parables, or stories, each with a message of how to live with each other, and ultimately how to love God by the way we treat each other. Let us listen now to a parable of Jesus that we hear during Ordinary time (John 6:32–35).

Reader 1: "So Jesus said to them, 'Amen, Amen, I say to you, it was not Moses who gave the bread from heaven; my Father gives you the true bread from heaven. For the bread of God is that which comes down from heaven and gives life to the world.'

So they said to him, 'Sir, give us this bread always.' Jesus said to them, 'I am the bread of life; whoever comes to me will never hunger, and whoever believes in me will never thirst.'"

Reader 2: Let us take a few minutes to think about this reading.

Reader 3: What did Jesus mean when he said, "it was not Moses who gave the bread from heaven; my Father gives you the true bread from heaven" (John 6:32).

Why is it important for us to receive the Eucharist? The symbol of the cross is often found on the host that we receive at Communion, a sign of Christ's love for us all.

As we pass around the cross, let us listen to the song "One Bread, One Body."

Listen to the song.

Leader: Let us pray: For the gift of Jesus, the Bread of Life.

All: We are one Body in this one Lord.

Reader 1: For the living Body of Christ in our home, school, church, and in the world.

All: We are one Body in this one Lord.

Reader 2: For the gift of the season of Ordinary time, a time to become disciples of Christ.

All: We are one Body in this one Lord.

Reader 3: We will now sing the song "One Bread, One Body."

All sing.

Leader: As we close our ritual prayer, let us offer each other a Sign of Peace.

Lesson 28

Portfolio

How does Jesus invite us into God's Kingdom?

Mini-Task

Ordinary Time gives the Church a chance to remind ourselves of everything we have learned from Jesus. We connect his love and teachings to what we do here and now. We find joy and celebration in the everyday and make the ordinary extraordinary.

Compare and connect the meaning and experience of Ordinary Time and an event in your life. What and how do we celebrate in each?

Compare and Contrast Chart Graphic Organizer

1. ______________________

2. ______________________

How are they alike?

____

____

____

____

How are they different?

______________________	______________________
______________________	______________________
______________________	______________________
______________________	______________________
______________________	______________________
______________________	______________________
______________________	______________________
______________________	______________________
______________________	______________________

Want to do more? Go to your Portfolio to continue this activity.

At Home

Pray with the saints tonight as a family. You might pray the Rosary or choose a devotion to a particular saint. Afterward, talk together about why the saints are examples for your family.

Unit 2: The Healing of the Servant

Unit 3: Paul Preaches to Love One Another

Welcome
to your *Christ In Us* Sourcebook

Here you will find:

Our Father

Our Father, who art in heaven,
hallowed be thy name;
thy kingdom come;
thy will be done on earth as
it is in heaven.
Give us this day our daily bread;
and forgive us our trespasses
as we forgive those who
trespass against us;
and lead us not into
temptation,
but deliver us from evil.
Amen.

Glory Be to the Father

Glory be to the Father
and to the Son
and to the Holy Spirit,
as it was in the beginning
is now, and ever shall be
world without end.
Amen.

Hail Mary

Hail Mary, full of grace,
the Lord is with you!
Blessed are you among women,
and blessed is the fruit of
your womb, Jesus.
Holy Mary, Mother of God,
pray for us sinners,
now and at the hour of our death.
Amen.

Gloria

Glory to God in the highest,
and on earth peace to people of good will.
We praise you,
we bless you,
we adore you,
we glorify you,
we give you thanks for your great glory,
Lord God, heavenly King,
O God, almighty Father.
Lord Jesus Christ, Only Begotten Son,
Lord God, Lamb of God, Son of the Father,
you take away the sins of the world,
have mercy on us;
you take away the sins of the world,
receive our prayer;
you are seated at the right hand of the Father,
have mercy on us.
For you alone are the Holy One,
you alone are the Lord,
you alone are the Most High,
Jesus Christ,
with the Holy Spirit,
in the glory of God the Father.
Amen.

Morning Offering

O Jesus, I offer you all my prayers, works, and sufferings of this day for all the intentions of your most Sacred Heart. Amen.

Evening Prayer

Dear God, before I sleep
I want to thank you for this day,
so full of your kindness
and your joy.
I close my eyes to rest
safe in your loving care.
Amen.

Apostles' Creed

I believe in God, the Father almighty,
Creator of heaven and earth,
and in Jesus Christ, his only Son,
our Lord,
who was conceived by the Holy Spirit,
born of the Virgin Mary,
suffered under Pontius Pilate,
was crucified, died and was buried;
he descended into hell;
on the third day he rose again
from the dead;
he ascended into heaven,
and is seated at the right hand
of God the Father almighty;
from there he will come to judge
the living and the dead.
I believe in the Holy Spirit,
the holy catholic Church,
the communion of saints,
the forgiveness of sins,
the resurrection of the body,
and life everlasting. Amen.

Act of Contrition

My God,
I am sorry for my sins with
all my heart.
In choosing to do wrong
and failing to do good,
I have sinned against you
whom I should love above
all things.
I firmly intend, with your help,
to do penance,
to sin no more,
and to avoid whatever
leads me to sin.
Our Savior Jesus Christ
suffered and died for us.
In his name, my God,
have mercy.
Amen.

Nicene Creed

I believe in one God,
the Father almighty,
maker of heaven and earth,
of all things visible and invisible.
I believe in one Lord Jesus Christ,
the Only Begotten Son of God,
born of the Father before all ages.
God from God, Light from Light,
true God from true God,
begotten, not made, consubstantial
with the Father;
through him all things were made.
For us men and for our salvation
he came down from heaven,
and by the Holy Spirit
was incarnate of the Virgin Mary,
and became man.
For our sake he was crucified
under Pontius Pilate,
he suffered death and was buried,
and rose again on the third day
in accordance with the Scriptures.
He ascended into heaven
and is seated at the right hand
of the Father.
He will come again in glory to judge
the living and the dead
and his kingdom will have no end.
I believe in the Holy Spirit, the Lord,
the giver of life,
who proceeds from the Father and the Son,
who with the Father and the Son is
adored and glorified,
who has spoken through the prophets.
I believe in one, holy, catholic
and apostolic Church.
I confess one Baptism for the
forgiveness of sins
and I look forward to the resurrection of the
dead and the life of the world to come.
Amen.

The Sanctuary

1 sanctuary the part of the church that includes the altar and the ambo. The word *sanctuary* means "*holy place*."

2 altar the special table that is the center of the celebration of the Liturgy of the Eucharist, also called the Table of the Lord.

3 crucifix a cross witha figure of Christ crucified, displayed in the sanctuary.

4 tabernacle the special place in the church in which the Most Blessed Sacrament is placed in reserve.

5 sanctuary lamp light or candle that is always lit near the tabernacle. It helps us to remember that Jesus is really present in the Most Blessed Sacrament.

6 ambo a sacred reading stand called the Table of the Word of God. The ambo is used only for proclamation of the Scripture in the Liturgy.

7 chalice the special cup into which the proest pours grape wine that becomes the Blood of Christ during the Liturgy of the Eucharist.

8 paten the special plate on which the priest places the wheat bread that becomes the Body of Christ during the Liturgy of the Eucharist.

9 cruets small glass jars that contain the water and the grape wine used at Mass.

10 presider's chair chair on which the priest who is celebrating Mass sits.

11 **processional cross** cross with a figure of Christ crucified that is carried in the entrance procesion and may also be carried during the Offertory procession and during recessional.

12 **Paschal Candle** a large candle that is blessed and lit every Easter. The lighted Paschal Candle represents the Risen Christ among us. The flame of the paschal Candle is used to light baptismal candles.

13 **baptismal font or pool** contains the water that is blessed and used during the Sacrament of Baptism.

14 **Stations of the Cross** fourteen pictures that help us to follow the footsteps of Jesus during his Passion and Death on the Cross.

15 **Reconciliation Room or confessional** a separate space for celebrating the Sacrament of Penence and Reconciliation. This is where you meet the priest for individual confession and absolution. You may sit and talk to him face-to-face or kneel behind a screen.

16 **stained glass** colorful windows that may show saints or scenes from Scripture.

17 **pews** where the assembly is seated during the celebration of Mass.

18 **statue of Mary** image of the Mother of God, our greatest saint. Statues of other saints may also be found in the church.

Celebrating the Mass

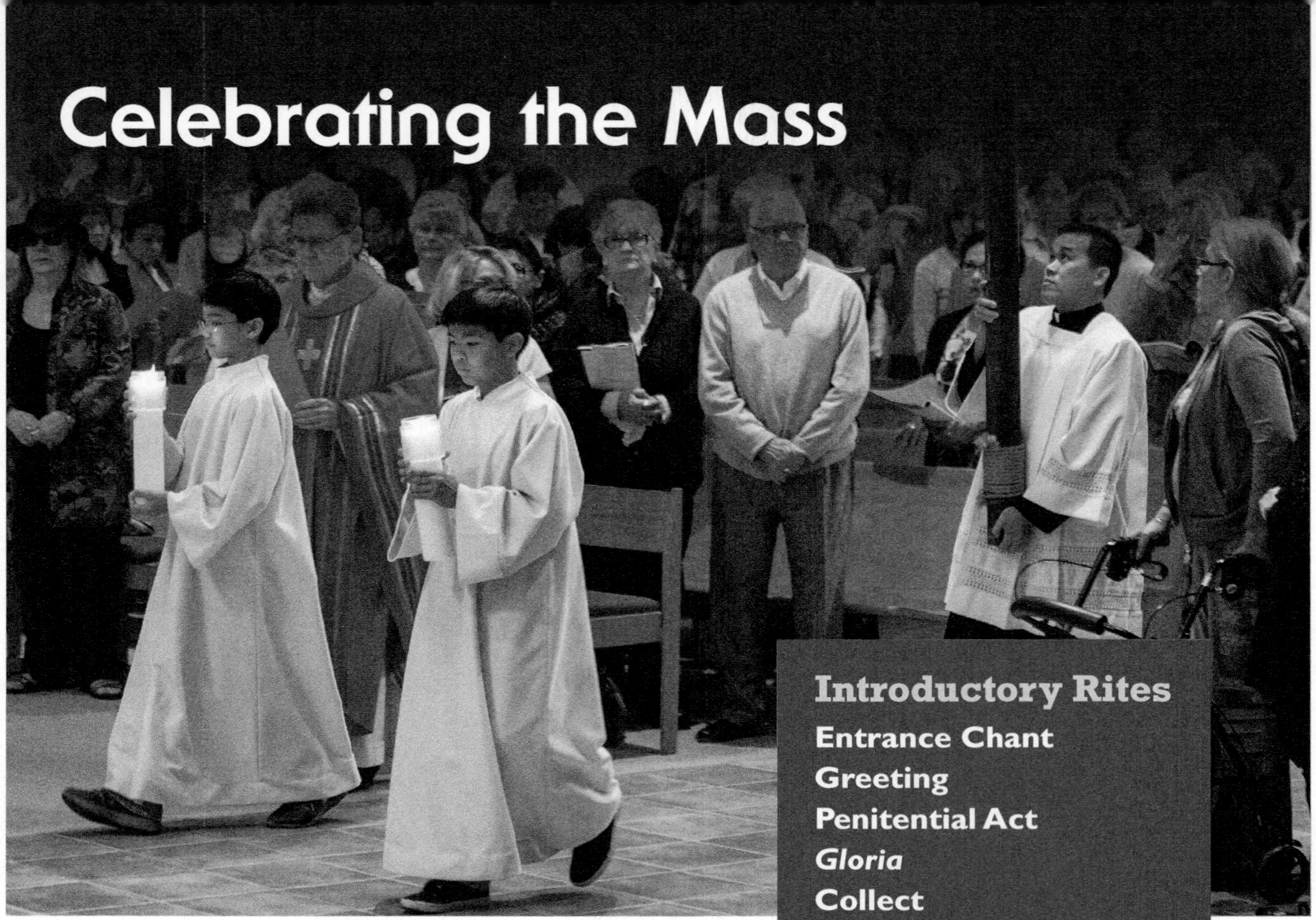

Introductory Rites

Entrance Chant
Greeting
Penitential Act
Gloria
Collect

Do you and your family sometimes wonder what the Mass is really all about? Here is a simple guide that brings awareness to the greatest prayer of the Catholic Church—the celebration of the Eucharist, or Mass.

Take a closer look at how the Mass begins and ends and at the two parts of the Mass—the Liturgy of the Word and the Liturgy of the Eucharist. All our prayers of praise and thanksgiving form one single act of worship. Share the meaning of these sacred moments with your family.

We Gather . . .

What better way to begin our worship than with an entrance song and a procession of the priest and other ministers! This shows our unity, for together we are the Body of Christ—the Church—gathered in God's name. Watch as the priest and deacon kiss the altar and bow. For it is on the altar, the table of the Lord, that the sacrifice of Christ is made present. We remember and make present the work of salvation accomplished by Jesus through his life, Death, Resurrection, and Ascension into heaven.

Together we pray, "In the name of the Father, and of the Son, and of the Holy Spirit." God is with us. In God's presence, we confess that we are not perfect; we have sinned. We pray for God's mercy and ask for the prayers of the community and all the saints. In this way, we prepare ourselves—mind, heart, and soul—to participate in the sacred mysteries of the Mass.

On most Sundays we pray an ancient hymn called the *Gloria*, first sung by the angels at the birth of Christ: "Glory to God in the highest . . . / For you alone are the Lord, / you alone are the Most High, / Jesus Christ, / with the Holy Spirit, / in the glory of God the Father." This hymn of praise speaks of the mystery of the Trinity, the Triune God, in whose name we gather.

The priest then prays the Collect, the opening prayer that expresses the theme of the celebration and the needs and hopes of the assembly.

Liturgy of the Word

God placed in each of our hearts a desire to know him better. At Mass we are invited to actively listen to the Word of God. In Scripture, God speaks to us of the wonders of salvation and of his love for all creation. Yet God also has a special message for each individual who hears his Word. What might that be for you or for members of your family?

Our response after listening to the First Reading, usually from the Old Testament, and the Second Reading, from the New Testament, is "Thanks be to God." God's Word is not merely a collection of past events. God continues to act in our lives today; God's Word has the power to transform us.

Between these readings is the Responsorial Psalm, which can be spoken or sung. Jesus himself prayed the psalms, which express every kind of emotion, as well as what we desire from God. The psalms are beloved prayers of the Bible in which we ask the Lord for many things, such as insight, renewal, guidance, strength, and protection.

Our dialogue with God continues as we prepare to encounter Christ in the Gospel. Now, though, we are standing, singing *Alleluia*, or other words of praise. Standing is a sign of honor for the Gospel, the Good News of Jesus Christ. This is the high point of the Liturgy of the Word. Jesus Christ, our Savior, speaks to us—comforting, strengthening, and calling us to live as his disciples. As the priest or deacon introduces the Gospel (Matthew, Mark, Luke, or John) our bodies are at prayer, too. We trace the sign of the cross on our forehead, lips, and heart. In this way, we ask that God's Word be in our thoughts and in the words we speak, and that it take root in our hearts, moving us to praise and bless the Lord and to do good in the world.

The homily that follows is to help us understand what God's Word means and to remind us that we are not alone. God's Word is within us, guiding us, and leading us to worship. The whole assembly then prays the Creed, stating aloud what we believe as members of the Church. In the Universal Prayer we pray for the needs of all God's people.

Liturgy of the Word

First Reading
Responsorial Psalm
Second Reading
Gospel Acclamation
Gospel
Homily
Profession of Faith
Universal Prayer

Liturgy of the Eucharist

Presentation of the Gifts
Prayer over the Offerings
Eucharistic Prayer
Communion Rite
- **Lord's Prayer**
- **Rite of Peace**
- **Breaking of the Bread**
- **Holy Communion**

Liturgy of the Eucharist

At the heart of the entire liturgical celebration is the Liturgy of the Eucharist. It begins with the Presentation of the Gifts of bread and wine, and a Prayer over the Offerings. This is a symbolic expression of joining ourselves with the sacrifice of Christ. We should offer not only what is positive in our lives, but also our struggles and sorrows. In essence, we unite our whole selves—everything we are and hope to be—with the sacrifice of Christ.

Now is the time for the high point of the entire celebration—the Eucharistic Prayer. We are on our knees, in quiet reverence. The priest, in our name, thanks God for all his works of salvation. Our resounding response of praise is: "Holy, Holy, Holy Lord God of hosts. / Heaven and earth are full of your glory."

We have come to the very heart of the Mass—the changing of the bread and wine into the Body and Blood of Christ. What a beautiful mystery of faith. Jesus is our high priest, and Jesus is present on the altar under the appearances of bread and wine. This is what makes the celebration of Mass the "perfect" act of worship. Jesus is offering the sacrifice through the ministry of the priest *and* is the one being offered. Listen. You can hear Jesus' words, as the Apostles' heard so long ago: "THIS IS MY BODY, WHICH WILL BE GIVEN UP FOR YOU . . . THIS IS THE CHALICE OF MY BLOOD . . . WHICH WILL BE POURED OUT FOR YOU AND FOR MANY FOR THE FORGIVENESS OF SINS." By the power of the Holy Spirit, our gifts of bread and wine have become the very Body and Blood of the risen Christ.

Jesus is truly present, even though the appearances of bread and wine remain. We prepare to receive Christ so that he may work in us. Together we pray the Lord's Prayer that Jesus taught us, and we pray that Christ's peace be with us always. We offer one another a sign of peace to show that we are united in Christ.

With your family, watch as the priest breaks the consecrated bread, the Body of Christ. Jesus also made this gesture—the Breaking of the Bread—at the Last Supper. It shows our unity, for in Holy Communion, we share in the one bread that is broken for us all. When we receive Holy Communion with faith and love, Christ can help us to become better, to become more patient and forgiving with a greater love and compassion for other people.

We Go in Peace . . .

In the Concluding Rites, the priest offers a final prayer and blesses us in the name of the Father, the Son, and the Holy Spirit. We hear these or other words of dismissal: "Go in peace, glorifying the Lord by your life." The Mass does not really end; it is meant to continue in our daily lives.

How will you and your family bring Christ to the world?

Concluding Rites

Greeting
Blessing
Dismissal

119 Luke, 10

Book

Chapter

Verse

Passage

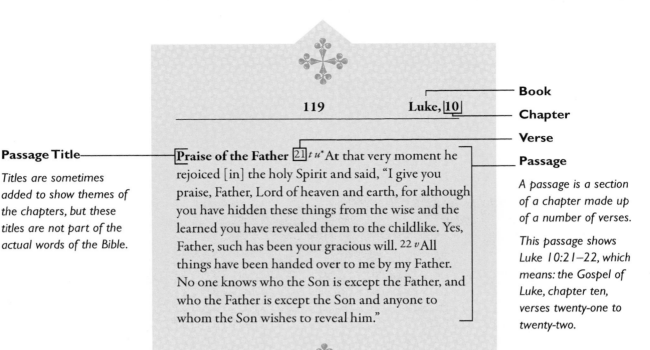

Passage Title

Titles are sometimes added to show themes of the chapters, but these titles are not part of the actual words of the Bible.

Praise of the Father 21 *t u** At that very moment he rejoiced [in] the holy Spirit and said, "I give you praise, Father, Lord of heaven and earth, for although you have hidden these things from the wise and the learned you have revealed them to the childlike. Yes, Father, such has been your gracious will. 22 *v* All things have been handed over to me by my Father. No one knows who the Son is except the Father, and who the Father is except the Son and anyone to whom the Son wishes to reveal him."

A passage is a section of a chapter made up of a number of verses.

This passage shows Luke 10:21–22, which means: the Gospel of Luke, chapter ten, verses twenty-one to twenty-two.

Reading the Bible . . . in Five Easy Steps

When you are given a Scripture passage to read, here are five easy steps that will help you to find it! With your child, follow these steps to look up **Lk 10:21–22.**

1. **Find the book.** When the name of the book is abbreviated, locate the meaning of the abbreviation on the contents pages at the beginning of your Bible. *Lk* stands for Luke, one of the four Gospels.

2. **Find the page.** Your Bible's contents pages will also show the page on which the book begins. Turn to that page within your Bible.

3. **Find the chapter.** Once you arrive at the page where the book begins, keep turning the pages forward until you find the right chapter. The image above shows you how a chapter number is usually displayed on a typical Bible page. You are looking for chapter **10** in Luke.

4. **Find the verses.** Once you find the right chapter, locate the verse or verses you need within the chapter. The image above also shows

Celebrating the Sacrament of Penance and Reconciliation

Individual confession

First, I examine my conscience.

The priest greets me.

We both make the Sign of the Cross.

The priest asks me to trust in God's mercy.

The priest or I may read from Scripture.

I talk with the priest and I confess my sins.

The priest talks to me about loving God and others.

He gives me an act of penance.

I pray an Act of Contrition.

In the name of God and the Church, the priest grants me absolution.

The priest extends his hand over my head.

I receive God's forgiveness of my sins through the words and actions of the priest.

Together, the priest and I give thanks for God's forgiveness.

I am sent to go in peace and to do the penance the priest gave me.

The Ten Commandments

1. I am the LORD your God: you shall not have strange gods before me.
2. You shall not take the name of the LORD your God in vain.
3. Remember to keep holy the LORD's Day.
4. Honor your father and your mother.
5. You shall not kill.
6. You shall not commit adultery.
7. You shall not steal.
8. You shall not bear false witness against your neighbor.
9. You shall not covet your neighbor's wife.
10. You shall not covet your neighbor's goods.

The Great Commandment

"You shall love the Lord, your God, with all your heart, with all your soul, and with all your mind. This is the greatest and the first commandment. The second is like it: You shall love your neighbor as yourself."

Matthew 22:37–39

The New Commandment

"I give you a new commandment: love one another. As I have loved you, so you also should love one another. This is how all will know that you are my disciples, if you have love for one another."

John 13:34–35

The Beatitudes

"Blessed are the poor in spirit,
for theirs is the kingdom of
heaven."

"Blessed are they who mourn,
for they will be comforted."

"Blessed are the meek,
for they will inherit the land."

"Blessed are they who hunger and
thirst for righteousness,
for they will be satisfied."

"Blessed are the merciful,"
for they will be shown mercy."

"Blessed are the clean of heart,
for they will see God."

"Blessed are the peacemakers,
for they will be called children
of God."

"Blessed are they who are persecuted
for the sake of righteousness, for
theirs in the kingdom of heaven."

Precepts of the Church

The pope and bishops have established some laws to help us know and fulfill our responsibilities as members of the Church. These laws are called the precepts of the Church.

It is helpful to think of the precepts as rules or principles intended as a guide for behavior. They teach us how we should act as members of the Church. These precepts also make sure that the Church has what it needs to serve its members and to grow.

1. You shall attend Mass on Sundays and holy days of obligation and rest from servile labor.
2. You shall confess your sins at least once a year.
3. You shall receive the Sacrament of the Eucharist at least during the Easter season.
4. You shall observe the days of fasting and abstinence by the Church.
5. You shall help to provide for the needs of the Church.

Holy Days of Obligation

Each Sunday of the liturgical year is a great celebration of the Church, or a solemnity. In addition to each Sunday, there are other solemnities in the liturgical year on which we are obliged to attend Mass to give special honor to Jesus Christ for the salvation he has given to us. These are called Holy Days of Obligation. Post this list of holy days in your home to remind everyone of them!

- **Solemnity of Mary, Mother of God** (January 1)
- **Ascension** (when celebrated on Thursday during the Easter season*)
- **Assumption of Mary** (August 15)
- **All Saints' Day** (November 1)
- **Immaculate Conception** (December 8)
- **Christmas** (December 25)

**Some dioceses celebrate the Ascension on the following Sunday.*

Catholic Social Teaching

There are seven themes of Catholic social teaching.

Life and Dignity of the Human Person

Human life is sacred because it is a gift from God. Because we are all God's children, we all share the same human dignity. As Christians we respect all people, even those we do not know.

Call to Family, Community, and Participation

We are all social. We need to be with others to grow and learn values. As Christians we are involved in our family life and community.

Rights and Responsibilities of the Human Person

Every person has a fundamental right to life. This includes the things we need to have a decent life: faith and family, work and education, health care and housing. We also have a responsibility to others and to society. We work to make sure the rights of all people are being protected.

Option for the Poor and Vulnerable

We have a special obligation to help those who are poor and in need. This includes those who cannot protect themselves because of their age or their health.

Dignity of Work and the Rights of Workers

Our work is a sign of our participation in God's work. People have the right to decent work, just wages, safe working conditions, and to participate in decisions about work.

Solidarity of the Human Family

Solidarity is a feeling of unity. It binds members of a group together. Each of us is a member of the one human family. The human family includes people of all racial and cultural backgrounds. We all suffer when one part of the human family suffers whether they live near or far away.

Care for God's Creation

God created us to be stewards, or caretakers, of his creation. We must care for and respect the environment. We have to protect it for future generations. When we care for creation, we show respect for God the Creator.

A Virtuous Life

The mark of a true disciple of Christ is one who believes, hopes, and loves. The theological virtues—faith, hope, and love—guide the way we live. These virtues are gifts from God. At times we may have doubts, or feel weak and want to give up hope. We may even act in unloving ways toward others. As a family, we participate in the sacramental life, and pray together for faith, hope, and love (also called charity). The theological and cardinal virtues unite us to God. Every disciple of Jesus is called to "put on" these virtues so that others can see Christ in us.

Cardinal Virtues

Prudence helps us to use reason to find the true good in every situation.

Justice helps us to respect other people and give them what is rightfully theirs.

Fortitude helps us to use strength or courage to use good judgment and behavior during difficult or challenging times.

Temperance helps us to use earthly goods in moderation.

Theological Virtues

Faith helps us to believe in God and all that the Church teaches us; it helps us believe all that God has told us about himself and all that he has done.

Hope helps us to trust in God's promise to share his life with us forever; it makes us confident in God's love and care for us.

Love helps us to love God and to love our neighbor; it is the greatest of all virtues.

Glossary

anoint (page 95) to apply oil to someone as a sign that God has chosen that person for a special mission

Anointing of the Sick (page 103) the sacrament by which God's grace and comfort are given to those who are seriously ill or suffering because of their age

Assumption (page 50) the belief that, when Mary's work on Earth was done, God brought her body and soul to live forever with the risen Christ

Baptism (page 93) the sacrament in which we are freed from sin, welcomed into the Church, and called to holiness

capital sins (page 159) the seven "deadly" sins

Cardinal Virtues (page 139) prudence, justice, fortitude, and temperance

Chosen People (page 146) a term for the Israelites, who were later called the Jewish people. God chose them to be his people, and he would be their God

Church (page 60) the community of believers, led by the Holy Spirit

common priesthood of the faithful (page 112) Christ's priestly mission shared by all those who are baptized

communal prayer (page 177) prayer we pray as a community

Communion of Saints (page 206) the whole communion of faith-filled people living now and united with those who have died but are are alive with God in heaen or in Purgatory

Confirmation (page 95) the sacrament in which we receive the Gift of the Holy Spirit in a special way

conscience (page 135) our ability to know the difference between good and evil, right and wrong

Consecration (page 98) the event at Mass in which the bread and wine become the Body and Blood of Christ

contemplation (page 201) wordless, silent prayer in which we focus entirely on God and his presence with us

conversion (page 164) a turning to God with all one's heart

Divine Revelation (page 20) the way God reveals himself to us

free will (page 124) the freedom to decide when and how to act

grace (page 60) a share in God's life

Holy Orders (page 113) the sacrament in which baptized men are ordained to serve the Church as deacons, priests, and bishops

Incarnation (page 51) the union of human and divine nature in one Person, God's Son

intention (page 197) the aim of our prayers or plan for them

justification (page 169) the action of God by which we are freed from sin and reconciled to God

Kingdom of God (page 219) God's reign of peace, justice, and love

laying on of hands (page 95) a sign of God's blessing that gives authority and grace in God's name

liturgical year (page 83) the calendar that guides the liturgies and prayers of the Church year

liturgy (page 72) the work and prayer of the whole Church

Liturgy of the Word (page 82) the part of the Mass in which we listen and respond to God's Word

Matrimony (page 115) the sacrament in which a baptized man and baptized woman become husband and wife and promise to be faithful to each other for the rest of their lives

meditation (page 201) wordless, silent prayer in which we seek to understand the "why" and "how" of being a Christian

mindful (page 187) attentive to or aware of God's presence

morality (page 125) the goodness or evil of our actions

mortal sin (page 157) very serious sin that breaks a person's friendship with God

mystery (page 20) something that is beyond our ability to understand

natural law (page 129) a rational awareness, a voice of reason, and a moral sense within us that together move us to naturally seek God and choose what is good and true

original holiness (page 43) the original state of being with God in total and complete happiness in which humans were created

original justice (page 43) the original state of living in perfect harmony and friendship with one another and with creation in which humans were created

Original Sin (page 154) the first sin that weakened human nature and brought ignorance, suffering, and death into the world; we all suffer from its effects

particular judgment (page 45) the judgment by God that each person will face at the moment of death

Paschal Mystery (page 53) the events of Jesus' birth, life, Passion, Death, Resurrection, and Ascension

People of God (page 60) a name for the Church and her members

prayer (page 176) raising our hearts and minds to God

precepts of the Church (page 149) laws that help us know and fulfill our responsibilities as members of the Body of Christ

Real Presence (page 98) the process by which the bread and wine become the Body and Blood of Christ

sacramentals (page 77) blessings, actions, and objects that help us respond to God's grace received in the sacraments

sacraments (page 73) effective signs given to us by Jesus through which we share in God's life

Sacraments at the Service of Communion (page 112) the Sacraments of Holy Orders and Matrimony

Sacraments of Christian Initiation (page 92) Baptism, Confirmation, and Eucharist. These sacraments make us members of the Church

Sacred Chrism (page 95) oil blessed by the bishop; it is used in the Sacraments of Baptism, Confirmation, Holy Orders, and Anointing of the Sick

Sacred Scripture (page 21) holy writings found in the Old Testament and New Testament in which God speaks to us in a human way

Sacred Tradition (page 25) the Revelation of the Good News of Jesus Christ as lived out in the Church, past and present

sanctified (page 30) made holy

sanctifying grace (page 167) the gift of sharing in God's life

sin (page 155) intentional thought, word, deed, or omission against God's law

society (page 140) a group of people bound together by a principle of unity that goes beyond any one individual. Its spiritual purpose is to fulfill the human vocation

solidarity (page 140) the Christian virtue that involves a love for all people and respects the needs of others and the common good

soul (page 40) the invisible spiritual reality that, along with our body, makes each of us human; the soul will never die

Theological Virtues (page 139) God's gifts of faith, hope, and charity

transubstantiation (page 98) the process by which the bread and wine become the Body and Blood of Christ

venial sin (page 158) less serious sin that damages a person's friendship with God

vice (page 159) a habit of sinful behavior

virtue (page 137) a good habit that helps us act according to God's love for us

Q: What is the mystery of God?

A: God is a mystery, which means that he is greater than the human mind's ability to understand. Words will never be enough to describe who God is. **CCC, 251, 260**

Q: What is Divine Revelation?

A: Divine Revelation is God's making himself known to us. Through Divine Revelation we come to know his plan of salvation for all people. **CCC, 51, 53, 68, 69, 230**

Q: What is Sacred Scripture?

A: Sacred Scripture is holy writings in which God speaks to us in a human way. God lovingly meets us and talks with us in Sacred Scripture. Sacred Scripture is God's Word to us. **CCC, 101, 104, 109**

Q: What is Sacred Tradition?

A: Sacred Tradition is the faith of the Church that has been passed on orally and in writing by the Apostles and their successors. **CCC, 76, 80**

Q: How can we know God?

A: We can know God through Creation and the Church. God created us with certain gifts to be able to know that He exists The Church uses the gifts of creation in her celebration of the sacraments. **CCC, 35, 47, 317**

Q: What is the Blessed Trinity?

A: The Blessed Trinity is God in Three Persons: the Father; the Son, Jesus Christ; and the Holy Spirit. It is the central mystery of the Christian faith. **CCC, 253, 261**

Q: What is the soul?

A: The soul is the invisible, spiritual reality within each of us that makes each of us human. The soul is immortal. It will never die. **CCC, 362, 363**

Q: What is faith?

A: Faith means believing that God has revealed himself to us through his words and actions, and most especially through Jesus Christ. Faith is a gift from God that guides how we live every day. The Church supports and nourishes our faith. **CCC, 1841, 1842**

CCC = Catechism of the Catholic Church

Q: What is the Assumption?

A: The Assumption of the Blessed Virgin marks the event in which Mary, at her death, was taken up by God, body and soul, into heaven. **CCC, 974**

Q: What is the Paschal Mystery?

A: The Paschal Mystery is what we celebrate in the Eucharist. The dying and rising of Jesus is made present to us in the Mass. Specifically, it is the life, Death, Resurrection and Ascension of Christ. **CCC, 654, 1085**

Q: What is the Incarnation?

A: The Incarnation is the mystery that Jesus became truly human while also remaining truly God. We can never totally understand its meaning. **CCC, 460, 464, 480**

Q: What is the People of God?

A: The People of God is the community of believers that make up the Church. We become members of Church when we are baptized. Jesus Christ is the head of the People of God and is led by the Holy Spirit. **CCC, 781, 695, 1267**

Q: What is grace?

A: Grace is God's gift of new life and friendship. It helps us grow as God's children. **CCC, 1996, 1997, 2000**

Q: How is the Church divinely sent?

A: The Church has a missionary mandate. This means that Jesus Christ has sent the Church out into the world to preach the Gospel to all people. **CCC, 849**

Q: What is the liturgy?

A: Liturgy is the work and prayer of the Church. Christ acts through the liturgy, particularly the sacraments, to communicate God's grace. **CCC, 1084, 1085**

Q: What are sacraments?

A: Sacraments are effective signs given to us by Jesus through which we share in God's life. The Holy Spirit prepares our hearts and minds to encounter Jesus when we celebrate the sacraments. **CCC, 1091, 1099**

Q: How does the Church share signs of God's grace?

A: The Church's Seven Sacraments are celebrations that are special signs of God's love, presence, and saving power. Jesus instituted, or began, the sacraments so that his saving work would continue for all time. We receive special graces from each of the sacraments when we celebrate them properly. **CCC, 1131**

Q: What are sacramentals?

A: Sacramentals are blessings, actions, and objects that help us respond to God's grace received in the sacraments. Sacramentals can help make every event in our lives holy. **CCC, 1670, 1671, 1677**

Q: What is the Liturgy of the Word?

A: The Liturgy of the Word is the part of the Mass in which we listen and respond to God's Word. **CCC, 1190**

Q: What is the liturgical year?

A: The liturgical year is the calendar that guides the liturgies and prayers of the Church year. During the liturgical year, we recall and celebrate the whole mystery of Christ. **CCC, 1168, 1194**

Q: Why is Apostolic Tradition important?

A: Apostolic Tradition is important because it means that we celebrate one faith received from the Apostles and passed down to the Church today. This is true even when the Church's style of worship and celebrations might be different in other areas of the world. The Church all over the world celebrates the same Paschal Mystery: the passion, Death, Resurrection, and Ascension of Jesus. **CCC, 1200–1202, 1209**

Q: What are the Sacraments of Initiation?

A: The Sacraments of Initiation are Baptism, Confirmation, and Eucharist. These sacraments of Christian initiation begin, strengthen, and nourish our life in the Church. **CCC, 1275**

Q: What is Baptism?

A: Baptism is the foundation of Christian life. It is the very first sacrament that we celebrate and leads us to the other two Sacraments of Christian Initiation, Confirmation and Eucharist. It is upon Baptism that we build our lives as followers of Christ. **CCC, 1256, 1258, 1260**

Q: What is Real Presence?

A: Real Presence is Christ's true and real presence in the Eucharist in the form of bread and wine. When we receive Holy communion, we are nourished by the Body and Blood of Christ. **CCC, 1410, 1413**

Q: What is Anointing of the Sick?

A: Anointing of the Sick is the sacrament by which God's grace and comfort are given to those who are seriously ill or suffering because of their old age. In this sacrament, we recall that by his own suffering, Death, and Resurrection, Jesus saves us. **CCC, 1518,1527, 1528**

Q: What is the common priesthood of the faithful?

A: The common priesthood of the faithful is Christ's priestly mission in which all those who are baptized share. Each of us is called to worship god, spread the good News of Jesus Christ, and serve one another and the Church. **CCC, 1533, 1535, 1591**

Q: What are the Sacraments at the Service of Communion?

A: The Sacraments at the Service of Communion are the Sacraments of Holy Orders and Matrimony. Those who celebrate them help the Church grow in holiness through the ministerial priesthood and through married life. **CCC, 1534**

Q: What is free will?

A: Free will is the freedom and ability to choose. God created each of us with an intellect and free will. These gifts mean we can freely choose to cooperate with God's action in our lives and God's plan for us. **CCC, 1711, 2025**

Q: What is morality?

A: Morality is the goodness or evil of our actions. There are three parts to every moral choice or act we make: the objective act (what we do); the intention (why we do the act); and the situation (such as where, when, with whom, and how). **CCC, 1750-1754**

Q: What is natural law?

A: Natural law is a rational awareness or voice of reason, and a moral sense within us that moves us to seek God and choose what is good and true. We have this awareness of what is good and true because we are created in God's image. **CCC, 1955, 1956**

Q: What is conscience?

A: Conscience is our ability to know the difference between good and evil, right and wrong. Educating our conscience about what is right and what is wrong is a life-long task. **CCC, 1713, 1776, 1796**

Q: What is virtue?

A: Virtue is a good habit that helps us act according to God's love for us. A person who is virtuous makes these habits or virtues a part of his or her life. **CCC, 1803, 1804, 1830**

Q: What are the Cardinal Virtues?

A: The moral or Cardinal Virtues are habits that come about by our own efforts. The Cardinal Virtues are the virtues of prudence, justice, fortitude, and temperance. **CCC, 1804, 1805**

Q: What is the New Law?

A: The New Law, or Law of the Gospel, is the work of Christ. In the Sermon on the Mount, Christ taught us a way of living, a low of love for God, self, and neighbor. It shows us the way to achieve eternal life. **CCC, 1949, 1950, 1965, 1966, 1983**

Q: What are the Ten Commandments?

A: The Ten Commandments strengthen our relationship with him. God's purpose in giving us the commandments was to teach us how to live in right relationship with him. God gives us the grace we need to follow his commandments. **CCC, 2082, 2085**

Q: What are the precepts of the Church?

A: The precepts of the Church are laws that help us know and fulfill our responsibilities as members of the Church. They are positive laws that present the minimum of what a Catholic should do in order to grow in love of God and neighbor. **CCC, 2041, 2042, 2043**

Q: What is Original Sin?

A: Original Sin is the first sin that weakened human nature and brought ignorance, suffering and death into the world; we all suffer from its effects. Baptism frees us from Original Sin. **CCC, 1707, 1714**

Q: What is sin?

A: Sin is an offense against God. When we sin, we turn our hearts away from God's love and choose that which we know is wrong. The choices we make weaken God's life in us. Sin is a thought, word, deed, or omission against God's law. **CCC, 1871, 1872**

Q: What is venial sin?

A: Venial sin is less serious sin that weakens our friendship with God. Even though venial sins do not turn us completely away from God, they still hurt others, ourselves, and the Church. **CCC, 1855, 1863**

Q: What is communal prayer?

A: Communal prayer is prayer we pray as a community. Like personal prayer, communal prayer helps to feel and remember God's presence. **CCC, 2566, 2567, 2591**

Q: What is contemplation?

A: Contemplation is wordless, silent prayer in which we focus entirely on God and his presence in us. **CCC, 2705, 2708, 2721**

Q: What is the Communion of Saints?

A: The Communion of Saints is the whole community of faith-filled people living now united with those who have died but are alive with God in heaven or in Purgatory To profess that we are a part of the Communion of Saints is to say that we are connected to all faithful people living and who have died. **CCC, 960, 1055**

Q: What are the liturgical seasons?

A: Seasons in the calendar year that celebrate special people and events in our Church. The liturgical seasons are Advent, Christmas, Ordinary Time, Lent, the Triduum, and Easter. **CCC, 1158-1173**

Q: Why do we celebrate Advent?

A: Advent is that time of year when we remember and celebrate the fact that Jesus Christ will come again in glory. No one knows the day or the hour when Christ will return. Therefore, we must be ready to meet him whenever he comes, our hearts filled with wonder, love, and praise. **CCC, 524**

Q: Why do we celebrate Christmas?

A: We celebrate Christmas because it is the feast of the Incarnation, when God was made flesh in his Son, Jesus Christ. The Incarnation strengthens Catholics in the belief that God works through the material world rather than remaining far apart from it. **CCC, 525, 526, 1171**

Q: Why do we celebrate Lent?

A: Lent is a season in which we renew our faith. Just as Jesus went out into the desert and fasted for forty days to prepare for his mission, so we renew our call to faith each year, during the forty days of Lent. **CCC, 1438**

Q: What is the Triduum?

A: The Triduum is the high point of the whole Church year. It is three special days in which we recall the Last Supper, the Death of Jesus on the cross, and God raising Jesus from the dead. **CCC, 1168**

Q: Why do we celebrate Easter?

A: We celebrate Easter because it is the season in the liturgical year in which we remember the Resurrection of Jesus Christ and renew our life in Christ. **CCC, 1169**

Q: What is Pentecost?

A: Pentecost is the day the Church celebrates the descent of the Holy Spirit on the disciples of Jesus after his Ascension. It is held on the seventh Sunday after Easter. The Church celebrates the way in which the Holy Spirit fulfills the promises of Jesus and showers gifts on us. **CCC, 696, 715, 731**

Q: What is Ordinary Time?

A: The season of Ordinary Time is a time for the Church to reflect on Christ's life and to grow in faithfulness to his teachings. Ordinary Time gives the Church a chance to remind ourselves of everything we have learned from Jesus. **CCC, 495, 508**

Index